To
Michael
Happy Christmas
2011
Love from
Christine, Len, Eleanor
&
Matthew

GOT, NOT GOT

The A-Z of Lost Football Culture, Treasures & Pleasures

Derek Hammond & Gary Silke

As seen on
Mirror
Football
www.MirrorFootball.co.uk

Pitch Publishing Ltd
A2 Yeoman Gate
Yeoman Way
Durrington
BN13 3QZ

Email: info@pitchpublishing.co.uk
Web: www.pitchpublishing.co.uk

First published by Pitch Publishing 2011
Text © 2011 Derek Hammond and Gary Silke

2

A CIP catalogue record for this book is available from the British Library.

13-digit ISBN: 9781908051141
Design and typesetting by Brilliant Orange Sports Management.
Printed in Malta. Manufacturing managed by Jellyfish Print Solutions Ltd.

Can I have my ball back, Mister?
I want to stand, not sit,
Nor advertise some oligarch
On a redesigned replica kit.

Can I have my ball back, Mister,
And rise above the tripe
Of multinational money-men
And dodgy agents' hype?

Can I have my ball back, Mister,
And suffer no more WAGs,
Nor read of sordid episodes
Of strikers' tawdry shags?

Can I have my ball back, Mister?
And I'll rebrand the sport,
To substitute the sheikhs and fakes
Who count but don't support.

Can I have my ball back, Mister?
I'll launder their ordure,
To launch it in the hellish pit
Of Lucifer's manure.

Can I have my ball back, Mister?
What arrogance, what shame,
What cynic stole such innocence?
I want another game.

Dermot Carney – 'Can I Have My Ball Back, Mister?'

*"I would also think that the action replay
showed it to be worse than it actually was."*

Ron Atkinson

Saturday's kids

At Sunday lunchtime, we took our seats in a flat-pack football ground on an out-of-town industrial estate. All cheers and applause were drowned out by the roar of the 'matchday experience' soundtrack while, out on the pitch, teenage millionaires clapped the crowd with gloved hands. Both teams were time-wasting from kick-off in their wrong-coloured kits – scared to lose a precious point, but ever mindful of their OPTA step-over statistics.

"Things have changed," I said.

"Yeah," my fellow platinum customer nodded, "you used to get change from fifty quid out of a Saturday."

On ten minutes, our chippy optimism began to feel misplaced. Despite our boys' heroic touchline dispute, the assistant referee couldn't be stared point-blank into reviewing their goalscorer's passive secondary-phase status.

"Modern players, eh? Kissing their badges, logos and adverts…"

"And then they're on their way as soon as their agent gets them a better offer. I'd love to see this lot play on a good old mudbath, against some proper cloggers. Against the Seventies team." Gary paused, perhaps wary of

the CCTV cameras and security tank tops raking the stands for banter. "Here," he added in a more distant tone, "how come we never get passed down over the heads of the crowd any more, so we can sit on the wall at the front of the Kop?"

It was a moment of unique clarity, fogged only by a vision of a football match played in the days before choreographed celebrations, when a gaggle of small children would run harmlessly on to the pitch to pat the goalscorer's back.

"Kids today don't support their local teams," I upped the odds with a sweet generalisation, "or even the underdogs in the Cup. They just support whoever won the League last season."

"A clip round the ear from a proper copper, in a hat like a tit…"

"Floodlight pylons, so you could find your way to away grounds…"

"Leeds United sock tags."

"Football," I couldn't stop myself blurting out, "*used to be better in the past.*"

And it's a fact.

"Modern players, eh? Kissing their badges, logos and adverts…"

We've got page after page of proof that's as conclusive as a big muddy ball mark on a lumbering stopper's shirt sleeve. Evidence as hard and fast as a Hot Shot Hamish net-buster, capable of lifting a goalie off his feet and making him say "Oof!" We've been collecting it up ever since half-time that day, when we began scribbling excited notes on the back of a fag packet, feeling like forty-something freedom fighters just whispering the words.

Once there was a time when we kicked a ball against the garage door and saw Wembley.

Down in our miniature, carpet-level world of football, tiddlywink players took on the attributes of real-life heroes. It wasn't just the fact that we were ten: football back then was a simple, innocent game touched with everyday magic.

In the intervening years, a mushrooming number of fans have decided they're falling out of love with football, although it isn't that easy to cut and run from unconditional love. You've probably heard them complaining that their local toilet-roll magnate has been ousted as chairman by a Bond villain; that it's somehow become illegal to wave their scarf above their head like a helicopter.

It was twenty years ago today, the beginning of the end. That's when the self-appointed custodians of our game hit upon the idea of branching out from fumbling with their velvet ball-bags, and allowed football to be sold down the river to the highest corporate bidder – most often an unvetted international playboy, stroking a fluffy white cat on his lap. Henchmen talked of bigger gates and a 'family atmosphere', but now the game was win or die. The out-of-puff

5,000

2
CHELSEA
£4,500

£100

3-4
BLACKPOOL
£1,500

defender with big rosy thighs was soon replaced by slick new technology. Without our say-so, our old home grounds were demolished to make way for football theme parks. You can't even buy a humble boiled burger at half-time, these days – and our quest goes on for the last blow football set on sale in Britain.

We hope you enjoy this journey through the Lost World of Football, with many a memory rekindled and heartstring tugged along the way.

However, our aim here isn't just to grumble about everything that has gone missing from the game. Instead of simply wallowing in our bittersweet mirage of a Golden Era, we're going to get up off our bottoms and do something about it.

We want to bring back into our footballing lives some of the magic from the magic sponge

of yore; some of the mud, the marvel, the Melchester Rovers.

We've been spreading our ideas at grass-roots level, holding a series of important inter-club fan summits (we've been grumbling and exaggerating about childhood matches down the pub). And, across the country, fellow fans are taking up the clarion call (well, they're certainly grumbling and exaggerating about childhood matches down the pub).

Week after week, fans are echoing the same demands to the portly Cockneys who run radio phone-ins, and shouting them at football bigwigs whenever they're in earshot. Some people we don't know have even emailed in to our *Mirror* blog. Next stop: the FA and the Premier League.

Football used to be better in the past. It's our game, not theirs. So let's *take it back*.

Thirty years would be good for starters.

Shock and awe: it's yer actual Bobby Moore.

**2
CAMBRIDGE UTD
£4,500**

Once there was a time when we kicked a ball against the garage door and saw Wembley.

1
MANCHESTER U
£15,000

9

A&BC

A&BC Chewing Gum of Romford, Essex, holds a special place in the hearts of millions of big kids. Back in the 1950s, it was Douglas Coakley (the 'C' in the company name) who came up with the idea of packaging football cards with a thin slab of chewy, a combination which proved a natural winner. Throughout the 1960s and into the 1970s they produced a yearly set of football cards, as well as other stickers, tattoos and card series covering everything from the Beatles to *Star Trek* – and American sports and TV-related cards bound for the US via partner company, Topps.

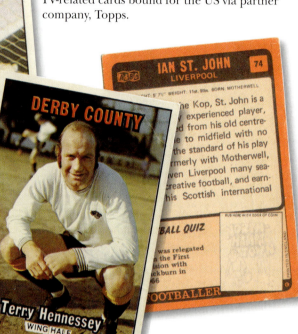

But, for some reason, it isn't easy to put out of your mind stray memories of football's long-lost people and places, the youthful obsessions and outdated rituals that seemed so important back in the day – and, in a strange way, still do. It might be a name on an email that you immediately associate with a recoloured kit on a card, and think: 'Not got.' Or just a vacant moment when you're driving at 80mph down the motorway, when you find yourself wondering… whatever happened to Terry Hennessey?

It isn't everyone who could possibly understand.

Rock-faced Tommy Smith valued his image rights at more than a tenner. **And A&BC dared to argue.**

Every British footballer who ever appeared on an A&BC card was paid a tenner image rights, and got to tell a company agent how tall they were and how much they cost from St. Mirren, for the blurb on the back. In 1969, George Best and his agent tried to up the ante to £1,000, with predictable results. Liverpool's Tommy Smith also reckoned his rocklike features were worth more, but after a phone call explaining that the fee was no indication of star stature, and a useful little earner for many of the checklist's lesser lights, 'The Anfield Iron' signed up with good grace.

In 1974, A&BC lost a long-simmering legal battle and was taken over by Topps-Bazooka. End of story.

ACTION MAN

They don't make boys' toys like Action Man any more. As hard as plastic nails, he was a soldier of fortune without fear or morals. A battle-scarred killer, he'd shoot playmates in the knees just for fun and inspire just-pretend explosions in the shrubbery. What kind of lessons would this eight-inch terrorist provide for any child today, teaching them the un-PC joys of deadly weapons?

An Action Man Tottenham badge given away with the original kit pack sold last year to a collector for £626.

Make no mistake, Action Man was a ruthless mercenary. He thought nothing of changing out of his moulded rubber French Resistance beret and straight into full Nazi Stormtrooper regalia. You might call him an opportunist or an early multitasker: one minute he was in the bath togged up as a Navy frogman, the next he was a Canadian Mountie or an astronaut.

Only now does it begin to make sense how this multi-skilled, determinedly unattached iceman should have chosen to spend his home leave – slipping into his football kit and turning out for your favourite Division One team.

Unfortunately, that's when our vicious little accomplice became a complete bore. Whether you had one Action Man or 22, there just wasn't a game you could base around his non-existent ball skills. The specific types of 'action' mastered by 'the movable fighting man' were limited to bending at the joints and being blown into the air. There was only so much fun you could have dressing a doll – yes, let's use the word – in football kit, especially as it exposed his shattered-looking kneecaps. The final straw was the orthopaedic stand which he needed to balance on one leg, hovering over

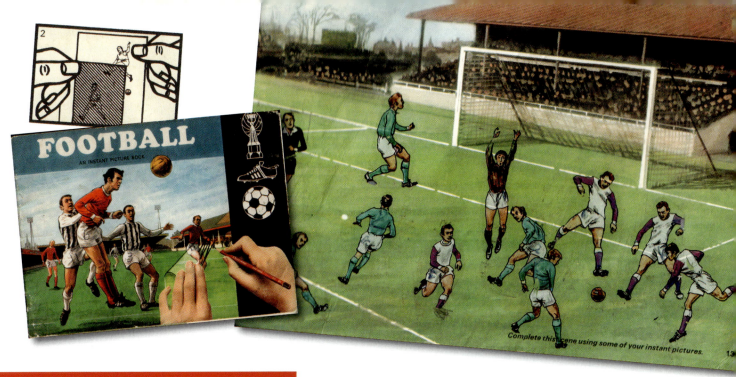

FOOTBALL
AN INSTANT PICTURE BOOK

Complete this scene using some of your instant pictures.

13

the ball in a sorry personification of inaction.

Because most Action Man enthusiasts kept their figures strictly military, the scarcity value of the football range has more recently seen eBay prices soaring. Right now, there's a Villa kit on the auction site with a bid of £480, which hasn't yet met the reserve price. An Action Man Tottenham badge given away with the original kit pack sold last year to a collector for £626. If you'd kept them, your two-inch-long Wolves socks could now pay for a decent night out.

But best be careful in your dealings with this dangerous figure. Witness the shocking case of my brother-in-law, who fell foul of Action Man when he was left playing alone, bathing in the kitchen sink (he was small; this was Scotland, 1972). Suddenly, a piercing scream shook the house; "MAAAAAAAAAAM! AH'VE GOT MAH TOODLE CAUGHT IN MAH ACTION MAN!" Even today, a mention of those evil elasticated joints brings tears to the eyes of one scarred Border brave.

Neither gripping hands nor an 'Eagle Eye' for goal got Action Man off the subs' bench.

ACTION TRANSFERS

This is easy. All you have to do is scribble the transfers off their greaseproof-paper backing on to the empty pitch in front of the Kop, and soon you'll have an action-packed Instant Picture™ of a match as good as anything a photographer could produce.

Now then. Let's 'peel away backing paper' and kick off with one of the White-and-Violet team realistically booting the ball upfield. While his goalie jumps around out of his area. And one of the Turquoises throws a dummy on the edge of the box. While another one goes for a diving header sitting on his team-mate's shoulders.

It's no use the Letraset bods flagging up the deadly danger of failing to 'slide backing paper under other pictures to avoid accidental transfer' – it's already too late for the centre-forward's head. What we really need is more players just hanging around, like in real life, gossing and blowing on their hands and doing leg stretches...

Scribble art: Never mind the Pollocks, here's the Patterson Blick Instant Picture Book.

11

Admiral modelled by Cov, Currie and Kevin Keegan, the Captain of our Ship.

dive into the box and rummage around for brightly coloured treasure… Norwich, Sheffield United, West Ham, Tottenham and Manchester United (though never Leicester City) kits, all bearing the jaunty yellow Admiral label.

There was no school uniform at Huncote Primary School, so virtually every boy in Junior 4 sported an Admiral shirt to top off their baggy, flared trousers. As Mr. Hughes' eye passed over his class he would have seen a riot of colour fit to shame the parrot cage at Twycross Zoo. Luton Town's orange, Coventry's sky blue, Leeds' yellow away and the red England away shirt (though I doubt he would have recognised them as such, being more interested in folk singing than footy).

The shirts you wore had no bearing on the team you supported. I was an all-blue, match-going Leicester fan, but I was happy to wear West Ham's claret and light-blue chevrons on my chest. Alan had never been to Luton but sported their lairy Day-Glo with the white-and-navy stripe down one side. Richard did support

273 ENGLAND HOME
ALL SIZES

ADMIRAL SPORTSWEAR

Firstly, we had to fund the expedition.

Somehow, the princely sum of two pounds, which amounted to ten weeks' pocket money, had to be scraped together. Washing a car or two might get you 10p, if you were lucky. And if an uncle visited you might even get a shiny 50p pressed into your palm, if he was trying to look better than your dad.

Steve wasn't Welsh, as far as he knew, but was seldom seen without his gaudy red, yellow and green international shirt.

When enough of us had the necessary, off we would go. It was a mile and a half to the hardware shop in the next village. We weren't interested in the racks of brooms or buckets or saws. We were wholly focused on the large cardboard box in the corner, marked 'Shirts £2, Shorts £1'.

To us, it was a source of great pleasure, stuffed with more highly fashionable cloth than any Milan catwalk. It was the 'Admiral Seconds' box.

The shop owner had a connection at the Admiral factory in Wigston, and this early version of TK Maxx was created – highly desirable labels at affordable prices.

Just as wannabe WAGs now fall upon labels like Gucci and Missoni, we would

Leeds, but the shirt came before the affiliation. Steve wasn't Welsh, as far as he knew, but was seldom seen without his gaudy red, yellow and green international shirt. Mitchell was a Leicester fan but would carefully line up the tram lines on his Coventry shirt and shorts.

And we all did this because, for just a couple of years, Admiral was IT!

The Admiral brand could be traced back to 1914 when it was used by the Leicester underwear concern, ABC Hosiery Ltd. By the 1970s the company were called Cook & Hurst Ltd., based in the suburb of Wigston.

At this time the first manufacturers' logos were beginning to appear on football shirts, and it was Admiral who seized on

WALES HOME
SIZES

the possibilities of commercialising strips. Bert Patrick, Cook & Hurst chairman, had formed an idea born out of England's 1966 World Cup win and the advent of colour TV. If kits could be uniquely designed and visibly branded then contracts with clubs could be signed, and the parents of young football fans would have to buy Admiral kit rather than the plain, generic shirts currently available. With a young, go-getting sales force, Admiral set about conquering the domestic market.

Don Revie's fondness for making a bit of brass to supplement his salary at Leeds was a big help in the early days. Leeds were the first to wear the nautical trademark. Then, when Revie became England boss, a £16,000 deal was cut and England's traditional plain white shirt was suddenly adorned with red-and-blue sleeve stripes and a yellow logo, much to the horror of traditionalists and to the delight of schoolboys across the nation. That shirt was the must-have item of 1975, and when Manchester United were also signed up, Admiral had the 'Big Three'. The rest quickly fell into line.

The Admiral agents had an eye for an opportunity. When Southampton beat Manchester United in the 1976 FA Cup Final they wore an Admiral strip that had been designed and manufactured since their semi-final victory, and

the multiple logos down sleeves and shorts were exposed to a huge global TV audience.

Although Admiral had kitted out local club Leicester City for a few seasons, only one logo had been on show. The enterprising Peter Shilton had signed his own deal and wore a 'PS' Admiral design on his otherwise gleaming white strip. In 1976, the outfield players also got to sport logos, and plenty of them. My dad recoiled with horror when he saw Admiral's typically unrestrained design. It was the end of football as we knew it, he reckoned. And he was

Operating from a modest financial base, they had to be sharp to retain their market share now other firms were breathing down their necks. Umbro diamonds were being worn by Arsenal, Liverpool, Chelsea, Manchester City, Everton, Derby and Scotland, while Ipswich Town, QPR, Birmingham and Nottingham Forest sported Adidas stripes.

Inevitably, Adidas, Umbro and Le Coq Sportif caught up with, and overtook, the pioneering Admiral. By the early Eighties, they'd lost their roster of bigger clubs, and the

Don 'The Don' Revie: an offer he couldn't refuse...

"My object is to focus attention on the undesirable practices of certain sports equipment manufacturers. The most unpleasant aspect is that

children are being exploited."

probably right. But we loved it and, after I got it for Christmas 1976, I seldom wore anything else.

In every copy of *Shoot!* there would be a full-page colour advert showing their latest designs; there was an *Admiral Annual* which showed only photos of games in which both sides wore the approved brand; and you could send away for a giant poster which displayed the company's growing roster of clubs from Aberdeen and Dundee to Orient and Eintracht Frankfurt.

In commercial terms, Admiral had done such a great job by 1977, they were hauled over the coals in Parliament by Newport MP Roy Hughes:

"My object is to focus attention on the undesirable practices of certain sports equipment manufacturers," he complained. "The most unpleasant aspect is that children are being exploited. One of the principal offenders appears to be the Leicester firm of Cook & Hurst, the chairman of which is Mr. Bert Patrick and their trade name is 'Admiral'. The attitude of that firm is arrogant... The English football team now has 'Admiral' emblazoned on its tracksuits. The firm of Cook & Hurst says that it has exclusive rights to use the English lion emblem on its products. It relies for that on the Copyright Act 1968 and its predecessors. That is an abuse of those Acts, which were intended for such items as jewellery and motor-car accessories... Star-struck youngsters who wish to wear the colours of their favourite teams are having to pay through the nose for the pleasure."

The general opinion of the Commons was that it was all a jolly rotten do, but there was nothing they could do about it. But Admiral, having lived by the sword of commerce, would soon die by it.

England contract, the biggest in world football, had moved to Umbro. Its brief Golden Age over, the company sadly went bust.

Although the logo has occasionally resurfaced, Admiral has never again been a force in the kit market. But every time I see Nike or Umbro proudly unveiling their latest minor rearrangement of stripes and collars as if it were a fashion revolution, then I think back to a small firm from Leicester who did it first and did it best.

AFTER THE MATCH

Programme advertisers used to care a great deal about fans' plans for after the match, and would fling regular, helpful ideas our way in case we hadn't yet made arrangements. A bite to eat or a celebratory/consolation sherbet were common suggestions. Care for a read or a listen? Take in a stage show or drop by for high tea; but please do not feed the kangaroos…

Belle Vue Zoo Park set out an enviable array of options for Man City fans, with performing sea lions, dancing and Wrestling Tonight ('Another Sensational Bill of 4 All-Star Contests – 5,000 Seats') high on the bill. At Brighton, 'An Action-Packed Night Out at the Races' beckoned 'just 400 yards from the Goldstone Ground as the Seagull flies'. For humans, there was a handy little map showing the way around the corner to the dogs.

After-the-match entertainment was clearly big business. In Bournemouth, Tony Cascarino upped the odds by offering nosh both before kick-off *and* after Ted MacDougall had done his stuff – only to be trumped by a competitor touting Florida as a pre- and post-match option…

ANIMALS ON THE PITCH

Even men with steel hearts love to see a dog on the pitch,
It generates a warmth around the ground that augurs well for mankind,
And that's what life's about,
Trouble is, these days you never see a dog on the pitch…

Half Man Half Biscuit

And HMHB are right, as they so often are.

Nothing used to bring a smile to the face so easily as a dog cavorting around the field, evading your goalkeeper's best efforts to capture him.

"Hurrah!" goes the crowd, every time he body-swerves out of his grasp.

"Sign him up!" shouts the wag. "BOOOOO!" we thunder, as he's eventually tethered.

But you don't see dogs on the pitch any more, and I think I know why. Those modern turnstiles where the bars go from head to toe… you can't jump over them, and dogs can't nip in under them.

Possibly the greatest four-legged turf encroacher was Bi, who invaded the pitch during the 1962 World Cup quarter-final between Brazil and England in Chile. After the usual 'Hurrah/Sign him on/BOOO!' scenario (but in Spanish, obviously), Bi was scooped up into the arms of England goal machine Jimmy Greaves, who was rewarded with a stream of canine urine down his shirt.

The Brazilian coach took charge of the incontinent mutt, and when no owner could be traced, he was raffled off among the Brazil side. Garrincha won, named the stray and gave him a home for the rest of his life.

Less heartwarming, if you're a Lincoln City fan, is the story of Bryn the Alsatian, who caused the Imps to be relegated out of the Football League in 1987. The old 'Applying for Re-election' system had, by now, been abandoned in favour of automatic promotion and relegation, and on the last day of the season it was either Lincoln or Torquay who were going to take a catastrophic and historic drop into the icy waters of non-League football.

Two-nil down at home to Crewe, it was Torquay who were hammering on the trapdoor when Jim Nicholl pulled a goal back for the Gulls. Charging toward the corner flag to retrieve a pass, he was then given a nasty bite by police-dog Bryn, who had assumed the player was attacking his handler. Nicholl's treatment lasted five minutes… and Torquay equalised in the injury time added on, thus relegating Lincoln in their stead.

Rammy the Ram: regimental mascot of the First Derby Militia. Derby County, too.

NORTH BANKERS IN THE FIRST TEAM

Arsenal

"Charlie George, Superstar, how many goals have you scored so far?" sang the Arsenal fans.

Every other club's fans sang: "Charlie George, Superstar, walks like a woman and he wears a bra." But they were just jealous.

Islington-born Charlie was a genuine Gooner as a kid and swiftly graduated from the North Bank to the first team. He looked the part, style guru Paolo Hewitt saying of him: "I remember Charlie George being interviewed on *Football Focus* with his brogues, Sta-Prests and a Fred Perry top, and I remember going, 'Wow, he's one of us'."

Sometimes George's suedehead past caught up with him. During the 1971-72 season Arsenal boss Bertie Mee had to discipline him for headbutting Liverpool's Kevin Keegan. Later in the same season he was in trouble again for flicking a V sign at the home supporters after he'd scored against Derby at the Baseball Ground. In this Mirrorcard from 1971, Pat Rice and Frank McLintock are trying to cover for Charlie's unexplained absence by balancing a portrait of him on their knees.

Charlie admitted that he never got on with Mee, which eventually led to a fall-out and the striker's exit to Derby, where they soon forgave him his rude gesture.

Meanwhile, Arsenal don't do local heroes any more. Their players come from Pamplona, Paris, Prague, Cancun, Sens, Douala, Rotterdam, Warsaw, Kostrzyn Nad Odra, Okazaki, Copenhagen, St. Petersburg, Abidjan and São Paulo… but not Islington.

APPLYING FOR RE-ELECTION

Fed up with football's dirty billions, its bloodsucking agents and bureaucrats, their blatant backhanders and bendy rulebook? Well, hard luck. An open season for double dealing is vital to grease the wheels of a new global industry driven by brands and celebrities. But, as one of the sad addicts who bankrolls the business, doesn't it make you yearn for some good old *small-time* football corruption, like we used to complain about in simpler times?

At the end of every season up until 1987, the chairmen of all the Football League clubs used to enjoy a cosy ritual. They'd get together for a jolly and a chinwag at the League's seaside HQ, all sucking on fat cigars and balloons of brandy. They'd consider a while, weighing the value of what the top non-League club might bring to the party – bigger crowds and better players – and then they'd wink and nod and shake hands, and agree to keep their little club exclusive for *just one more year*.

In the days before free promotion into and relegation out of the League, the champions of the Northern Premier and Southern Leagues would apply for election to the Fourth Division, while the club at the bottom of the basement applied for re-election. It was democracy in action – except for the old pals on Blackpool Prom and their comfortable unspoken pact: if you don't ever vote me out, then I won't ever vote you out. And now, gents, swiftly on to the resolution of item 23 on the agenda: what time are the strippers on?

And yet, despite the safeguards, the 1970s saw all the North West's minnows fall foul of backstabbing. Barrow, once home to Liverpool's Emlyn Hughes and Everton's Gary Stevens. Billy Bingham's Southport. Bill Shankly's Workington. A football hotbed snuffed out, and all to save on southern clubs' petrol money. Our unfortunate outliers joined Gateshead, Accrington Stanley and Bradford Park Avenue in making way for the more geographically acceptable Peterborough, Oxford, Cambridge, Hereford, Wimbledon and Wigan (best not make it too obvious, eh?).

Sadly, the North-West Three were ejected before the League chairmen dreamed up the line about potential new boys' grounds having to 'meet League requirements' retrospectively, a year before any application was made. That stroke of genius was enough to hold back the tide of progress until as late as 1997. By that time, most of the old 'Over My Dead Body' brigade had shuffled on, in any case, and it was left to their sons to assure fans in the local press that there were no plans whatsoever to sell the club's ground to supermarket developers.

Cheerio, cheerio, cheerio: Workington, Barrow and Southport go up in smoke.

ASTROTURF

Plastic turf is right up there alongside a punch on the nose for wearing the wrong coloured scarf when it comes to disappeared football stuff we're actually pleased to see the back of.

How I hated going up to Oldham, where Andy Ritchie and Roger Palmer would run rings round us on their lino pitch.

And how I loathed Luton, who not only played on Astroturf but also banned away fans. How much advantage did they need?

How I mourned when my favourite player, Alan Young, twisted his knee on the unyielding artificial grass at Loftus Road and was never quite the same again.

And how I cheered when I went to see QPR v. Aston Villa, and a Brummie fan marched down the terraces to the front wall and deposited a large square of genuine turf on top of the plastic pitch.

Nature knows best.

PS I Love You: Shilts' Scribble Sells For Small Fortune Shock.

Seventies punchline alert: "I don't know, I never smoked Astroturf..."

THE AUTOGRAPH BOOK

Gone out of existence. Withdrawn from the field. Abandoned. Missed. Passed by.

Everything we come across on this journey through football's Lost World is no more. They thought it was all over – and they were dead right.

The autograph book was unlike any other of its day. Its cartridge-paper pages were blank, devoid of words and lines, with the built-in compensation of alternate pastel shades – chalky blue, green, pink, yellow. The outer corners of the pages were missing, rounded off so as not to offend the hand of an honoured victim. The spine of the leather-bound booklet ran down the short side, so it lolled open invitingly.

On the cover of the book there was no author's name or title, just a single, golden word in a curly typeface. And then there was the vital loop of elastic to hold the book closed in the owner's back pocket, either encircling the whole precious volume, or just stretching over a single corner.

Lost. Let slip. No longer in our possession.

It isn't just the autograph book that has bitten the dust in recent years, but also the crowd of small boys hanging around the locked double door marked PLAYERS AND OFFICIALS

CENTENARY YEAR CENTEN

Official Matchday Magazine of Coventry City F.C.
Tuesday 13th March 1984 k.o. 7.30pm

Aston Villa

THE SKY BLUES

CENTENARY 40P

ONLY an hour after the match. The players are missing, too: men who didn't need a minder at their side to talk to a twelve-year-old about the afternoon's brawls and cannonballs. The kind of players whose personally signed message you'd want to treasure forever.

The warning signs came when first two, then three, and now four of the five attackers in every team were phased out, goalscoring deemed surplus to requirement. Local heroes fell out of fashion. Red-faced stoppers failed to evolve with changing times, and so soon became extinct. And the best player in every team of the Sixties and Seventies became the first called up to the great kickaround in the sky – Billy Bremner, George Best, Peter Osgood, Keith Weller, Bobby Moore.

All gone, but not forgotten.

In the intervening years, football magazines and club shops have churned out sheets of pre-printed (quite literally auto-) autographs to help save the all-important stars time and hassle. It's all a question of supply and demand, too? Autograph books have been replaced by handily pre-signed official postcards, and the gaggle of young fans outside the ground by eBay entrepreneurs.

"Hey Mister, will you sign this matchworn shirt/vintage electric guitar for me, and pose for an authentication shot?"

AVOIDING THE SCORE

The proliferation of live televised football has made the ancient art of avoiding the score almost redundant. Steering clear of a football result in order to enjoy highlights in the evening is seldom necessary these days.

There was a time when I had to take a felt-tip to my dad's copy of the *Sports Final*, and diligently scrub out the results of the two games that would be featured on *Match of the Day* that evening. And how many times have I stuffed my fingers in my ears and sung "La la la la la la" when an over-eager newsreader has nearly given the game away?

A whole episode of *Whatever Happened to the Likely Lads?* was given over to this phenomenon as Bob and Terry spent a day on the run from their friend Flint, who was only too aware of England's fate in Bulgaria that afternoon. Their schoolboy error: betting a fiver each that they could prolong their blissful ignorance until the TV highlights at 10.20pm.

Ooh, what happened to you? Whatever happened to me?

I diligently felt-penned out the scores in Dad's Sports Final

"You'll never make it," another mate reckoned. "There's the radio. Evening papers. Television news."

And, sure enough, Terry caught a glimpse of part of a TV headline that read: 'England F...'.

Ah well, that was obviously 'England Flop', wasn't it? Or it could have been 'England Fail'. Or 'England Fiasco'?

'England Fight Back After Early Setback'? 'England Five'? 'England Fade'?

For those of you who don't want to know the result, please look away now.

Aston Villa

THE FOOTBALL CATHEDRAL

Villa Park used to have a unique feel among football grounds, its palatial architecture and its setting under the hilltop gaze of a Jacobean stately home combining to reflect the belief that Aston Villa was no common club.

Opened in 1923, some time after the club's Victorian heyday, the Trinity Road Stand was the masterpiece of football's greatest architect, Archibald Leitch. The red-brick citadel not only embodied the club's stature but also perfectly echoed its historic surroundings. Yes, the beautifully overblown gables were designed in part to mirror those of Aston Hall, but that isn't to ignore the influence of the great Victorian funfair that had once sprawled over Aston Lower Grounds. The neighbouring Holte Hotel, a grand old gin palace and music hall built in that same sub-17th-century style, was one of three concert halls once set here amid gardens and fairground attractions. When Villa took up tenancy in 1897, the multi-purpose sports and showground had not only played host to Cup semi-finals and Test cricket, but also to Buffalo Bill Hickok's Wild West Show. The old pleasure grounds' bowling green stood in front of the Trinity Road Stand until 1966; the original aquarium and menagerie buildings were actually incorporated into Leitch's Villa Park as the club offices and gymnasium, and survived until the late Seventies.

That was the true beauty of Trinity Road: the grandeur of its stained-glass windows, its sweeping staircase and gold-leaf Italian mosaics could attract the future King George VI as ribbon-cutter; but there was also an element of fantasy on offer here, the promise of an escape from work into the possibilities of the weekend.

Villa Park's funfair menagerie survived until the 1970s

Sadly, at the end of the 1999-2000 season, Villa chairman 'Deadly' Doug Ellis unilaterally decided to bulldoze Trinity Road, and with it Villa Park's special aura. The stand had never been listed. Fans had naively imagined the most admired structure on any English football ground didn't need to be. The bulky replacement stand that now vaults right over Trinity Road is of neither interest nor value, having succeeded only in increasing Villa Park's capacity from 40,310 to 42,640.

Withe 'n' Shaw: not a Nickname Strike Duo, but a 'garden city' south of Manchester.

b

BALDIES
Extinct Football Species No. 1

No miracle cure has been developed for male pattern baldness – it's just that modern-day man has the option to say, "Oh, well," and shave away what remains of his last attempt at a hairdo. All gone, it's just another look.

But a few decades ago that opt-out simply wasn't available. Only Yul Brynner, Detective Lieutenant Theo Kojak and the baddy in *Thunderbirds* could get away with the full naked slap. Respectable adult males in the UK couldn't go around looking like yobboes or circus acts, they had to be more cunning.

Baldness was definitely seen as, if not quite a disease on a par with leprosy, then certainly a malady. Benny Hill spent most of his weekly show slapping little sidekick Jackie Wright* on his naked pate, and there was a playground song directed at any schoolmate who had his hair cut shorter than the long thatch we considered to be the ideal in the Seventies:

> *Ay up skinhead, over there,*
> *What's it like to have no hair?*
> *Is it hot or is it cold?*
> *What's it like to be bald?*

Even achieving the status of professional footballer didn't halt the jibes towards poor baldy. Leicester City's Andy Lochhead might have thought he was safe perusing *Goal* magazine's 1969 FA Cup Final Special... but no.

was quite alarming when it fell off onto his shoulder, before being hoisted back into place, so many times per game. The comb-over solution might have been okay for greengrocers or vicars, but for someone charging round a field and heading a football for a living... well, they weren't fooling anyone.

Similarly, the wig couldn't be considered, no glue on Earth being strong enough to risk the ignominy of it becoming dislodged during a keenly contested midfield tussle.

Terry Mancini of QPR and Arsenal seemed to shrug off his premature hair loss with a cheery grin, despite having a head like an ostrich's nest. He grew what was left round

I AM BALD!

"My secret is my Crown Topper. The small photograph shows how I used to look. Now I wear a Crown Topper." Absolutely undetectable! Even your barber won't know! As worn by film and TV stars. You can sleep in it and even enjoy sports in it. The Crown Topper makes you look and feel at least TEN YEARS younger. Send for illustrated brochure now (no obligation).

NAME
ADDRESS
COUNTY

CROWN TOPPER
130 Regent St. London W.1. Tel: REGent 7487.
Branches at Glasgow, Manchester, Leeds,
Bristol, Newcastle and Dublin.   F.L. (18/11)

Before and After: and not even your closest acquaintances will ever suspect.

Ay up skinhead, over there What's it like to have no hair? Is it hot or is it cold?

What's it like to be bald?

In the 'Meet the Teams' feature he is introduced thus: "ANDY LOCHHEAD... will be sporting the only bald head when the teams line up on Saturday..." No mention of his thundering header at Anfield which secured City's place in the quarter-finals, oh no.

So how to disguise that socially unacceptable naked scalp? Bobby Charlton of Manchester United and Ralph Coates of Tottenham both opted to grow the remaining sidey bit long and lay it over the drought area in the middle. Bobby's thin blonde strands managed to pull off a certain grace of their own, but Ralph's doormat

the outside and got on with his game. Brave pioneers like Terry helped get us to where we are today.

These days, baldness passes unnoticed and unremarked, and the likes of Stephen Ireland, Wayne Rooney and Zinédine Zidane have escaped the teasing and scorn handed out to their sparsely thatched predecessors.

Baldness is no longer a crime, which is a good job as otherwise this book would have to have been written from a prison cell.

* The uncle of Middlesbrough and Ireland centre-half Alan Kernaghan.

THE BANANA SHOT

Originating in South America in the 1950s, the so-called 'banana' shot was a Dastardly Foreign Trick in the form of a long-range effort on goal, clearly missing by some distance. It then magically bent in the air and dived inside the upright, making a decent defence and an honest netminder look ruddy foolish.

In the era of the modern 'ping-pong' football, big bananas are no longer anything to write home about. It's far harder to kick the thing straight.

And so the show-offs and showboaters of the 21st century have perfected a new-fangled *vertical* banana which appears to be ballooning into the stand before dipping quite unnaturally under the crossbar. This is accomplished by taking a funny sideways run-up and 'wrapping your foot around the ball'. Witchcraft.

Big bananas
are no longer anything to write home about

ÜBER ALLES

No one is quite sure why Birmingham City chose to adopt a sideways West German flag for a change shirt during the 1972-73 and 1973-74 seasons.

Rumour has is that a Blues director, on a pre-season tour of Germany, was impressed by the striking colour combination of black, red and amber displayed on the Bundesrepublik Deutschland flag, and decided to use it as an alternative colour scheme to City's classic blue-and-white 'penguin' kit of the time. It was only worn a handful of times, at places like QPR and West Brom, but seems to be looked upon favourably by the St. Andrews faithful old enough to remember it.

Watching footage of the kit in action can be quite disconcerting because the players take on a very different appearance depending on which direction they're running. It often looks as though there are three teams on the pitch.

Umbro briefly revived the broad penguin chest stripe for the 2007-08 home strip but, sadly, the 'German flag' didn't make a reappearance.

Maybe next season?

Birmingham City

For those of you watching in black-and-white, the yellows are kicking left to right.

"THE END OF THE ROAD"
THE TEAM OF '91

Side One

Bluenose Cassette 1

All rights of the owner of the recorded work reserved. Unauthorised public performance, broadcasting and copying of this tape prohibited.

23

Blackburn Rovers

UNCLE JACK'S TITLE

The dawn of the 1990s saw a cash bonanza promised to every club lucky enough to be Premier League material. And yet even as the go-getters' dream became reality, the most successful club owner of the day remained uninterested in profit margins and churn rates, despite a £600 million fortune founded in steel. Jack Walker was a football fan. When it came to his lifelong love, Blackburn Rovers, money was meaningless.

Roy Keane hadn't reneged on a done deal, to join United. But for 1994-95, the transfer record was topped again, bringing Chris Sutton from Norwich. And Rovers pulled off the big one.

Jack Walker goes down as the last of football's great local benefactors, the last hometown chairman ever to lift a club up by the bootlaces and bankroll them to the title. And all for £27 million, the same price as a modern star's packed lunch.

"He followed Rovers all his life and was a bread-and-butter fan," says Rovers legend Simon Garner of Walker, "who luckily had a lot of money."

For years, he'd slipped the club cash for the odd signing; but when he finally took over the helm in 1991, he reacted like a kid in a sweetshop, setting on ex-Liverpool boss Kenny Dalglish armed with a blank chequebook, and scraping into the big league via the play-offs, thanks to the likes of Colin Hendry, Mike Newell and David Speedie.

Having renovated Ewood Park and revitalised the town, 'Uncle Jack' set his sights yet higher for 1992-93, smashing the British transfer record to land 22-year-old Alan Shearer for £3.5 million – and finishing fourth. England regulars Tim Flowers, David Batty and Graeme Le Saux followed, and Rovers made runners-up behind Man U in '94.

They might have made it to the top even quicker had a bid for Gary Lineker paid off, or if

Blackpool

WHEN THE WIND BLEW

Whenever you visit Blackpool in the football season, you're lucky to see any sunshine. Only sadistic games masters and their families frolic in the Irish Sea as you walk the Golden Mile. But no matter how hard the sand is whistling around your soggy Hush Puppies and their stripy windbreaks, you'll always find the Blackpool Tower observation platform closed to the public.

"Too windy," the security guard/ringmaster will explain for the millionth time to every man, woman and child within earshot. "The wind's ten times stronger up there than it is down here."

Which is a shame, because a 518-foot remodelling of the Eiffel Tower was always the perfect place to see the vast adverts painted for that very purpose on the stand roofs at Bloomfield Road. From the observation platform, happily windblown generations looked down on Dutton's Beer's OH BE JOYFUL!, replaced in the 1970s by WHITBREAD TANKARD. COOL, REFRESHING FLAVOUR, and the long-surviving ISMAIL & CO. TEA AND COFFEE MERCHANTS. Pre Health & Safety, we braved all

weathers to stand on a thick pane of glass set in the floor – IN CASE OF EMERGENCY DO NOT BREAK GLASS – and imagine plummeting straight down to the Prom, 380 feet below.

Now the roof ads are long gone, along with any other distinguishing feature of Bloomfield Road, all inspired or enforced by the bracing local weather.

Four decades ago, the club was forced to rip the roof off the Kop before a stiff breeze beat them to it. As late as 1990, the wind demanded they lop twenty feet off their vintage floodlight pylons and, worse still, were ordered to postpone home matches if westerly gusts rose above 55mph – though only, mercifully, measured at ground level.

THIS IS THE MAYORESS LADS – SHE'S GOING TO AUTOGRAPH ONE OF YOUR BALLS!

BLOODIED BUT UNBOWED

In football's pantheon, the manly acts which now elevate a player to the status of a god hardly compare with those of the past. Despite being twenty times more skilful and ten times more muscly than any previous generation, footballers are now protected like babies in swaddling from doing anything that might affect their club's investment – sorry, their 'Health & Safety'. So: no more tackling; no more contact with fans; no playing on with a broken neck in the Cup Final – or even the slightest bump.

Compare and contrast with Terry Butcher's example in September 1989, in a World Cup qualifier against Sweden which saw the England centre-half walk off the pitch at the Råsunda Stadium looking like a casualty from the trenches.

England needed a draw to qualify for Italia 90 ahead of Poland, and a 0-0 draw is what they got, thanks in no small measure to Butcher's bravery. Early in the game he clashed heads in an aerial challenge and suffered a nasty gash to the forehead.

He was hastily patched up with seven stitches and a bandage and returned to the fray, courageously heading away a series of Swedish long balls and crosses even though it must have stung something awful. His wound re-opened and his bandage, shirt and even shorts were stained with blood as he donated pints to the cause.

It's an iconic image, but these days Terry wouldn't even get the chance to play Richard the Lionheart. At the first sign of claret, a player is whisked away from the action, taken down the tunnel and quarantined in case we all catch the AIDS. The flow has to be completely stemmed, all his kit incinerated and every piece of 'contaminated equipment' replaced before the player can return.

No more barging, or challenging the goalkeeper. No more opting to run off a twinge instead of flopping and calling for the trainer. No more bandages. No more heroes.

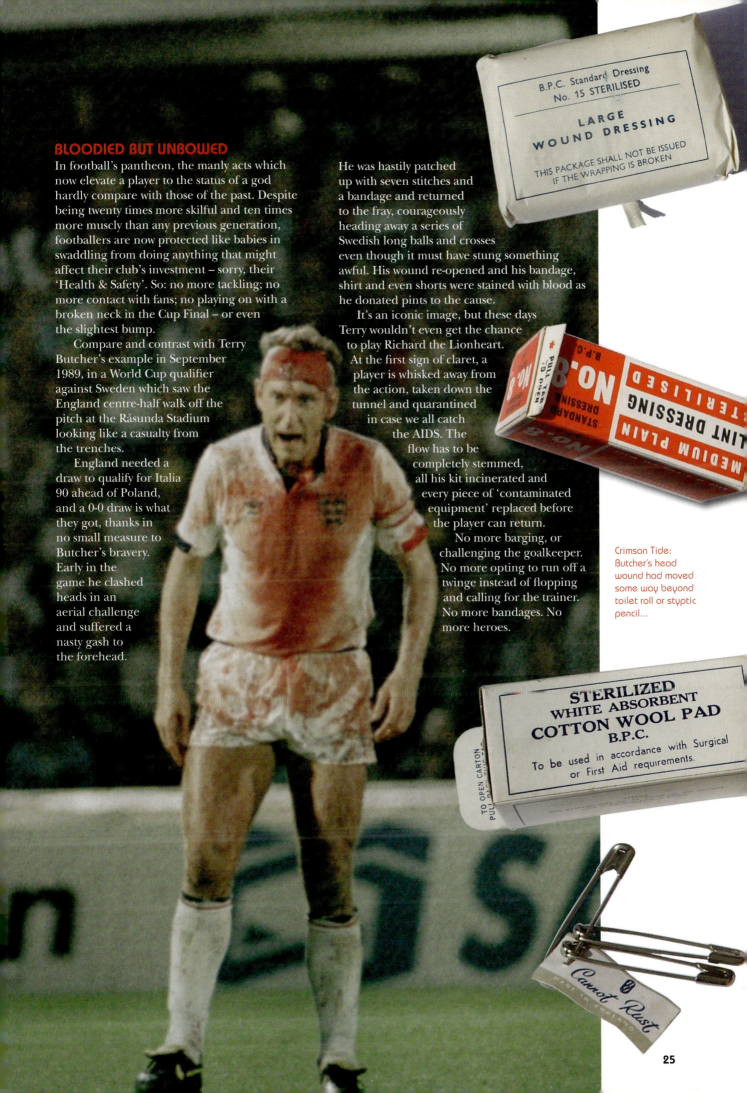

Crimson Tide: Butcher's head wound had moved some way beyond toilet roll or styptic pencil...

B.P.C. Standard Dressing No. 15 STERILISED

LARGE WOUND DRESSING

THIS PACKAGE SHALL NOT BE ISSUED IF THE WRAPPING IS BROKEN

NO. 8 STANDARD DRESSING B.P.C. PULL TO OPEN

MEDIUM PLAIN LINT DRESSING STERILISED

STERILIZED WHITE ABSORBENT COTTON WOOL PAD B.P.C.

To be used in accordance with Surgical or First Aid requirements.

TO OPEN CARTON PULL

Cannot Rust

Bolton Wanderers

GOAL OF THE CENTURY

Bolton Wanderers decided to get 'with-it' in 1979 and snaffle themselves one of those new-fangled foreign imports that everyone else was buying. Spurs had snapped up the Argentinian World Cup winners Ardiles and Villa; Ipswich had gone Dutch with Mühren and Thijssen. Trotters boss Ian Greaves, meanwhile, was working on less of a budget, and wasn't thinking in terms of bringing in a friend to hold his exotic superstar's hand. Having spotted Poland strolling their World Cup group before falling to Argentina, his sights alighted on Eastern European targets – not a member of the Argentina 1978 squad as such, but nevertheless a player with two Polish caps, by the name of Zdzislaw Tadeusz Nowak.

FRANK
WORTHINGTON
BOLTON WANDERERS

Imagine Tad's thoughts as he steps off the plane from dear old Polska. What will the football be like in England? Will I get a nickname as cool as 'Ferrari', like at Legia Warsaw? What will competition be like for a first-team place?

'Will I get a nickname as cool as 'Ferrari'?'

In Tad's first game – Ipswich at home, televised by ITV's *Big Match* – he is to find out. Frank Worthington is the competition. Frank is also a foreign import, in a way, holding dual citizenship of Planet Playboy and Football Talent Heaven.

Tad can only watch as the man with flowing rock-star locks gets the ball with his back to goal twenty yards out, juggles it for a bit, lobs it over his own head, turns and volleys it into the net.

Tad doesn't make it at Burnden, heading back to Poland after 24 games and a solitary goal.

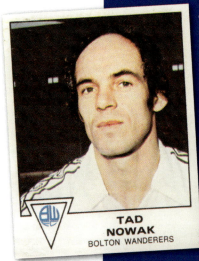

TAD
NOWAK
BOLTON WANDERERS

Tad: recent team-mate of ace playmaker Kazi Deyna, signed by Man City in 1978.

BRIGHTON & HOVE ALBION
And Smith Must Score

No, not the fanzine that ruined Seagulls fans' Saturdays for years to come, its sellers heaping ironic misery on themselves and all fellow Brightonians whenever they shouted those dread four words outside the Goldstone... No, we're talking about a classic Wembley Cup Final, and those three slow-motion seconds in 1983 which all too briefly had visions of a blue-ribboned FA Cup playing behind the eyelids of every fan in the country, followed inevitably by an open-top victory bus chugging down Brighton prom.

It was the moment when Brighton, already relegated from Division One that season, were destined to pull off one of the most romantic underdog acts in FA Cup history, following up their semis victory over champs Liverpool with the scalp of high-flying Man U. A team full of internationals – Wilkins, Mühren, McQueen – humbled by a side whose leading light was Liverpool old-boy Jimmy Case. Big Ron Atkinson, the epitome of big-club flash, outshone by clown-haired Jimmy Melia, his *Saturday Night Fever* suit and curious spats.

"And Smith *must* score," bellowed Peter Jones on Radio 2...

The Seagulls' record signing from Rangers,

"The Brighton fans were always great with me, and it was funny when they called their fanzine *And Smith Must Score*. When I spoke at Steve Foster's testimonial dinner last year, and started my speech by saying 'I don't know whether Brighton supporters will remember me', they saw the funny side."
Gordon Smith

AND SMITH MUST SCORE

THE FIRST MAN

WHO'S NEXT?

50p

SCOTTISH DIV 2

Welcome to
BRIGHTON
& HOVE ALBION
F.C.

HERE WE COME?

Gordon Smith had already given Brighton a first-half lead with a cool header; but United had hit back through Wilkins and Stapleton before an 87th-minute equaliser took the final to extra-time

As the clock ticked down the final seconds of the 120th minute, Case lobbed through to Mick Robinson, who coolly tricked and turned the United stoppers, and trickled an inviting pass across the box to the unmarked Gordon Smith. The perfect man for the job. Only Gary Bailey to beat.

"People still shout at me about the miss all the time," Smith admits, "when I'm getting out of taxis or going into a shop."

United went on to win the replay 4-0.

But Smith, until recently the chief exec of the Scottish FA, remains a Brighton hero.

LUCKY

THE ASHTON GATE EIGHT

The Robins' fall from grace was bewilderingly swift. In the late 1970s they were chomping away at the top table with the likes of Manchester United and Liverpool, but after four seasons in the top flight they were relegated to Division Two. The next season they were relegated again, and in 1982 their record plummet came to an end with a sticky splashdown in the sucking financial swamp of Division Four.

"People should never forget in this city that without those eight players there would not be a Bristol City Football Club here today. I don't think they've ever been given due recognition."
Jonathan Pearce

Bristol City

The Eight remembered: sorry to say they had to let themselves go...

With several players on lucrative deals signed during the good times, the club were on the brink of liquidation. To save the club, the desperate directors pleaded with the eight on long-term contracts to walk away with half their money.

In recent years we've seen players expecting a sainthood for giving up a couple of minute's worth of their £50,000 per week to keep the tea lady on, while the Ashton Gate Eight gave up far more to save their club.

The Voluntary Redundancy Roll of Honour reads: Peter Aitken, Julian Marshall, David Rodgers, Geoff Merrick, Gerry Sweeney, Trevor Tainton, Chris Garland and Jimmy Mann. Without whom...

BRISTOL CITY

OFFICIAL MATCH DAY PROGRAMME 40p

TUESDAY, 10th JAN. 1984

BRISTOL CITY v NOTTS CO.

F. A. Challenge Cup
3rd Round (Replay)

Bristol Rovers

THE NICKNAME STRIKE DUO

The warning signs came when first two, then three, and now four of the five attackers in every team were phased out, goalscoring deemed surplus to requirement.

In the era of the lone target-man, classic strike partnerships are about as fashionable as sheepskin car coats.

Historically, nonetheless, every top club has boasted classic flick-'em-on and bang-'em-in pairings, and every other has hoped to hit paydirt with an 'almost psychic' strike duo, most often in the 'Little & Large' mould. But precious few sides have had a dynamic duo so inseparable they were given a collective nickname, like Blackburn's 'SAS' pairing of Sutton & Shearer. Palace's Wright & Bright rhymed, but no cigar. Villa's Withe & Shaw is a sprawling housing estate in Manchester... but Bristol Rovers' 'Smash & Grab' were the real deal.

Alan Warboys was 'Smash', the human battering ram. Bruce Bannister was nippy 'Grab', thriving off the scraps and knockdowns. The two Yorkshiremen used to travel down to Bristol together: they loved the family atmosphere at Eastville and the old-school dog track around the pitch.

In the 1973-74 season they scored forty between them (Smash 22, Grab 18) to take Rovers up to Division Two, where their goals immediately sparked an unbeaten run of 32 games; but it was the 8-2 at Brian Clough's Brighton (Smash 4, Grab 3) that brought about the height of 'Smash & Grab' mania in the national press – and a Bristolian craze for Wild West-style posters and scarves.

Bruce Bannister cheerfully admits that he still treasures a 'Wanted' poster of himself and his old partner in crime.

Bristol Rovers All The Way
(3.07)
(Trad. Arr. Hull—Lyrics Murphy)
Redman Music Ltd.

Rod Hull, Emu & B.R. Football Team

Produced by Phyllis Rounce
A Sound Ventures Production
℗ 1974 Sound Ventures Ltd.

EMI 2734

All rights of the producer and of the owner of the recorded work reserved. Unauthorised public performance, broadcasting and copying of this record prohibited. Made in Gt. Britain

EMI 2734B

Emu meets The Gas – to the tune of 'She'll Be Coming Round The Mountain'.

**Emu's first one in the queue on Saturday,
'Cos he watches Rovers every time they play,
And when Smash 'n' Grab are scoring,
You ought to us roaring,
You can hear the noise a hundred miles away.**

Rod Hull, Emu and the Bristol Rovers Football Team

BULLY FOR ENGLAND
It Could Never Happen Now

Third Division player... picked for England... scores on debut.

You can almost see that storyline screwed up and sailing into the wastepaper bin during a brainstorming session at *Roy of the Rovers* comic. But in 1989 it really happened to a crop-haired goalbasher from Tipton by the name of Stephen George Bull.

Bully's rise was faster than meteoric. Aged twenty, he was still working gruelling thirteen-hour warehouse shifts, seven days a week.

"When I see footballers who don't give their all I feel like telling them to get down a factory and see how they like it. It might buck their ideas up a bit," he told *Shoot!* magazine.

His manager at Tipton Town recommended Bull to West Brom, where he made just six appearances and scored three goals. Despite a 1:2 scoring ratio, Ron Saunders offloaded Bull after fifteen months – big mistake, and it gets worse – to bitter local rivals Wolves for a bargain £35,000.

Bull scored nineteen goals in his first season, even though he didn't arrive until November – and then he really got his shooting boots on in 1987-88, scoring an incredible 52 goals in all competitions as Wolves romped to the Division Four title. Just to prove it wasn't a fluke he then scored another fifty the next season as Wolves topped the Third.

The England set-up was alerted to this emerging goal machine and Bull was fast-tracked through the England Under-21 side, despite being over-age.

On Saturday 27 May 1989, England played Scotland at Hampden Park. They were 1-0 up through a Chris Waddle header when John Fashanu limped off before half-time, replaced by the bristling debutant. The man who had spent his season terrorising defences from Exeter to Darlington now did the same in front of 63,000 Scotsmen on the international stage.

With ten minutes remaining, Gary Stevens launched a long ball forward, Bull leapt up for an aerial challenge and the ball skidded off his back. In a split second he'd turned and fired a blistering shot past Jim Leighton in the Scots goal. As the tartan masses hit the exits, Bull was congratulated by Bryan Robson, Chris Waddle and Paul Gascoigne. He must have thought he was going to wake up back in that warehouse at any minute.

As it turned out, Bull's international career was short-lived, his fourteenth and final cap coming against Poland in October 1990. He paid

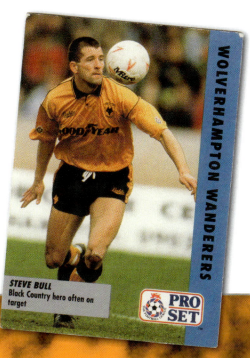

WOLVERHAMPTON WANDERERS

STEVE BULL
Black Country hero often on target

PRO SET™

the price for his loyalty, sticking with Wolves who had stalled in Division Two.

Bully wasn't the first Third Division player to pull on an England shirt – Tommy Lawton of Notts County did it in 1947-48; Coventry's Reg Matthews got five caps in the mid Fifties; Crystal Palace's Johnny Byrne played one game in the early Sixties, and Peter Taylor, also of Palace, got four caps in 1975-76 – but in the days when oversize Premier squads Hoover up all the available talent, he'll almost certainly be the last.

The Tipton Terrier: pedigree goalbanger.

"When I see footballers who don't give their all I feel like telling them to get down a factory and see how they like it. It might buck their ideas up a bit."

Burnley

THE FOOTBALL FACTORY

Back in the 1950s, visionary chairman Bob Lord hatched a cunning plan. Although a healthy fraction of Burnley's then 80,000 population was turning out at Turf Moor, it was never going to be enough to compete with so many local Division One outfits. These were the days when gate money was the overwhelming contributor to a club's coffers, with no TV, marketing or corporate cash coming in. So Lord established a production line of talent which became known as the 'Football Factory', with local players lined up by super-scout Dave Blakey, coached by the great Jimmy Adamson and bossed by Harry Potts.

Perhaps surprisingly, the factory conveyor belt wasn't in the cobbled backstreets of Burnley, but instead at 17th-century Gawthorpe Hall, outside the mill town. Just when you might have been expecting the Hovis theme, the Clarets go all *Brideshead Revisited* on you, their training ground nestling by a stunning Elizabethan country house set amongst woodlands and landscaped gardens.

The great scouts, the coaching set-up and attractive tearooms coaxed many talented youngsters to Burnley's country pile. In 1960 they became the smallest town ever to win the League. And from then on in, whenever the funds were low, they sold off a chunk of the family silver.

It seemed never ending, and allowed the club to punch way above their weight for almost two

The Clarets break for elevenses on their Elizabethan country estate.

decades; but it was a balancing act, and eventually it came crashing down in the mid 1970s when the big clubs eventually wised up on scouting, and Burnley could no longer unearth the number of rough diamonds they once had.

Just over a decade later they escaped the drop into non-League football by the skin of their teeth. But, even so, the Clarets' experience is enough to give us high expectations of a team from a similar-sized town – Wigan, say – winning next year's Premier League title with a side packed with local talent.

MIRRORCARD

BURNLEY

26

STAR SOCCER SIDES

SERIES OF 100

Buy the *Mirror* regularly to complete your series

Back row (*l. to r.*): Bellamy, Kindon, Waiters, Waldron, Mellor, Nulty and Angus. Front row (*l. to r.*): Collins, Thomas, Casper, Dobson, Probert, Fletcher and Docherty.

SCORE BOARD

URNLEY

Ground:
urf Moor,
Burnley.

FACTORY PRODUCT

Straight off the end of the Burnley conveyor belt: for equivalent modern prices, add two noughts...

Andy Lochhead	Leicester City	£70,000
Willie Morgan	Manchester Utd.	£117,000
Brian O'Neill	Southampton	£75,000
Ralph Coates	Tottenham	£190,000
Steve Kindon	Wolves	£100,000
Dave Thomas	QPR	£165,000
Martin Dobson	Everton	£300,000
Geoff Nulty	Newcastle Utd.	£120,000
Leighton James	Derby County	£310,000
Ray Hankin	Leeds Utd.	£200,000
Brian Flynn	Leeds Utd.	£175,000

C

It makes you fear
for the day when
the blanket ban
on home comforts
will be extended,
all too literally, to
the tartan vacuum's
time-honoured twin,

the car rug.

THE CAR BLANKET

There's now a warning sign by every turnstile block with a long list of all the things you're not allowed to take into the ground. Some of the banned items make a certain amount of sense: knives, guns, cats and dogs that might break free from their leash or carrying basket and run on the pitch, much to everyone's amusement. Others seem a bit petty.

They don't want you to take drinks in, purely so that you'll be forced to buy theirs. Umbrellas are banned, which is harsh when it's tipping down. Even vacuum flasks now get the big thumbs-down from the two luminous security men employed to check your ticket long before you reach the old turnstile bloke who's no longer permitted to take your money and pocket 25 per cent because he hasn't passed the necessary security checks and hospitality exams.

I wonder when the last ugly flask-related incident happened at a football match. Also, when the last first-degree burns were caused by an unfurled banner setting alight. There must surely be some horrific precedent at Leicester City as, believe it or not, all banners and flags now need to be checked and registered *before matchday* by both home and away fans, to ensure they comply with fire safety regulations.

Now they've gone and banned banners and flasks, I fear for the day when the blanket ban on home comforts will be extended, all too literally, to the tartan vacuum's time-honoured partner, the car rug.

In response to the bans, like everyone else, my dad just puts his flask in his inside jacket pocket, and ignores the jobsworths. I haven't asked, but I don't think he's considering checking his car blanket to see if it's made from flammable material. He's a rebel like that.

I like to think he takes his car-blanket lead from Villa and Birmingham City's old hardman boss, Ron Saunders – no quarter given on the training pitch, eyes like pissholes in the snow – who was never without his snug tartan companion in a blustery dugout.

That's the kind of image I'm certain me and my dad project, all tucked up in the East Stand, sipping that lovely milky plasticky coffee that only Mum can make.

Enjoy the little luxuries while you still can.

		Home					Away					
	P	W	D	L	F	A	W	D	L	F	A	Pts
Carlisle	3	1	0	0	1	2	2	0	0	4	2	6
Ipswich	3	1	1	0	2	1	1	0	0	2	1	6
Liverpool	3	1	1	0	2	0	1	1	0	2	2	5
Wolves	3	1	1	0	4	2	1	0	1	2	3	5
Everton	3	1	1	0	2	1	1	0	1	1	2	5
Arsenal	3	1	1	0	3	1	1	0	1	2	1	4
Derby	3	1	0	0	1	0	0	1	1	2	3	4
Stoke	3	1	0	0	3	1	0	1	1	0	2	4
Man. City	3	1	2	0	3	1	0	0	1	0	3	3

JEKYLL & HYDE ADVENTURES IN EUROPE

For a few years in the Sixties and Seventies, Cardiff City led a double life... a struggling Second Division side by day, European trail-blazers by night.

In those days, Welsh clubs plying their trade in the English leagues were allowed to enter the Welsh Cup. With no one bigger than Swansea, Wrexham and Bangor City standing in their way, the Bluebirds frequently made it into the European Cup Winners' Cup via this route, enjoying ten European campaigns between 1964-65 and 1976-77.

In 1967-68, emerging star John Toshack helped brush aside Shamrock Rovers, Breda and Torpedo Moscow for a semi-final meeting with Hamburg. Although the Welsh side drew 1-1 in Germany, the Germans edged the second leg in Cardiff 3-2, earning the right to lose to AC Milan in the final.

The Bluebirds began their famous 1970-71 Euro campaign by thrashing the Cypriot side Pezoporikos Larnaca 8-0 at Ninian Park, and trouncing Nantes 7-2 on aggregate. However, in the four-month winterval before their quarter-final against Real Madrid, John Toshack (already scorer of five goals in that season's competition) was sold to Liverpool. Even so, Cardiff beat the Spanish giants 1-0 in front of almost 50,000 at Ninian Park. It remains one of the Bluebirds' finest moments, despite Real turning the tide to win 2-0 back at the Bernabéu.

Sadly, Cardiff's gateway to Europe was closed and padlocked in 1996, when a rule change meant that only clubs from the Welsh leagues were allowed to enter the Welsh Cup. Ah well, at least they can concentrate on the League now...

Seventeen-year-old Nigel Rees, about to drop a perfect cross on goalscorer Brian Clark's head.

Cardiff City

CARDIFF CITY
SEASON 1970-71
OFFICIAL PROGRAMME

WEDNESDAY, 10th MARCH, 1971
VERSUS
REAL MADRID
KICK-OFF 7.30 p.m.
1/-
BLUEBIRDS
JOURNAL 5p

SOUTH WALES ECHO
REAL MADRID
SPECIAL

5p

ON TOP OF THE WORLD

Just for a moment, Carlisle United were on top of the world, Ma.

Like James Cagney's gangster, Cody Jarrett, balanced on the globe-shaped gas-holder in the classic *White Heat.*

Or like Edmund Hillary and Tenzing Norgay standing astride the previously unconquered summit of Mount Everest.

Early in the 1974-75 season, Carlisle United sat at the very top of English football – and not just in the usual geographical sense.

The ascent had begun in 1963 when Alan Ashman brought instant success to English football's North-Western outpost with successive promotions to the Third and Second Divisions – alas, only for the star boss to be whisked away by West Brom.

Carlisle trod water until Ashman's return five years later, when he quickly picked up where he'd left off. In front of gates of 8,000, with a cut-price team, he inspired promotion to the top flight. Former Carlisle boss Bill Shankly proclaimed it as "the greatest achievement in the history of football."

"The greatest achievement in the history of football." Bill Shankly

The *Match of the Day* cameras were at Stamford Bridge on the opening day of the season to see Ashman's £200,000 side shock Chelsea with a 2-0 win. The following Tuesday, United travelled to Ayresome Park and beat Middlesbrough 2-0. And then, on Saturday 24 August, 1974, they beat Tottenham 1-0 in their first home game, Chris Balderstone converting a penalty past Pat Jennings to place Carlisle at the top of the first published league tables of the season.

Sadly, they were shot down faster than Jimmy Cagney, finishing the season bottom of Division One, and by 1987 they had returned to base camp, Division Four.

But no one can ever take away the Sunday newspaper cuttings of that league table...

Carlisle United

CARLISLE UNITED

Founded: 1904; Ground:
Brunton Park; Manager:
Alan Ashman

CHRIS BALDERSTONE

PETER CARR

FRANK CLARKE

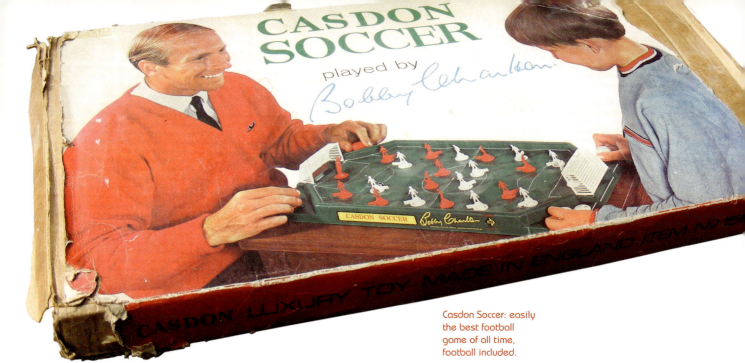

Casdon Soccer: easily the best football game of all time, football included.

CASDON SOCCER

"Casdon Soccer – played by Bobby Charlton," the box proudly proclaims. And there is Bobby, resplendent in scarlet Slazenger V-neck pully, leaving his defence wide open as the little boy (representing you and me) launches an offensive.

Bobby's grinning in a convincing enough manner, and the blurb on the underside of the box reinforces his commitment: "Bobby Charlton says it is the nearest thing to English soccer it is possible to experience in one's own home, and has spent many hours playing with his own family."

"Bobby has spent many hours playing with his own family..."

Really real: Bobby Charlton takes on brother Jackie in the 1965 FA Cup semi-final replay.

What a delicious thought, brother Jackie coming round to play with Bobby. No arguments about who would be white and who would be red.

This system of pirouetting players, ball-bearing ball and wildly undulating pitch surface was a big seller over the years, and Casdon's 'Item No. 150' went through several rebrands. Kenny Dalglish put his name to it after Bobby's retirement, and then in the Eighties it became the England Squad Soccer Game with Paul Mariner, Kevin Keegan, Bryan Robson and Garry Birtles challenging the rules of perspective by crowding round the playing surface along with two small children on the box photo.

According to the online Casdon Toy Museum, "Some say it was probably the best football game of all time" – although that bumpy pitch and the crude one-colour players both intruded into the game's proudly touted 'realism'.

I'll admit that a pitch consisting of dramatic troughs and peaks wasn't something that taxed my imagination too much. Our school pitch was sited on a field that had been employed for strip farming during medieval times. Several centuries after the enclosure of England's land our field of dreams still stubbornly consisted of ridges and furrows. A charge down the right wing was literally an up-and-down experience, and particularly small full-backs standing in particularly deep furrows could almost be hidden from view. A useful, if underhand, ambush tactic.

I don't think Bobby would have endorsed that.

Estadio Nacional: six miles west of Lisbon, deep in the Caixas Woods.

Celtic

WINNING IN A WOOD

When Celtic's 'Lisbon Lions' defeated Internazionale of Milan in the 1967 European Cup final, they could hardly have done so in more beautiful surroundings. The Hoops' unlikely 2-1 victory – which brought the trophy to Northern Europe for the first time in thirteen attempts – was played out against the elegant backdrop of Lisbon's Estadio Nacional, built on a dreamy wooded hill overlooking the Atlantic Ocean.

Dating back to World War II, the arena looked more like something left over from the Roman Empire. Bare stone benches were provided for spectators, a classy white colonnade topped the West Side, and there were no floodlights to intrude on the tree line. Neither was there an east side to the ground, which opened out on to a grand ceremonial approach, although the temporary press stand erected here gave many fans back home the impression the final was played in some humble lower-league ground.

Meanwhile, for the 10,000 trailblazing fans that made the trip, mostly in one massive motorcade, the true impact of the stadium, their first taste of foreign travel... and sunshine... was unforgettable.

Time may not have entirely bypassed this enchanted forest clearing, with plastic seats, ugly floodlights and a new sports complex diluting the idyll; but when green-and-white-hooped pilgrims look up at the *Ben Hur*-style colonnade (never mind its tacky new plastic cover), they'll still see Billy McNeill receiving the trophy like a gift from the gods.

Heaven sent: See 'Mind the Gap' for Jinky on Gods vs. Mere Mortals.

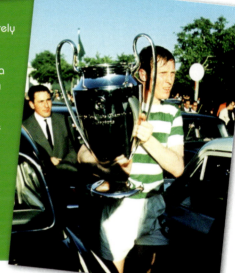

CHANCER CHAIRMEN

Before Bond villains and venture capitalists took over the world of football, it was a more parochial class of self-made men who were left to do everything from picking the team of a weekend to helping Mrs. Chairman cut the ribbon on the new Popular Side hospitality boxes. And these old chancers didn't get where they were by listening to footballers and their bloody ridiculous wage demands.

"The answer is no," was the small-time big man's catchphrase. "Take the extra three pounds a week or sling your hook, lad."

A pillar of the local community, Mr. Chairman doled out jobs for life in his palatial nut-and-bolt factory in the middle of town, drove a Jag with a carphone and had the Football League in his shiny waistcoat pocket.

"No budget for players. No new stand roof. And, no, I won't be selling up to some consortium of bloody outsiders."

Perhaps unkindly, it is Michael Knighton – a Derbyshire property trader domiciled in the Isle of Man, with a frustrated yearning to play keepy-uppy in front of the Stretford End – who is commonly remembered as the ultimate chancer to don a new club scarf over a big suit and tie. We may laugh now, but his £20 million bid for Manchester United in 1989 was a British record at the time. And it was even rubber-stamped by the United board before his backers

"I could sit down with any coaches at any level and I'd be astonished if their considered opinion was: This man is an egotist."

Michael Knighton, Carlisle United chairman-manager

got cold feet, forcing the one-time Everton apprentice to move on and attempt set up a rival global brand at Carlisle United.

True to historical form, it wasn't long before the chancer had installed himself as head coach, informed the *Sunday Mirror*, "What I am doing here has nothing to do with megalomania," and led the club into administration.

CHARLES BUCHAN'S FOOTBALL MONTHLY

It was the world's first monthly football magazine, unleashed on Britain's thrill-starved youth in September 1951 – and, despite missing the start of his debut season, *Charlie Buchan's* proved an instant hit.

Here, at last, was some colour to brighten the grey post-war landscape covered by the monochrome grown-up media. At least, bright pastel colours were daubed over black-and-white photos to vivid effect. And, in an era when kids were only expected to speak when spoken to, Charlie undid the top button of his sports jacket and did his best to address the herberts.

Even from the standpoint of sixty years on, the magazine's format is strikingly familiar, suggesting Charlie's editorial team got it pretty much right first time. There's analysis and tips from ex-pros and other enthusiastic scribblers; there's page-size posters for the bedroom wall, and interviews with players who aren't allowed to say anything.

Thumbing now through Charlie's back pages, he provides a unique window into an unrecognisable world of side partings and V-neck shirts, of rugby boots and weirdly recoloured violet irises.

From the magazine's perspective, football was steering into choppy waters when Buchan himself died in 1960, leaving the *Monthly* rudderless in the face of tidal changes such as footballers demanding a minimum wage, and suddenly not all agreeing to sport leather hair.

Personally, I never even knew who Charles Buchan was as I flicked through the pictures in the *Charles Buchan's Soccer Gift Book* annuals handed down by my elder cousins – and even now it's a bit

of a shock to discover he played for Sunderland *before* the First World War, as well as for Arsenal in the 1920s. By the time I got to consume these reprinted magazine pages third-hand, the mag itself had long dropped its originator's name from the title, struggling for an audience even in the aftermath of a World Cup victory that was sparking the rise of whole new peripheral football industries.

Still, I'm sure it's very different if you actually remember players like Liverpool's Ron Yeast, from a time when the Reds wore funny white shorts and Bill Shankly looked... exactly the same as he always did.

Although it limped on until 1974, *Football Monthly* never stood a chance against the new generation of marginally more readable comics and magazines put together by people who had heard of the Rolling Stones. Mud, even, eventually.

If it proves anything, it's probably that in retrospect every age seems like a Golden Age, provided you were ten.

Fifty years ago today: The World's Greatest Soccer Annual, yours for 52½p.

BACK HOME TO THE VALLEY

Funny bugger, home. If it came down to take it or leave it, you'd always take it; but, even then, mostly for granted.

Home is a place of routines and rituals acted out by you and yours, none of which seem all that important until they're taken away. And then you begin to miss them. The place, the people; home comforts, even the privations of the Valley's blustery terraces on a day when the east wind was blowing straight down the Thames from Siberia. And once you've left home behind – or your home has left you behind – the iron rule of football's Lost World kicks in, and there's no way you can ever go back.

That's why what happened to Charlton fans back in the Eighties and Nineties struck a chord with so many football fans from outside south-east London.

Initially, in September 1985, it was easy to sympathise with their dread feelings of homelessness, never mind their having to suffer a period in limbo playing in the hell-hole (unless you're a Palace fan, or course) of their local rivals' Selhurst Park. The Wilderness Years ticked on, the Valley's derelict stands strewn with rubble and wild shrubberies, bringing to mind nothing but images of Bradford Park Avenue's Peel Park. Even with the tantalising promise of a return home after six years, an initial refusal of planning permission, a 'Valley Party' election campaign, yet more financial troubles and the delay of building work meant prolonged agony, this time exiled to Upton Park.

But then, in December 1992, the impossible happened. The Addicks were reprieved, somehow allowed to break the immutable law of time and return to what had seemed lost forever. For fans of other clubs whose homes lay buried beneath branches of Asda, the overriding emotions were wonderment and jealousy.

Into The Valley: Ahoy! Ahoy! Land, weeds and sky...

THERE'S NO PLACE LIKE HOME.

A warm welcome back to your local ground from your local building society.

WOOLWICH

CHEAP ADMISSION

Cheap admission? Okay, we'd have to concede that this entry isn't so much funny – it's more what Radio 1 DJ Dave Lee Travis might have called a 'true story'…

In 1950, the typical price of admission to a higher-league football match was around 3 shillings (15p), or 1.7 per cent of average national weekly take-home pay.

By 1980, admission was £1.50, again around 1.7 per cent of disposable weekly income.

Moving on another thirty years, it comes as something of an eye-opener to work backwards from an average 2010 salary of around £25K – and 1.7 per cent of the average £400 per week take-home – to discover that the average price of admission rebased to traditional, twentieth-century spending levels should have been no more than £6.50.

Admission charges remain the same: well, give or take a thousand per cent hike.

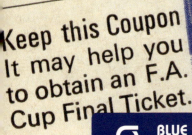

Chelsea

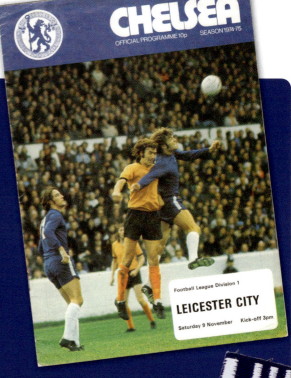

BLUE IS THE COLOUR

Ask any snugbarful of football fans of a certain age and, irrespective of club loyalties, they'll tell you 'Blue Is the Colour' was not only one of the best club football songs ever to become a *Top of the Pops* fixture, but also the first.

Ask anyone the occasion of the recording and they'll reply in a shot. It was the classic 1970 Cup Final between Chelsea and Leeds United, when a whole generation cried on the settee because the cheerful, fun-loving Goodies (Chelsea, never mind the ankle-snapping presence of Ron Harris) had fallen behind to the evil panto-villain Baddies (Leeds, although Peter Lorimer was all right).

We sang it in the playground, non-stop, on the occasion of the first ever Cup Final replay. Milkmen whistled it. Coh, I remember when Chelsea Village were all fields, me...

Disappointingly, however, 'Blue Is the Colour' actually marked Chelsea's forgotten 1972 League Cup Final failure against Stoke – and, as for originality, it was five years behind West Brom's equally unmemorable FA Cup Final single of 1967. Still, there can be no more enjoyable way to waste six minutes than to Google the title and watch British

Pathé's newsreel footage of the Chelsea boys' debut recording session. With Alan Hudson and Ossie, their arms draped in turn around every available team-mate. With Dave Webb and his unfeasible dimple. And Charlie Cooke, heading straight for the nerve-busting crate of beer... all, even according to Pathé's notes, in sunny 1970.

That's our answer, and we're sticking with it.

Fair comment: Chelsea's labelmates included Dutch one-hit wonders, Shocking Blue...

THE CLOGGER
Extinct Football Species No. 2

1966 is remembered for glorious, golden images of a grinning, red-shirted Bobby Moore, carried on his team-mates' shoulders, holding aloft the Jules Rimet trophy. However, from a non-English point of view, the tournament saw world football reach a nadir of cynical foul play. It's known across the footballing globe as the 'Dirty World Cup'.

There's a slow-motion sequence of Pelé continually being hacked down by Portuguese defenders in the Group Three game at Goodison Park. As he falls to the turf in agony with his arms outstretched to a classical score there are echoes of Sergeant Elias's harrowing death scene from *Platoon*. Thus the world's most talented player limped off the field and out of the tournament, denied his stage and his

moment for another four years.

It was a time when defenders appeared to have free rein to hoof lumps out of strikers, who were given virtually no protection from referees. Full-backs had grown tired of being made to look like monkeys by the likes of Stanley Matthews and had discovered that there was more than one way to stop a tricky winger.

The nominated hard man of each club was almost as celebrated as the star strikers they sought to bruise: Ron 'Chopper' Harris of Chelsea; Liverpool's Tommy Smith, 'The Anfield Iron'; Leeds United's Norman 'Bites Yer Legs' Hunter (and a few more besides); Nobby Stiles of Manchester United (his name was Norbert and he wore big glasses – he had to be hard); Tottenham's Dave Mackay...

There seemed to be a complicit

The nominated hard man of each club was almost as celebrated as the star strikers they sought to bruise.

understanding between roughneck and referee whereby no one could be booked in the opening five minutes of a game. He was allowed one free, 'welcoming' clog on an opposing forward's calf, 'just to let them know I'm here'.

The second, Achilles-crunching challenge might warrant a brief word of warning from the ref. The third might occasionally earn a booking, at which the defender would present a picture of outraged innocence.

By this stage, the talented striker had completely lost:
1 – stomach for the contest; or,
2 – all feeling below the waist,
  and the job was a good 'un.

Between then and now, FIFA's gradual aim has been the emasculation of the defender and the increased protection of the forward for an end product of more goals.

Look at you now, you poor modern-day defenders. Arms outstretched, as if crucified, to prove that you aren't pushing or pulling the delicate, fleet-footed little striker haring through the penalty area. Forever treading a tightrope between daring to attempt a tentative tackle or letting him walk round you and score. One split second late and you know

he'll tumble over, whether you connected with him or not. And a penalty will be won, and the game lost, and you'll have picked up your seventeenth yellow card of the season... and once, just once, you'd love to rake your studs down his shin and hear his anguished cry and watch him squirm as the ref yells: "PLAY ON!"

What Happened Next?
Clue: it involves Greavsie and the greyhound track.

What Happened Next?
Clue: it involves Norman Hunter, someone's shin and tomato ketchup.

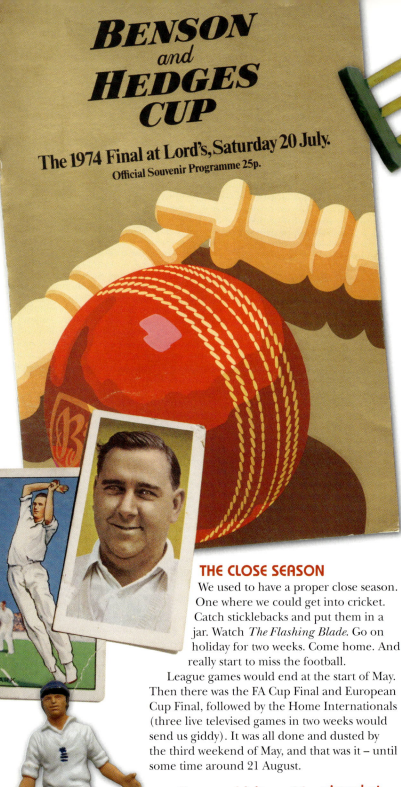

BENSON and HEDGES CUP

The 1974 Final at Lord's, Saturday 20 July.
Official Souvenir Programme 25p.

Cricket So Boring Fielder Finds Time To Go Fishing Shock.

THE CLOSE SEASON

We used to have a proper close season. One where we could get into cricket. Catch sticklebacks and put them in a jar. Watch *The Flashing Blade*. Go on holiday for two weeks. Come home. And really start to miss the football.

League games would end at the start of May. Then there was the FA Cup Final and European Cup Final, followed by the Home Internationals (three live televised games in two weeks would send us giddy). It was all done and dusted by the third weekend of May, and that was it – until some time around 21 August.

You wouldn't want to miss what 'Wantaway' Clive Goodyear had

allegedly denied this morning...

The close season has now been nibbled away at both ends and is threatening to disappear altogether.

May is all about the play-offs, while the sprawling UEFA Europa League kicks off its Qualifying Round on 1 July, and the Football League usually times its 'Big Kick-off' in the first week of August.

What was once three months is now one. Weren't football's greedy boys ever taught that you can have too much of a good thing?

CLUBCALL

We don't always recognise how lucky we are, to have, in the internet, an instant, 24-7, universally available source of dubious information about our favourite club.

Back in the Eighties and Nineties, by comparison, we were still trapped in a lengthy tailback waiting to join the Information Superhighway at Junction 1. And while we waited, we dialled up Clubcall a bare minimum of three times a day. Just in case, like…

All was well if we happened to live or work within radio range of our hometown, but wander further afield than the last newsagent to stock the Blackthorpe *Gazette* or the Everpool *Examiner*, and we were knackered for the kind of rumour and tittle-tattle that would never make a regional sporting news round-up on TV.

It was the sheer unavailability of the info that made it so tantalising. You wouldn't want everyone else to know that Carlton Fairweather had a hammy, would you? – not if you were still thinking he might be playing Saturday. You wouldn't want to miss what 'Wantaway' Clive Goodyear had allegedly denied this morning – or boss Bobby Gould's counter-denials of any new striker rumours. Ahh, the rumours...

The Clubcall service came as a blessing for all exiled fans, and for many more trapped at work without up-to-the-minute info, but with the benefit of a free phone to avoid the disgraceful premium call rates.

At the end of the line – literally – was a local newspaper stringer (or at least an Ansafone recording of him) summing up the back-page stories from yesterday's evening paper. To deliver value for money, he also used to make up juicy filler on the spot, and read it out. S-l-o-w-l-y.

"Hello... and it's a big... Pilgrims... welcome... to your exclusive... front-line... Clubcall service for... Plymouth Argyle... Football... Club.

"Listen to... Clubcall... for all the latest... news... and... information..."

Because we were paying by the minute.

COFFER

The chances are, if you wore football-related jewellery in the medallion-man 1970s, then it was made by Coffer Sports.

In the days when no item of bling was complete without a little football badge, Northampton- and London-based Coffer were the jewellers to a nation of kids.

They had a wonderful range of pendants, identity bracelets, rings, sew-on patches, lapel badges and key-rings, all tastefully* crowned with enamel club badges. The epitome of mid-Seventies cool was undoubtedly Leeds United's iconic 'Smiley' necklace, which somehow almost atoned for the 'Scowling' sins of McQueen, Bremner, Giles and Hunter.

A&R Coffer Ltd. started up in the souvenir business just after the war and early boosts to the, er, coffers included the Coronation of Queen Elizabeth II and Beatlemania. However, after England's World Cup win in 1966, football soon overtook royal shindigs and pop idols.

"Metal club badges are probably our biggest selling line," Arthur Coffer explained to the *Football League Review* in 1973. "For many fans the collecting of these lapel badges has developed into almost a cult. But rosettes are not far behind. We make more than half a million of them a year, in all sizes and all colours, and I cannot see them losing their appeal even though there are signs that the soccer souvenir market is slowly changing."

Perhaps realising that the 'slow change' was towards replica shirts, Coffer entered the competitive world of kit manufacture in the early Eighties, producing strips for Swindon Town, Bristol City and Rochdale. And then, sadly, they went bust.

"This highly successful souvenir depicts enamelled colourful crests of all leading clubs in a high-quality product. Popular with male and female supporters. Attractively carded."

The 'Smiley' necklace

* According to our taste in the Seventies.

Enamoured with enamel: last one with a space on their denim jacket is a cissy.

COMIC UNDERDOGS

Football's comic-strip heroes of the 1960s-80s split neatly into two categories. In one camp were the world-beating supermen in green-and-purple chevrons who scored pile-driving goals every week, on the way to Skillchester Athletic's 25th consecutive championship. They were okay for the Liverpool fans who expected success every season, and for children with healthy aspirations.

**"Gah, the cross is too high. But wait...
The half-naked flanker is leaping to head it.**

No... to volley it into the net..."

And then there were the more improbable heroes, the impossible underdogs aimed at kids who had realised early on that football would always be less about winning than about moaning and cursing and hoping.

Now maybe it was just me, but I always felt Billy Dane out of *Scorcher's* 'Billy's Boots' – your typical football-obsessed pre-teen, born with two left feet – was somehow *undeserving* when he found ex-England ace 'Dead-Shot' Keen's magical old boots in his gran's attic. Bring on the bullies, I used to mutter, to pinch Billy's boots for the umpteenth time. And this time let him be exposed as a fraud in the District Schools Cup Final, and *not* get his magic boots back at half bloody time.

I wasn't keen on my heroes being successful, let alone averagely lucky. Nipper Lawrence fitted the bill, an orphan who lived on the bleak dockside of Blackport with his landlady and pig-ugly bulldog, Stumpy. Penned in superb DirtyVision to signify Northernness and social squalor, times were hard for Nipper – but then

he went and got picked for England and started wearing a white suit. It could hardly have been more upsetting if the prison team in *Tiger's* 'Lags Eleven' had escaped and won the Costa del Crime Premiera Liga.

The *Valiant's* 'Raven On The Wing' was drawn in the same sooty style as *Scorcher & Score's* 'Nipper', with a healthy dash of social injustice thrown into the mix as our favourite lightning-fast gypsy boy risked injury and ridicule playing barefoot for Highboro United. So what did he want? Pity?

I was just as uncomfortable with 'The Boy in the Velvet Mask' out of *Roy of the Rovers* comic. Alan Hemmings was the son of a one-time England goalie paralysed in the line of duty, and was understandably forbidden from having anything to do with football. It wasn't enough to stop him donning a superhero mask and turning out for Lynchester United.

Still, I couldn't help feeling the Hemmings lad was an attention-seeking showboater rather than a genuine underdog – and that was one accusation that no one could ever throw at my all-time *Scorcher* favourite, 'The Kangaroo Kid', who was brilliant and heartbreakingly rubbish in just the right proportions…

Second Division Redstone Rovers were on a pre-season tour of Australia when they spotted a feral teen frolicking with a flock of kangaroos in the outback. When he clocked the half-naked wildman's party tricks with a stray practice ball, manager Barney Patch had only one thought: Secret Weapon.

The Kid's League debut: a voice in the crowd: "Gah, the cross is too high. *But wait*, the wild-haired substitute is leaping to head it. No… to *volley* it into the net…"

The Kid raises a powerful forepaw and punches the sky. Kangaroo buddies Tarkil and Darga go ape in the dugout.

Raised as a marsupial in a pouchful of regular joeys, yet destined to take the steps of Wembley in a single bounce. Now that's what I call rags to riches.

Tommy's Troubles: the young striker's main worry was a plot straight out of 'Billy's Boots'.

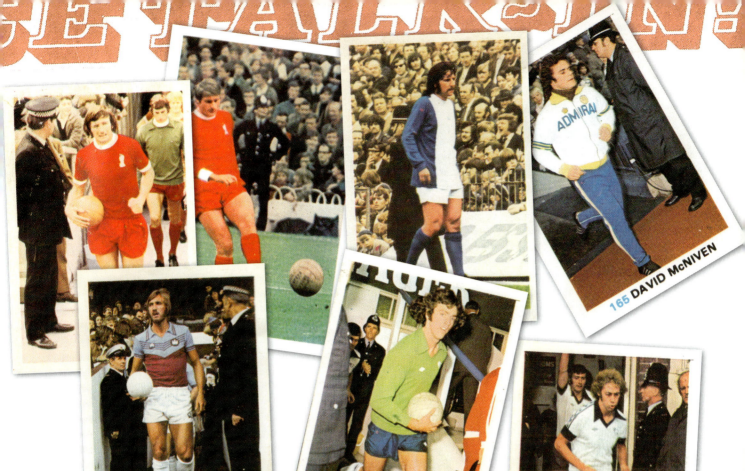

165 DAVID McNIVEN

363 BILLY BONDS

123 GRAHAM MOSELEY

117 CHARLIE GEORGE

THE COPPER

Although the football sticker album had been knocking about for years on the Continent and even in South America, it wasn't until after the wake-up call of 1966 that anyone thought of introducing the idea to Britain. Incredibly, even though we'd had football cards taking up the cigarette-card slack in the final years of the Fifties, not a single manufacturer thought to produce a card or sticker set to mark the little matter of England staging the World Cup Finals.

When FKS finally produced their *Wonderful World of Soccer Stars* album and sticker set for a regional trial run in 1967, it's as if they were casting around for a method to stamp some Britishness on the very European feel of stickers, set against our good old cardboard oblongs. Deciding against introducing any actual stickiness to the self-styled sticker format – cue a million albums ruined by fumbly fingers trying to 'apply adhesive here' along the thin top strip on the reverse of the paper stickers – they apparently opted instead to include in the photo backgrounds as many good old-fashioned Bobbies as possible.

Dome-helmeted coppers staunchly patrolled the tunnel and touchlines, clearly watching the match instead of even pretending to keep an eye on the crowd. These were uniquely un-European football stickers, full of muddy kickaround action from old agency stock with cut-and-pasted heads – plus that vital ingredient of reassuring, trustworthy PC Plod.

It could never happen today, where all that's allowed into a card shot is a player's head and shoulders, with even club colours and badges blanked out unless all the correct merchandising licences have been fully paid up.

And even if the odd fluorescent-jacketed cop did manage to sneak into shot, the effect just wouldn't be the same, with contemporary RoboBobs all weighed down by visors and pepper sprays, side-handled batons and laptop computers in the face of a silent, all-seated crowd of club clients.

There were no heat-sensitive cameras showing up in the background of even the most offensive perm and 'tache moments of the Seventies and Eighties; no helicopters taking to the air at the first sign of Arsenal's Peter 'Horror' Storey.

Cops on the Kop: some people will do anything to get a decent view of the match.

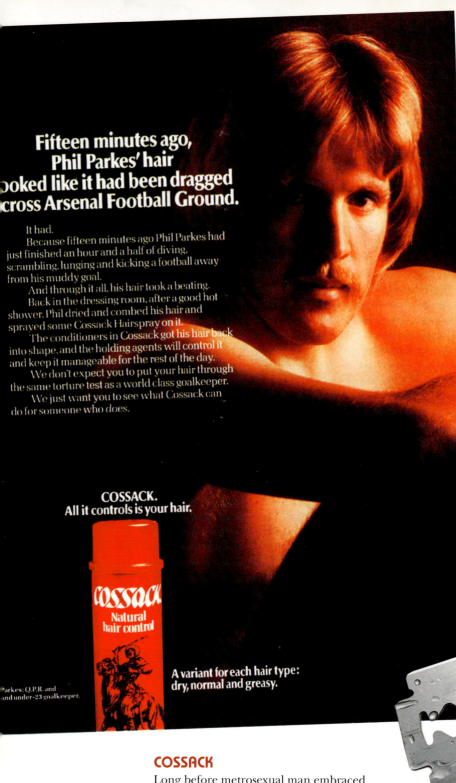

Fifteen minutes ago, Phil Parkes' hair looked like it had been dragged cross Arsenal Football Ground.

It had.

Because fifteen minutes ago Phil Parkes had just finished an hour and a half of diving, scrambling, lunging and kicking a football away from his muddy goal.

And through it all, his hair took a beating.

Back in the dressing room, after a good hot shower, Phil dried and combed his hair and sprayed some Cossack Hairspray on it.

The conditioners in Cossack got his hair back into shape, and the holding agents will control it and keep it manageable for the rest of the day.

We don't expect you to put your hair through the same torture test as a world class goalkeeper.

We just want you to see what Cossack can do for someone who does.

COSSACK.
All it controls is your hair.

cossack
Natural
hair control

A variant for each hair type:
dry, normal and greasy.

Parkes: Q.P.R. and
and under-23 goalkeeper.

COSSACK

Long before metrosexual man embraced toiletry and grooming products up to and including moisturiser, defoliant and facial scrub, advertisers were forced to approach the subject with extreme caution.

In 1977, the average male half of the bathroom cabinet will have housed the following:

1 – A plastic green bottle of Brut 33, a birthday present from two years ago (acceptable, because Henry Cooper and Kevin Keegan advertised it);

2 – A small, tapering, white plastic bottle of Old Spice with a greening, crusty 'gold' lid, a Christmas present from five years ago (acceptable, because of all the surfing);

3 – One of those deadly old 'safety' razors where you had to unscrew the handle until the blunt, rusty razor could be extracted and a new one carefully pushed in;

4 – A three-quarters empty bottle of TCP in case of bad shaves, wasp stings or cycling accidents;

5 – Nothing else.

Now Cossack wanted to introduce hairspray to our cabinets. But how to get us defensive, pre-blokey teenagers used to the idea when it appeared to be the first step on the road to spraying our handkerchiefs with lavender and mincing around like John Inman?

The cunning solution was to employ Queens Park Rangers and England Under-23 goalie Phil Parkes, who only resorted to 'hair control' because he had "just finished an hour and a half of diving, scrambling, lunging and kicking a football away from his muddy goal."

Surely, there was no way dishy, auburn-moustached Phil would ever endorse anything dead puffy?

"Back in the dressing room, after a good hot shower, Phil dried and combed his hair and sprayed some Cossack hairspray on it…"

The 'safety' razor: facial lacerations were easy to hide with tufts of bloody toilet tissue.

But just in case anyone thought showering sportsmen and attention to looks jeopardised Cossack's status as a true man's product, best name it after a bunch of hard bastards from the southern steppes of Asiatic Russia, renowned for their horsemanship and military excellence.

Rest assured, one squib of 'greasy hair formula' swordsman's sex glue on your barnet and you'd be quite literally knocking the ladies dead.

44

COTTON

It's the sensual associations that come bundled with cotton that make it such a rich source of minor, if largely subconscious, pleasure.

Ahh, the smell of a new cotton T-shirt being pulled on over your head on a Friday night. The slow fade of a favourite shirt, laundered a hundred times by your mum. Cotton next to the skin – warm against the winter cold, cool in summer...

In 150 years, the only negatives against cotton were an association with hippie cheesecloth and, ah yes, the institutionalised horrors of the slave trade.

Cotton isn't just perfect for clothes because it's easy to take care of and to wash. It's soft because it's made out of perfectly natural fluff. And it's cheap because the fluff grows on trees.

And so some tiresome bean counter inevitably decided to put about the idea that cotton is altogether second rate. Wear it for sports and it apparently now soaks up sweat in a way that you wouldn't want it to be soaked up. Cotton isn't stretchy enough, and it needs ironing, unlike a certain artificial wonder-fabric. They even tried to convince us that shell-suit bottoms were cooler and more comfortable than jeans.

Now, it just so happens that while cotton is cheap, polyester is cheaper. So much cheaper, it's practically free.

Polyester is an artificial plastic made from the acids and alcohol produced when you torch petroleum – in other words, from exhaust fumes.

Polyester is hard wearing primarily because it's hard. It's rough to the touch, keeps you cold in winter and hot in summer. Wear it in summer, or for sports, and it will make you smell like you've been dead for a week.

Once a shirt manufacturer has successfully cooked up a small blob of pungent plastic, all they need to do is dye it, extrude it into plastic yarn and run it through a plastic knitting machine. Then children in Southeast Asia are generally used to sew the things together. Their labour is cheap.

Manufacturers are shy about letting on how much it costs to turn their little blob of oily cack (or eight recycled Coke bottles) into a new plastic shirt, allegedly hiding the figures in shame from even from the most hard-nosed City analysts.

Polyester is an artificial plastic made from the acids and alcohol produced when you torch petroleum – in other words, from exhaust fumes.

Let's guess it costs a manufacturer around 10p to make a replica shirt. Ooh, but then there are labour costs to factor in, and the balancing eco cost of shipping old rubbish halfway across the world. Call it 20p, all in?

Let's then guess that the manufacturers sell the shirts to our football clubs for around £10.00. At that point, clubs are able to factor in the revenue they make by using their players and fans as human advertising space, which subsidises the net cost of a replica shirt. And then they sell them to us for £39.99.

You might think the Football Association, as part of their remit of looking after football on the fans' behalf, would be keeping an eye on any potential profiteering. But, unforgivably, the FA themselves, along with four top British league clubs, were among thirteen businesses found guilty of illegal price-fixing by the UK Office of Fair Trading in 2003. Ten were fined, including many leading sportswear firms and retailers, eventually paying fines totalling £16 million.

Strange, but we don't remember the price of replica football shirts subsequently being slashed to tuppence.

Coventry City

Let's all sing together,
Play up Sky Blues,
While we sing together we will never lose.
Proud Posh or Cobblers,
Oysters or anyone,
They can't defeat us,
We'll fight 'til the game is won.

The Sky Blue Song
Tune: The Eton Boating Song; Lyrics: Jimmy Hill

SKY BLUE REVOLUTION

Best remembered by the kids of the Seventies, Eighties and Nineties for his thirty-year run as the opinionated presenter of BBC's *Match of the Day*, Jimmy Hill is just as often recalled with a shake of the head by older fans who think of him as the bolshie type/player of principle who stood up and demanded a minimum wage for himself and his mukkas around the dawn of the Sixties. And yet in-between times, as manager of Coventry City, Hill undertook an influential, self-proclaimed football revolution for which he's rarely given credit.

Taking over late in 1961, the great moderniser began a PR onslaught, introducing Britain's first continental-style one-colour kit, changing the club nickname from boring Bantams to mod-sounding Sky Blues, and leading the Third Division also-rans on a six-season romp up the leagues.

"Between us, we took excitement into the Third Division towns throughout England," he wrote in his 1966 New Year programme notes. "We turned League matches into Cup ties, drab monotony into fervent patriotism. The strains of 'The Sky Blue Song' and the chants of 'Coventry City Cha-Cha-Cha' often woke up local fans to reply just as noisily..."

Hill introduced the Sky Blue Express supporters train, and organised the first big-screen beambacks to Highfield Road as early as 1965. He rode a white horse around the Highfield Road pitch – mercifully his only Lady Godiva reference – personally overseeing the doling out free Bovril and tea at half-time from Sky Blue backpacks.

"We had started a revolution which was to reverberate around football. Some clubs wagged jealous tongues and ridiculed our so-called gimmicks; some journalists, too, who had willingly used our kinky stories in the headlines..."

He arranged 'pop and crisp' days for local kids to meet the stars, and took the lead in corporate entertainment, signing up 'leading local business people' as Vice President's Club members. Before the match and at half-time, Sky Blue Radio rocked the tinny PA system: yet another famous first that was destined to catch on.

Job done, Hill quit for a career in the hot new arena of TV football two days before the Sky Blues' debut in the top flight.

"The strains of 'The Sky Blue Song' and chants of 'Coventry City Cha-Cha-Cha' often woke up opposition fans..."

Part of the Union: from minimum wage to £100K a week, all thanks to Jimmy Hill...

COVENTRY CITY
OFFICIAL PROGRAMME
SIX PENCE

Crystal Palace

THE FEDORA

Managers today don't wear fedoras, and they don't suck habitually on big cigars. Not like Big Mal.

They don't get to change the club nickname, either. 'The Glaziers' was old-fashioned in Malcolm Allison's urgent opinion; he much preferred Benfica's nickname of 'The Eagles'. So he nicked it, as soon as he took over at Selhurst Park in 1973.

The flamboyant new boss also liked the look of Barcelona's kit – red-and-blue stripes were groovier than claret and blue, due a rest after 68 years. Well, the strategy had worked wonders at Man City a few years earlier, when Mal had switched them into AC Milan's red-and-black stripes, and lifted the European Cup Winners' Cup.

Only Mal could have received an FA disrepute charge for inviting notorious actress Fiona Richmond to share the team bath back in 1976. And then he kicked off the next season early, bossing a team of Playboy Club bunny girls against a team of assorted chimps and orang-utans from the film *Battle for the Planet of the Apes*.

Best of all, Mal employed a hypnotist-psychic called Romark (Ronald Markham, strictly speaking) to lift an ancient curse on Selhurst Park. However, the pair fell out, and the illusionist ended up helping Lawrie McMenemy's Southampton side beat Third Division Palace in the 1976 FA Cup semi – or maybe they were just destined for glory...

"I was in the bath with all the players and we heard the whisper that she was coming down the corridor. We all leapt out and hid, because we knew there'd be photos and that wouldn't go down too well. Malcolm and Fiona dropped everything and got in the bath."

Terry Venables

Psychic illusionists today don't prove their skills by driving blindfold through Ilford town centre. And they don't crash into the back of a police van after 20 yards...

vocalion

The outrageous exploits of Britain's most liberated lady ...!

Miss Fiona Richmond

James Clarke's soundtrack from the film 'Hardcore' (1977) and selected music from the films 'Exposé' (1975) and 'Let's Get Laid!' (1977)

HARDCORE

Mal's giant-killing fedora claimed the scalps of Leeds, Chelsea and Sunderland in the '76 FA Cup.

22
23
24

CRYSTAL PALACE F.C.

CUFF CLUTCHING

In the late Sixties and early Seventies, the trend for long-sleeved shirts led to an outbreak of cuff clutching.

Denis Law was mostly to blame. Whether straining to reach for a diving header, performing an acrobatic signature scissor-kick or saluting one of his many goals, Law always kept the white cuff of his red (or navy) sleeve stretched into his palm, clutched as tightly as a pushchair-bound infant grips his security blanket.

But a million mothers' chorused complaints of "You're STRETCHING it!" soon dried up when the cuff-clutching movement suffered two body blows: first , the trend for short-sleeved football shirts returned, and then chief protagonist, The Lawman, sadly hung up his boots after the 1974 World Cup.

Even the statue outside Old Trafford – the 'Trinity' which set Law on a plinth with George Best and Bobby Charlton – portrays two inches of bronze cuff tucked under three fingers of his skyward-pointing hand.

Cue a million mothers' chorused complaints of

"You're S-T-R-E-T-C-H-I-N-G it!"

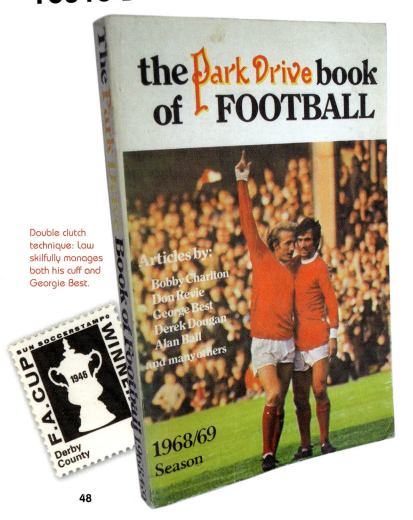

Double clutch technique: Law skilfully manages both his cuff and Georgie Best.

CUP FINAL BUILD-UP

It's difficult now to place exactly where the FA Cup Final used to sit in our calendar of red-letter days. It wasn't quite up there with Christmas or a birthday, but it was bigger than Bonfire Night and the first day of the summer holidays, and made the frankly overrated Easter seem a very sick puppy. More than merely the climax of the season, it was also a super-rare chance to see a live match on TV.

It was one of those days when you'd wake up with a rush of anticipation...

The trip to the shop to buy essential supplies had to be made early to avoid missing any of the extensive TV build-up. I always considered a pint of milk to be the Cup Final drink, as players were always interviewed slugging cow juice after the match; the *Radio Times* Cup Final edition was also a must – along with a starter, (candy shrimps), a main course (Monster Munch) and dessert (Mars bar).

The *Radio Times* would be arranged on one side of the telly, and the Cup Final edition of *Shoot!* on the other, and then – with the game still five hours away – we'd be ready for the off, flicking between *Cup Final Grandstand* and *Cup Final World of Sport*.

Cup Final It's a Knockout saw Stuart Hall's usual brand of physical tomfoolery contested between supporters of the two competing clubs with the odd celebrity fan and ex-player thrown in. *Cup Final Mastermind* was another regular BBC programme given a going-over with the silver polish for the big day, along with *Jim'll Fix It* and *A Question of Sport*. Meanwhile, ITV adapted a football blooper-laden *It'll Be Alright on the Day*, hosted by the supernaturally smug Denis Norden, and *Cup Final Punchlines*, a game show patrolled by former comedian Lennie Bennett.

Every now and again we'd catch up with the teams 'relaxing' in their hotels, getting to see Gordon Hill do his Norman Wisdom impression, and the Manchester United players laugh nervously (hey, maybe Southampton have got a chance, after all). This was not to be confused with our chance to 'meet' the stars (not forgetting the two subs, slightly resentful, mooching around like spare parts), and to examine them for signs of heroic potential.

It was one of those days when you'd wake up with a rush of anticipation...

As Wembley Way began to fill up, Fred Dineage performed saintly acts as the 'Man in the Crowd', handing over miraculous freebies to the ticketless fans who looked the most down in the dumps. And so the teams would finally leave their hotels, cheered on to the coaches by hotel staff and local kids, their progress followed by helicopter as they were escorted through the North London streets toward the Twin Towers.

And the comedians... so many comedians. Eric Morecambe. Mel Smith. Billy Connolly. Griff Rhys Jones and Pamela Stephenson, too. The football signalled an open season for what used to be called Male Chauvinist Pigs, and worse. Warren Mitchell got to 'do' Alf Garnett. Michael Barrymore got to 'do' John Barnes. Freddie Starr dressed as Hitler and goose-stepped around the hallowed centre-circle, and we were all treated to highlights of the Women's FA Cup Final.

After the teams emerged from their Cup Final coaches in their Cup Final suits, they'd stroll out onto the Cup Final pitch to be collared by Martin Tyler for a 'quick word'.

Just as you were beginning to flag under the strain of so much build-up, Jimmy Tarbuck and Gloria Hunniford's *Celebrity Party* would reach fever pitch – with the arrival of Paul Robinson out of *Neighbours*.

At last, it was time for 'Abide With Me', and soon the teams, led by their managers, would stride from the tunnel in their posh new Cup Final tracky tops, and we were only a royal handshake away from kick-off.

With apologies to Brian Moore, we went along with two-thirds of the viewing public in our house, and it always had to be the BBC for the actual match.

The Monster Munches were long gone, the milk bottle was empty, and the *Radio Times* had fallen down behind the telly.

Let's hope it's a cracker...

d

DIY

DIY is all about originality, personalised team colours and sending out an individual message. Like hot pants, mini-skirts and cotton football tops, it's not just a sad old nostalgia kick but a groovy retro look for the 21st century. You dig?

Knitting was an ancient craft not dissimilar to today's recycling craze, and just as popular in the olden days. It involved taking a pile of fluff found on a sheep's back, twisting it into 300 yards of yarn and then painstakingly twisting this single length into a giant knot shaped like a bobble hat.

Why buy a baseball cap 'off the shelf' (or off a dodgy stall outside the ground) unless you're attempting to mimic the street style of an octogenarian Alabaman redneck? Get yourself a nice bobble instead. You might not be able to knit it yourself, but your gran will set you up with two cardboard rings and another 300 yards of wool and you can feel the DIY joy of spending seven creative hours winding yourself a giant fluffy bobble as big as your head.

Don't throw away those football socks, shorts and shirts just because they're ripped or worn out. Get darning with a needle and some not-quite-the-right-colour thread, and your mum will soon reassure you that they're 'as good as new'.

Why not crochet yourself an adult-sized football romper suit in your club colours?

Why buy a nylon scarf emblazoned with an 'unofficial' version of your team badge (a clip-art Ram, a clip-art Shrimp, a clip-art, er, Gill?) and an unimaginative phrase such as 'Up the Blues', or 'Gillingham FC'.

Instead, get knitting and purling (ask Gran) and you too can look a proper bobby-dazzler in a big stripy scarf with a custom message direct from your heart. Something like 'Up' in one white stripe, and 'For The Cup' in another. Or 'Frankie Prince Ate My Hamster'. The sky's the limit. You'll probably end up crocheting yourself a complete adult football romper suit in your club colours.

And, finally, don't even consider one of those off-the-stall banners on a flimsy balsa-wood stick, which in all probability hasn't even passed its Health & Safety flammability test.

Simply strip a sheet off the bed, make with the felt-pens and bingo! NORMAN BITES YER LEGS.

Up For The... Cup: Roberto Mancini and family.

TRACK SUITS
Millington

DANGEROUS TRAINING

"There was no specialist goalkeeper training then," Gordon Banks explained to us. "I had to do the outfield training. Run the laps, do all the exercises, and then we'd finish up with five-a-side..."

Banksy wasn't recalling ancient history for our benefit, but a time just before he won the World Cup with England. A dark age when footballers were put through training regimes that would make a modern-day risk assessment officer fall backwards off his chair.

"When I was at Rangers, we used to dread going to Gullane beach and just running and running and running. Jock Wallace and John Greig would push you hard. Along with all the running on the beach and the sand dunes, they used to make us run up what was called

'Murder Hill'...

"But because we didn't have an actual training ground then," Gordon added delightedly, "we had to play on the car park! I couldn't dive about on that surface so I didn't go in goal, I played outfield!"

In the early Sixties, many clubs didn't have a training pitch, and would utilise whatever they had to get their players fit. As well as a car park, most clubs were also in possession of a set of good old-fashioned circus strongman weights that looked more likely to give you a double hernia than bulging biceps. And a trainer would think nothing of sending the most valuable members of the playing staff running up and down concrete terraces or the steep steps of the stands.

But in these times of £30 million strikers, you can't really take a chance on them tripping on step Y and finally rolling to a halt on step D.

Best let them out for a gentle trot on the soft, lush turf of the training ground, or invite them into the air-conditioned gym for a spot of TRX Suspension Training. Safer still, a virtual spin round the block on the Trixter Xdream bike, to keep the insurance premiums down.

"The last exercise of the day was just running up and down it and, on the last leg of it, we had to run to the top, come half way down, go round a pole and then go back up to the top. Some of the boys would be on their hands and knees trying to get back to the top."

Craig Paterson, Rangers survivor, 1982-86

Great pretender: the Argentine's wily guile seemingly knew no bounds.

"I'd played for the England Under-23s a couple of times, but I'd never met anybody like that before. It was a different world, the way they played – standing on your toes and catching hold of your shirt when the ball was nowhere near you. One thing they did do was get really angry – just to put you off your game. They were very clever with it. Niggly wasn't the word for it."

As told to us by Don Rogers, Swindon Town

Vicious hair tug

"British competitors agree it's smart to shy away from any goodwill gesture," Trevillion suggests. "A pat on the cheek will, if the hand is held rigid, carry a violent slap. A playful hair ruffle can – if the fingers are suddenly closed tight – result in a vicious hair tug." That Alan Gilzean should think himself lucky.

Sickening ear dig

There's no room for complacency, even for the sprightly Spurs inside-forward: "The friendly face pat will, if one finger is bent inwards, produce a sickening dig in the inner ear."

Stiff-arm in the face

Each alarming accusation is proven to be accurate by Trevillion's own accompanying illustrations of biffs, tugs and pokes. Best get your retaliation in first, or you'll end up with a stiff-arm in the face like Wolves' Dave Wagstaffe, who suffered a rip to the inside of his right cheek (see 'After the Match', when you can read all about it in the *Sporting Star*).

The imaginary gash

Look out for the clever shirt-jerk manoeuvre which befell Celtic's Jimmy Johnstone, which resulted in Jinky apparently delivering a Glasgow kiss to the oppo's nose. The feigned injury was then attended to by a crooked trainer, who was ready to stick a plaster across the imaginary gash.

Cheats' charter

But surely the all-time lowest of the low must be German netminder Sepp Maier and his cunning invention of giant goalie gloves big enough to rest against both posts at once, effectively blocking all shots at goal. A version of this 'cheats' charter' was later imported to Blighty and used by fun-loving fans as amusing 'foam hands'.

DASTARDLY FOREIGN TRICKS

If you're thinking of travelling abroad this summer, best bear in mind the warnings of this chilling article ripped out of the *Sunday Express* some time around the dawn of the 1970s. Devised and drawn by cartoonist Paul 'Roy of the Rovers' Trevillion, 'Watch These Dirty Dodges' detailed a whole catalogue of liberties being taken by Continentals – and, rest assured, we're not just talking away goals counting double.

"Europeans work well on the blind side of referees, especially in crowded goalmouths. They nudge you off balance, pull your shirt, pinch and grab. They tackle more effectively with their hands than their feet – they should wear shin pads on their arms!"

Alan Gilzean, Spurs and Scotland.

Derby County

BRING BACK CLOUGHIE

Do you remember this? Whatever happened to that? Bring back the other! To anyone who isn't up to their neck in British football, it might seem we're all obsessed with the distant past. But that isn't an accusation anyone could aim at the Derby County faithful back in 1973, when fans and players worked together in a rare pincer movement, desperately attempting to turn back the clock just a matter of days.

The object of their concern, almost inevitably, was Ol' Big 'Ead – the manager who had led the club to the Second Division championship, then the First Division title and the semi-final of the European Cup.

Events were set in motion when Brian Clough and his assistant Peter Taylor sensationally resigned their positions following the Rams' 1-0 away win against Manchester United. The idea was a grand double-bluff, forcing a power struggle designed to dislodge director Jack Kirkland and egotistical chairman Sam Longson, who resented his protégé's growing media celebrity.

While the players went on lightning strike, fans produced a snowstorm of stickers, posters and leaflets (remember banda sheets? Whatever happened to banda sheets? Bring back banda sheets!) in support of the 'Bring Back Cloughie and Taylor' campaign.

But with Longson revelling in his re-emergence as top dog, there was no going back on what Clough called "the worst decision I ever made" – now not just the stuff of legend, but fiction and film, too.

DIVISIONS ONE TO FOUR

It was a simple, effective system of nomenclature which could hardly have been bettered. Divisions One to Four. Perfect. Every division did exactly what it said on the tin.

Division One was the top league, in which the finest teams could be found competing for overall top spot in a four-league system. Accordingly, the side that finished in first place were known as League Champions. It didn't trouble anyone when Division One was referred to by its alternate title, the First Division, because only a fool would manage to confuse the number 1 with any lower-ranked league.

Unfortunately, thanks to the instigation of an exclusive, breakaway league in the 1990s, we're all now made to sound like fools on a weekly basis.

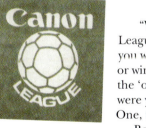

"What do you mean, you 'won the League Championship'? Do you mean you were English League champions, or winners of the Championship, the 'old' Second Division? Or were you champions of League One, the 'old' Division Three?"

Best follow the lead of fans down the leagues, and revert unilaterally to the previous, working system, in an unspoken pact never again to waste time using the suffix 'old' before a named division.

Let the sponsors stand in front of their logo boards and call the leagues whatever they like. Meanwhile, Division Three is, and will always be, the third tier of English football, aka the Third Division...

27	DEC. 4	11	18	25/27	TOTAL
			X		7
		X	X		11
					2
					5
			X		5
					6
		X	X		7
	X				5
	X				5
X					6
	X				10
X	X				10
					4
					6
			X	X	8
		X			8
X	X				6
	X				9
					7
		X			9
	X				8
X					6
			X		8
X					2
X					6
		X			10
		X	X		6
					4
	X				6
					6
X					7
					7
		X			6
	X				2
	X		X		6
X				X	6
X					4
X	X				2
X					2
					2
7	11	9	10	12	12

DOING THE POOLS

Doing the pools was a bit like surviving on the *Titanic*. Men did it by skill, women and children by luck.

The idea was simple. You might say deceptively so. All you had to do was run your eye – or pin, if you were a lady – down the list of Saturday's matches in the coupon's left-hand column, and mark with a Biro 'X' in the grid of tiny squares those that would result in a draw. Correctly forecast seven or eight in a single line of guesses, and you'd be set up for life. By the mid Seventies, the record pools win had topped half a million: enough to buy your very own Bob Latchford off Birmingham City.

Today, it's hard to imagine how central the pools were to our hopes and dreams, before the old companies were crippled by the first skill-free spin of the National Lottery machine in 1994 – ironically, the very weekend of the highest ever pools win: £2,924,622. The fascination and intrigue surrounding the pools was once equivalent to all that generated today by fixed-odds betting, online gambling, the National Lottery, *Big Brother* and *The X Factor* combined. The ultimate promise was for one undeserving, talentless nobody to be elevated into the big time for doing bugger-all. You didn't even have to do a karaoke turn to get to Spend! Spend! Spend!

Pools culture used to run deep. Everyone was in hot pursuit of a 'divvie', desperate to avoid a 'coupon-buster' upset on the 'Treble Chance'. Tabloid small-ads were awash with proven winning 'systems' invented by mathematical geniuses who then chose to sell them on for 20p instead of simply winning every week.

On Tuesday dinnertimes, Dad would study his coupon with one eye on the tipsters' choices printed in the morning paper. All he needed was eight draws. *If* it proved to be a jackpot week, that is, with no more than seven or eight score-draws (which scored 3 points), and maybe a sprinkling of no-score draws (2 pts). *Provided* he invested in a relatively expensive 'full perm' instead of a cheap, enticing 'plan' promising a Cash Cascade. And *given* that he didn't have to share the prize with too many other shrewd, insightful punters – or lucky factory-girl syndicates.

As if divining the future weren't a big enough ask, Dad then had to flex his knowledge of applied factorial equations, scribbling something incomprehensible down the side of his coupon like 'Perm any 8 from 11, 30 goes per penny x 930 lines = £0.75 new pence'.

At Saturday teatime, James Alexander Gordon would tip the wink after he'd finished reciting the results on *Sports Report*. "And the pools forecast," he'd intone. "Very good. Telephone claims are required for 23½ points."

And someone, somewhere, might get more points than anyone else: a top dividend.

For us, neither Mum's lucky numbers nor the 'Millionaire-Maker' Plan ever worked their magic; but somehow we always took solace from the fact that we'd at least ticked the little box marked 'no publicity'.

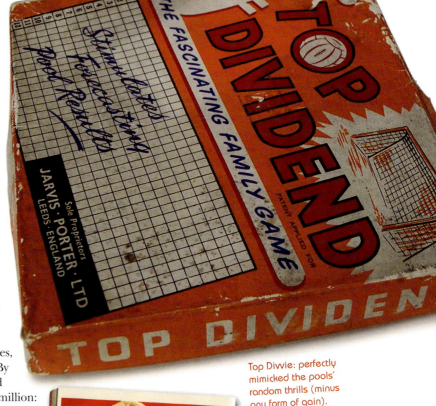

TOP DIVIDEND — THE FASCINATING FAMILY GAME — PATENT APPLIED FOR — Stimulates Forecasting Pool Results — Sole Proprietors JARVIS · PORTER · LTD LEEDS · ENGLAND

Top Divvie: perfectly mimicked the pools' random thrills (minus any form of gain).

The best of both worlds DOUBLE ENTRIES

A Lit-Plan or a Full Perm? It's a question most pools investors have pondered. A Full Perm makes all your Score-Draws count, yet the wider scope of a Lit-Plan is tempting too. That's why so many investors use both on the same coupon. Try a Double Entry yourself and double your winning chances. See overleaf.

P. Harrison's Double Entry won £331,196

FULL PERMS FOR FULL COVER

A Full Perm won Mr Frank Reed £355,329

LADIES COUPON — LITTLEWOODS TREBLE CHANCE

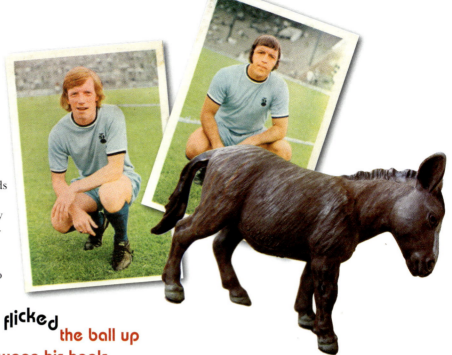

THE DONKEY KICK
It Could Never Happen Now:
Goal of the Season, 1970-71

"An out-of-puff Everton defender upends Cattlin with a groin-high tackle...

"A swift talking-to, and now Coventry have a free-kick 25 yards out. It's ginger-haired Willie Carr standing astride the ball, while moustachioed Ernie Hunt, looking like a Mexican bandit, shapes to pang one goalward.

"But, my gracious! Carr has *flicked* the ball up *backwards* between his heels...

Hunt has let fly with a looping rasper... and YES!

"But, my gracious! Carr has flicked the ball up backwards between his heels... Hunt has let fly with a looping rasper... and YES! Right into the corner of the net over goalkeeper West!

"What a sensational trick, every schoolboy in the Midlands will be trying out the 'Donkey Drop' tomorrow lunchtime...

"But hold on. The referee is receiving a message from the fourth official on his headset. He's disallowed the goal, brought back play, and has booked Carr for touching the ball twice."

DO'S AND DON'TS

Imagine a world where footballers were governed by grown-ups with the foresight to dissuade them from setting fire to £50 notes in front of people with proper jobs.

Almost incredibly, such a world did exist, and not so very long ago.

Training Rules and Instructions to Players was an West Ham United publication containing emergency hotline phone numbers – including one direct to boss Ron Greenwood's bedside table – for the very purpose of steering potentially errant Hammers, out on the lash, back on to the straight and narrow.

A few simple rules might work a treat today at any Premier League club, reminding players of their responsibilities regarding driving a Baby Bentley at 160mph, and wearing electrical headphones during TV interviews:

Training

All players will attend the grounds for training at 9.45am daily (except match days) and shall be under the orders of the management for the rest of the day.

Motor Cars

Players are not prohibited from running a motor car, but it must be clearly understood that they do so at their own risk. Wages will be forfeited during the time of incapacity for any injury which is resultant through accidents in this pastime.

Damage to Club Property

No loose balls will be allowed in the Gymnasium.

Electrical Equipment

In no circumstances must any player use or manipulate any electrical apparatus or instruments. The operation of such equipment will be controlled and carried out by qualified members of staff.

HOME TELEPHONE Nos.

E. CHAPMAN ... Upminster 3346
R. GREENWOOD Loughton 1246
B. JENKINS ... Grangewood 5366
and Grangewood 0057 (Clinic)

A. WALKER ... Crescent 8298
W. ST. PIER ... Ingrebourne 44568
E. GREGORY ... Seven Kings 5186

❋

BOLEYN GROUND
TELEPHONE Nos.
Grangewood 0704
Grangewood 2740

❋

These numbers are for your personal use and **must not** be disclosed to unauthorised persons.

2

All facilities at the Boleyn ground are for your benefit and to help make you absolutely fit for your profession. Physical and mental fitness are of vital importance to success, and it should be a point of honour with you to conduct yourself in a manner which will ensure you taking the field in a perfectly balanced mental and physical condition, thus enhancing your own and the Club's reputation.

Members of the Staff are available at all times to assist you in any playing or domestic problems you may have. Do not hesitate to call upon them.

3

THE DUGOUT

The bench used to be just that. A bench. A modest wooden affair made to seat a maximum of four people. The manager. The trainer, armed with his bucket of cold water and a sponge. The lone substitute, often wearing a sleeping bag in the winter months. Another bloke. Perhaps an injured player wearing a trendy suit. Or an assistant manager wearing a comfortable, battered old tracky top and Rumplestiltskin bottoms.

Dugouts were once quite literally pits, dug down to thigh level so as to afford the backroom boys

a rubbish view of the match.

Subbuteo had it about right with their C114 Bench Set. A beige wooden bench with just three figures on it. No bucket though.

Dugouts were once such modest affairs, they were quite literally pits, dug down to thigh level so as to afford the unimportant backroom boys a rubbish view of the match. They were the historical equivalent of those thin, plastic cushions that ball-boys are now lowered to squat on, down

on the cinder track. What mattered most was that paying members of the public could see clearly over their heads.

But times have changed.

These days, the dugouts are part of the technical area, which takes up a prize chunk of Main Stand real estate at least as big as the Directors' Box. They have airline-style seats with headrests, and Perspex covers so the fans directly behind are forced to try and make out the pitch through a giant wobbly lens.

There are dozens of people who qualify to sit there – so many, in fact, that many recent Second Division matches have seen the gathering in visitors' dugout exceed the crowd in the away end. First up, there's the manager (who's now called a coach). Then there's the coach (who's now called the physio). The trainer (who's now the dietician, or is that the assistant coach?). The warmdown supervisor, who's now, erm… Five substitutes. Or maybe seven. And the rest of the squad, hordes of them, chatting amongst themselves in their all-black pro presentation tracksuits with their initials on. Plotting and planning. Up to no good, left to their own devices. Like kids on the back seat of the school bus – a breeding ground for unrest.

"You know how much my mate gets for appearance bonus at Charlton? Go on, guess…"

In the old days, the lone sub had no one to plot with. If he was an old has-been, he'd sit there, smothered in liniment to keep the cold out of his joints, hoping he wouldn't be called upon. If he was a promising young lad, he'd sit there with growing resentment.

"If I'm not on by the 70th minute, I'll be handing in a transfer request Monday morning…"

Then he'd look at the Gaffer, with his sheepskin coat and tie and tortured expression, and think: "Well, maybe give it another week…"

"You know how much my mate gets for appearance bonus at Charlton? Go on, guess…"

DUTCH COURAGE

The merest suggestion of a bottle of beer is now enough to send the club dietician into a dead faint, but it wasn't always so.

Brian Clough seemed to subscribe to the theory that it was better to be drunk and relaxed rather than sober and nervous.

Sensing some 'nerves' as his Forest side travelled up to Liverpool for a 1978 European Cup tie, Cloughie ordered the coach driver to stop at a pub. After this unscheduled lunchtime session the Forest players had a relaxing afternoon in the hotel before drawing 0-0 at Anfield and progressing into the next round with a 2-0 aggregate win.

Later that season Clough carried out another experiment, unconventionally opting for Champagne *before* the League Cup Final against Southampton.

The Forest boss ordered his team into a private room at their hotel, locked the door and told them no one was leaving until all the bubbly was history – preferring his players to be hung over at the breakfast table rather than lying awake worrying. Cloughie's vindication for the benefits of booze? Forest 3-2 Saints.

In the same era, Scotland's Gordon McQueen only had to breathe whisky fumes on Mick Mills in the Wembley tunnel to win the Home Internationals' psychological battle. But still we're not allowed to report that alcohol is a performance-enhancing wonder drug. On New Year's Day 1971, West Ham travelled to Blackpool for a FA Cup Third Round tie, the icy weather

promising only a wasted overnight stop on the Golden Mile... so Bobby Moore, Jimmy Greaves, Brian Dear and Clyde Best toddled along to ex-heavyweight champ Brian 'The Blackpool Rock' London's 007 Club. It was hardly a monumental session, just a few pints and wine with a meal (and young Bestie stuck to Vimto, bless him) but it caught the attention of a Hammers fan who was displeased to see them out drinking before a game. Cue a surprise thaw, an off day for Moore, and a 4-0 drubbing by the Tangerines.

On Monday morning, the angry fan was in Ron Greenwood's office, and the press soon got hold of the story. As a result, Greavsie, Mooro and Dearie (Dearo?) were each fined a week's wages and dropped for two games.

There's no pictorial evidence that Jimmy and Bobby were wearing 'Kiss Me Quick' hats on the pitch, with their arms round each other, swearing that they were best mates, but it's an enduring image.

Every one a winner

Bass Charrington (North West) Limited.

Glass half full? Ann Field checks her progress against that of Gwladys Street...

ENGLAND 4-2 WEST GERMANY
The 1966 World Cup Final:
It Could Never Happen Now

"Some people are on the pitch! They think it's all over… It is now!

"The referee has communicated with his assistants and the fourth official via their headsets and, yes, he's quite rightly calling the players off the field for their own safety, while stewards and police set about arresting the three irresponsible individuals – the sick so-called fans who have spoiled this great occasion for the players, for the 99,997 decent people in the crowd, for Her Majesty the Queen and the millions watching worldwide.

"The game might be restarted at some point later today, though after this shocking pitch invasion the Germans would be quite within their rights to demand a replay.

"And FIFA's Health & Safety Executive will be lobbying hard to ensure it's played behind closed doors."

Winged victory: the figure on the Jules Rimet Trophy is the Greek goddess of pricey plastic boots.

JULES RIMET CUP
WORLD CHAMPIONSHIP
ENGLAND 1966 JULY 11-30
WEMBLEY · EVERTON · SHEFFIELD · SUNDERLAND · ASTON VILLA · MANCHESTER · MIDDLESBROUGH · WHITE CITY

OFFICIAL SOUVENIR PROGRAMME

PRICE

WORLD CUP!

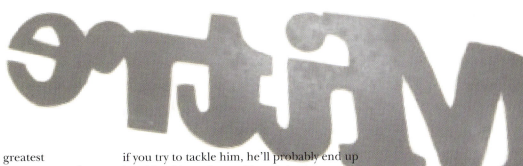

ERTIM

Psychologists reckon one of the greatest evolutionary attributes of the human memory is our inability to remember pain.

Well, it's obvious they've never been involved in a hectic game of Subbuteo, where your dashing left winger gets flicked clean off the pitch and into Row K of the Swirly Psychedelic Axminster Carpet Stand, where he's in danger of being lost or forgotten...

Until, thirty seconds later, you dive into the attack after a pitch-length clearance from Mick Mills (the one-inch tall version, balancing on his immense saucer) which falls right at the feet of Paul Mariner (ditto).

And that's when Eric Gates re-emerges in the plot, sinking his head, his needle-sharp elbow and unyielding podium into the soft gristle right up under your kneecap.

It's the most searing agony known to man, involving technical stuff like ligaments and cartilage and swear-words your mum never knew you even knew.

if you try to tackle him, he'll probably end up breaking his neck – and he might drag you down with him on to the icy ridges.

Luckily, before you have time to react, the kid drops a shoulder, jinks and lets rip. A rocket. Right down the middle.

You move to turn your back, but it's too late. The ball hits you plum on the tender skin of your inner thigh. The smacking noise alone is enough to make you feel physically sick, never mind the wet, bitter-cold slap of pain – and all your team-mates within earshot are laughing as the ball rolls off for a corner.

Mr. Parkin trots on with his bucket of water as you hop and cry. He unbends you expertly on the frozen ground and reaches to dab the magic sponge on the pink weals made even angrier by your pre-match experiment with deep-heat liniment.

"'Ere, it says 'ertiM'," the trainer grimaces, reading your inner thigh.

You should coco.

"That's when Eric Gates suddenly re-emerges in the plot, sinking his head and his needle-sharp elbow into the soft gristle under your kneecap.

Subbuteo kneecap makes the minor twinge of childbirth seem like a walk in the park.

And, unfortunately for anyone who has read this far, you only need to be reminded of the pain in order to feel it all over again, stirred up from among the dentist's drills and teenage heartbreaks – you thought she hadn't noticed you, but in fact she was laughing at the very idea – deliberately hidden away in the deepest, sickest recesses of your mind.

There's only one pain that even comes close.

It's a bright, frosty January morning. You're playing away at Johnstone's Hosiery Under-14s, and you're 3-0 down after five minutes.

It's weird how these flashy top-of-the-league types thought to bring their trainers, instead of just grabbing their duffle bag full of last week's muddy kit and boots from the cupboard under the stairs.

It's like playing in ungainly platform soles, clacking around on the frozen mud. You're losing the feeling in your feet, flapping your arms, breathing smoke. Above all, you're wary of going down in the box, where the icy mud looks as sharp as razor-blades – like miniature mountain ranges, if you half-close your eyes and imagine you're in a plane over the Alps.

Now people are shouting your name, telling you to wake up. A kid with long hair is ten yards away, flying in your direction. Trouble is,

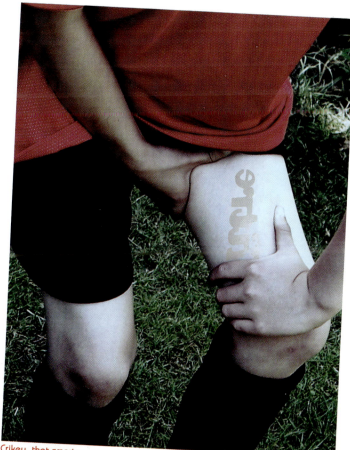

Crikey, that smarts: luckily, a freezing sponge is at hand.

ESCAPE TO VICTORY

Just a hundred or so years late, film-makers finally caught up with the pacifist musing of every schoolkid who ever kicked a ball around a playground. Why send millions of ordinary blokes to death just to settle an argument between a bunch of pushy politicians and posh generals? *Why not settle all the world's differences with a game of football?*

At last, in the shape of 1981's landmark *Escape to Victory*, an answer was provided for the optimistic dreamers who had asked the great conflict-quashing question about World War II:

Because it wouldn't work.

Not even as a fanciful plot device, never mind as a serious ploy in international diplomacy.

Or would it?

Famous footballer Michael Caine is a Prisoner of War, the natural choice to put together a team to play the Nazis, who fancy a day off from jackboots and genocide. Sylvester Stallone is here too – and would you believe the big lunk wants to play in goals? But that bit of bad luck is balanced by the incarceration of the entire Ipswich Town side of the late Seventies.

Behind the scenes, it was sheer genius to rope in Gordon Banks, the one man capable of training Rocky up to the requisite shot-stopping standard to give the Germans another good old 1966ing. On camera, Michael Caine squeezes his gut into a vintage football top and almost seamlessly morphs into Ipswich skipper Kevin Beattie during match scenes. And what a masterstroke to cast Pelé, quite against type, as a footballer from Trinidad... because Brazil didn't join the Allies until 1944, see? And that's just the kind of slip that could have undermined the whole plot.

It's this kind attention to detail that lent the film such credibility, ultimately winning director John Huston his Nobel Peace Prize for the global eradication of armed conflict since the last ever war, in the Falklands.

THE EUROPEAN CUP WINNERS CUP

Didn't you used to love those European nights when you cheered on the British teams against the 'Continentals' almost as passionately as you supported your own side? Tuning in to Radio 2's *Midweek Sports Special*, second-half commentary always commenced promptly at 8.02pm, with Peter Jones forced to compete with the constant blare of klaxons from some far-flung stadium.

Of all the annoying, unnecessary, self-justifying crimes by football's tinkering élite, their record on European club competitions is perhaps most heinous of all. The fate of the European Cup, the Cup Winners' Cup and the UEFA Cup reveals a classic case of fixing, fixing and fixing again something that wasn't broken in the first place.

The European Cup was a proud and prestigious tournament, breathtakingly simple in its purpose. The league champions of each European country played a knockout tournament to find out who was the best. That was it.

And it worked, too. The biggest and best clubs in Europe repeatedly lifted the biggest trophy, whose trail around the EEC – from Madrid and Milan to Amsterdam, Munich, Liverpool and Nottingham – reflected the rise and fall of so many little empires.

Then, in the early 1990s, it was decided that there weren't enough games to satisfy television and corporate sponsors, so UEFA introduced a group stage. Next came their worst decision ever, ignoring Freddie Mercury's heartfelt warning – "No time for losers, 'cos We Are the Champions" – to allow runners-up to compete, and boost up the numbers.

Once the Champions League was no longer solely for Champions, greedy logic served up a no-

brainer: let in the third-place teams. And – hell, why not? – the fourth-placed losers, too.

These were the traditional qualifying places for another once-respected European trophy, the UEFA Cup, which inevitably suffered from the knock-on effect. It was converted into the Europa League: a competition designed to clutter up the fixture list, to rake in money, and to discover who's the best fifth-placed side in Europe.

The European Cup Winners' Cup, once a straight knockout tournament for the winners of each domestic club trophy, suffered what was arguably a yet more ignominious fate. In 1999 it was considered surplus to requirements. Another victim of the ever-expanding Champions League, it was taken outside and shot like a scrapyard dog.

It had been a well-loved competition in its 39 years – a chance for glory for clubs such as Tottenham, West Ham and Chelsea, who couldn't summon the consistency required to win a League title, but could manage a cup run. When they extinguished the ECWC's flame they took a lot of the shine off the FA Cup and, presumably, every other domestic cup in Europe.

Personally, I gave up on it all when they introduced a further group stage to the now morbidly obese Champions League. It was painful for a while, but I knew I'd quit for good when Chelsea faced Manchester United in the 2008 Champions League Final and I couldn't be bothered to wheedle my way out of a School Governors' meeting planned for the same night.

My eleven-year-old self – who would probably have done a little wee of excitement in anticipation of an all-British final – wouldn't have recognised me. But then neither would he have recognised what's left of our once-wonderful European club competitions.

Ticket trail: Manchester City's path to the 1970 ECWC Final.

1—1 — 2—0

0—0 2—0 2—4 1—0 2—0

3—2 0—0 0—1 1—0

0 3—2 0—0

0 3—0

—1 3—0

—2 2—0

3—1 2—1 2

2—4 3—2

4—0 2—

HITCHING ABROAD

Back in the days before we started taking the jet engine for granted, the world was a much bigger place. Greece, for instance, was bloody miles away. But that didn't stop Scouse teenagers Frank Keegan and George Quinn hitch-hiking to Athens to see Everton's European Cup quarter-final against Panathinaikos in March 1971. They couldn't afford to fly on the official travel package at a whopping £34, so they walked down to the East Lancs Road and got their thumbs out... and just ten days later, there they were in Athens.

With all the optimism of youth, Frank and 'Gubba' took sleeping bags and slept in whatever shelter they could find. Under a lorry in Southampton, in a car port in Cologne. The third

and fourth days afforded them the luxury of hostels in Munich and Salzburg, while Day 5 saw them sleeping in a VW van they had inherited (though which, sadly, neither of them could drive). Day 6 saw them in a hostel in Villach near the Austria-Yugoslavia border, but problems arose when they tried to break through the Iron Curtain, next morning.

Gotta Lotta Bottle: one more for your Everton jean jacket.

Official magazine 10p
Everton v Panathinaikos
European Champions Cup
Quarter Final—first leg
Tuesday 9th March '71

Everton
IN EUROPE

Unable to thumb a lift, they headed for the border on foot, not realising it was 21km away, high in the mountains. A blizzard descended and it took nine hours to reach the checkpoint. The Austrians let them out, but the Yugoslavians wouldn't let them in. Then the Austrians wouldn't let them back, leaving them standing in the dark in no-man's-land, soaked and shivering.

Luckily, a Good Samaritan then happened along, offering them a lift and shouting down the border guards' objections. He paid for the intrepid duo's accommodation and food for the night and the next day took them as far as Zagreb. After nights spent in the back of a lorry in Belgrade and, accidentally, a crypt in Skopje, a lift through Greek bandit country finally deposited the pair in Athens – though their joy was tempered by Gubba's discovery that he'd lost his match ticket.

Happily, word of Frank and George's big adventure soon got round the travelling Evertonians who arranged not only a replacement ticket – a goalless bore-draw followed the 1-1 draw at Goodison, sending Everton out on away goals – but two welcome seats on the plane home.

The lads' return journey took four hours.

EXOTIC IMPORTS Extinct Football Species No. 3

Ooh, the sheer thrill of the very idea: a player *from abroad*, eh?

I'd never seen one before, not in a British team's colours, so to spot a group of four squatting together on *The Victor* comic's 'Football Favourites' poster greatly pricked my curiosity. It was like getting to tick off a bittern, a reed warbler, a lapwing and a corncrake in my *Observer's Book of Birds*, all at once. Mindblowing, in a mindblowingly modest way.

The reason I'd never seen a foreign player? This was England, around the turn of the Seventies. Except now here were Bjarne Jensen, Preben Arentoft, Borge Thorup and Per Bartram, crouched in Morton's hoopy

socks like... like a hoop of hoopoes. Over the years, the ten Danish amateurs snapped up by Morton in the Sixties fanned out to Newcastle (Arentoft), Glasgow Rangers (Johansen), and Crystal Palace (Thorup and Bartram)... but Greenock's cosmopolitan lead didn't stop there.

Wafted in on a warm Bermudan wind, West Ham's Clyde Best became the first black and/ or non-British player I'd seen on a football pitch (tick, tick); but the burly West Indian was as disappointing as a cuckoo in real life. Good in the air, he played like a common-or-garden domestic centre-forward, when I'd been hoping for otherworldly trickery. Lots of the other fans were upset with him, too.

Orient winger John Chiedozie was more like it: a skilful featherweight, eminently hackable. Aged twelve in 1972, John had arrived in London as a refugee from Biafra, practised in barefoot football and dodging bullets – and made his League debut just four years later. Fellow Nigerian Tunji Banjo followed. And the Africans contributed in a small way to making the top clubs seem old-fashioned in their blinkered geographical choice of players.

After the 1978 World Cup, Spurs boss Keith Burkinshaw made the victorious Argentinians Ossie Ardiles and Ricky Villa the first big foreign signings of the Seventies (though technically they were pipped by Southampton's popular Yugoslavian full-back Ivan Golac). Both

were brilliant, at the vanguard of bringing a welcome, sexy difference to spice up the English game. Meanwhile Birmingham City also went Argentinian with combustible full-back Alberto Tarantini. He lasted just 23 League matches before jumping into the crowd to punch a fan who had probably shouted something ill-advised about his legendary afro... or his temper.

The two Africans made the top clubs seem blinkered in their choice of players.

Ipswich Town's 'double Dutch' engine room of Arnold Mühren and Frans Thijssen memorably lit up Division One with two-elevenths of Total Football; but Sheffield United came close to going one better when Harry Haslam took Argentine kid Diego Maradona on trial. However, the £400,000 asking fee seemed a bit steep to the Blades' board, so they landed Alejandro 'Who?' Sabella for £160,000 instead...

Ossie's going to Wembley, his knees have gone all trembly...

THE FA TACTICAL GURU

For approximately two hours, nearly fifty years ago, English football was given ample reason to believe that it was on top of the world. Manager Alf Ramsey took the technical plaudits for his 'wingless wonders" victory in 1966 – using what history now tells us were stifling tactics and negative 'enforcers' – though some of the glory/shame also fell on the Football Association's assistant director of coaching, Charles Hughes.

Just as controversially as Ramsey pulling out all the stops against tricksy opposition, the FA's tactical guru was an advocate of the direct, long-ball game.

Hughes 1974 masterwork *Football Tactics and Teamwork* built on the stats-based theory of Wing Commander Charles Reep, a previous power behind English football's throne. Twenty years before, Reep had analysed thousands of matches and made the discovery that "over 80 per cent of goals result from moves of three passes or less"; also that "60 per cent of all goalscoring moves begin 35 yards from an opponent's goal."

No time for fancy stuff like dribbling or passing. Cut to the chase. Lump it into the mixer, sharpish.

Biff, bang, 1-0 to the goodies.

That's why the long-ball game was used as the model for English football: because it appeared to lead to goals.

No time for fancy stuff like dribbling or passing. Cut to the chase. Lump it into the mixer, sharpish. Biff, bang, 1-0 to the goodies.

The controversy escalated in 1980 when Hughes wrote the *FA Coaching Book of Soccer Tactics and Skills* – the official national coaching manual – in which seven pages appeared under the heading 'Passing Techniques – Lofted Passes', versus two pages allotted to 'Improvisation and Inventive Play'. Unfortunately, by now, foreign teams had learned to counter England's masterplan by passing rings around them.

'Route One' was widely considered a curse, with players and coaches speaking out against the training methods rubber-stamped by the FA

Even so, Hughes was promoted to FA Director of Coaching as late as 1990, when he hit back at his critics with *The Winning Formula*, in which he called possession football a 'misguided attacking strategy', leading to nothing but a lot of inconsequential midfield play and all the excitement and goal action steadily draining out of world football over the past thirty years.

While practically every successful contemporary coach believed that holding on to the ball led to goals, Hughes insisted that, "the overwhelming evidence is that the proponents of possession play are mistaken". Why? Because "time is always on the side of the defenders."

Even after Hughes's resignation in 1997, the statistical evidence remains stubbornly compelling (provided you don't count a long pass as a 50 per cent chance of losing the ball). In an analytical sample of 109 international matches played over twenty years, 87 per cent of goals scored came from move of five passes or less. Interceptions, rebounds and shooting from set plays were massively more productive than playing keep-ball.

The great Brazilian side of the Seventies – prime exponents of possession play – scored two-thirds of their goals from moves involving five consecutive passes or less.

In the Eighties, nine out of ten Argentina's World Cup-winning goals came from five-pass moves or less.

"The strategy of direct play is far preferable to that of possession football," the now discredited tactical guru insisted. "The facts are irrefutable and the evidence overwhelming."

The Football Association Coaching Book of
SOCCER
TACTICS AND SKILLS

CHARLES HUGHES

Charles Hughes: a Marmite kind of football theorist...

THE FANCY-DRESS PHOTO OP

There was a time when even the country's top footballers were subject to the whim and fancy of any magazine or newspaper photographer who had a barmy idea.

Here, Liverpool's John Toshack and Kevin Keegan have been asked to pose as 'Deadly Duo' Batman and Robin. Seemingly powerless to say no, they don distinctly low-budget approximations of the superheroes' costumes. Putting aside all dignity, they strike a pose for the snapper.

Further examination of other photos taken during this humiliation of British football's most potent strike force reveal that the 'R' on Robin's costume had been written with a marker pen, while Batman's shorts look as though they were made by somebody's mum.

King Charles of North London fares a bit better. At least his costume and throne are of BBC Props Dept. standard, although he does still look like a bit of a plank.

Can you imagine, for one moment, trying to collar one of today's superstars after training and trying to get them dressed up as a historical figure, or as a camp, baggy superhero for a newspaper shoot?

You'd be lucky if they even heard the request past their massive Beyerdynamic DT770 PRO Headset 250-Ohm earphones, before you were politely told to eff off. By their minder. Through a security fence.

Keggy and Tosh as Del-Boy and plonker Rodney as Batman and Robin.

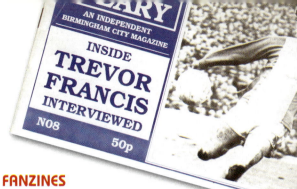

FANZINES

In 1976, punk fanzine *Sideburns* featured three diagrams of finger positions on a guitar, hand-drawn across a page – an E, an A and a rudimentary G.

"This is a chord... This is another... This is a third... NOW FORM A BAND."

It took a little while for the revolutionary DIY ethic to catch on in the world of football, but eventually fans took to their cranky old typewriters, hunting and pecking and ker-chinging out their frustrations, and learning all-new reprographic skills along the way.

They were tired of hearing 'The Fans' View' expressed second hand in the media, where the final word, the final edit, was always predictably happy and safe. Before the 1980s, every word written about football came from an industry perspective – tapped out by writers who were paid by newspapers, magazines, television companies or club programmes, which were in turn reliant on the FA, the League or the clubs themselves.

It's a tough job, running the back page of a local paper without access to news information, player interviews or pictures.

Up on the Roof: As peaceful as can be, the world below can't bother me...

FANS ON THE ROOF

When all else had failed, and you were locked out of the big match, ticketless and distraught, there was always one final guerrilla option available – provided you'd just popped a personal Party Seven on a long motorway journey, and had a silk scarf ready tied to each wrist as a climbing aid.

In that case, simply find your way round to the lowest stand, sneak through somebody's back garden and reach for the stars via a rusty Edwardian drainpipe. The only rule on the subject (other than 'Do Not') stated that there must be at least three of you involved, for purposes of egging on, passing beer up drainpipes and flicking the Vs at stewards craning their necks on the touchline.

Ignoring any warning signs about the corrugated roofing not being designed to bear any weight, inch your way along until you have a perfect view of the whole pitch. Ignore the Bobbies shouting at you to get down: they aren't going to follow you up there, although they may have a word in your ear when you bump back to earth at the bottom of that drainpipe.

For now, you're perfectly safe as long as you don't jump up and down when your team score. After all, nobody ever fell through a football stand roof.

Except that Man United fan at Norwich... and that Wolves fan at Scarborough. And they were both okay, eventually.

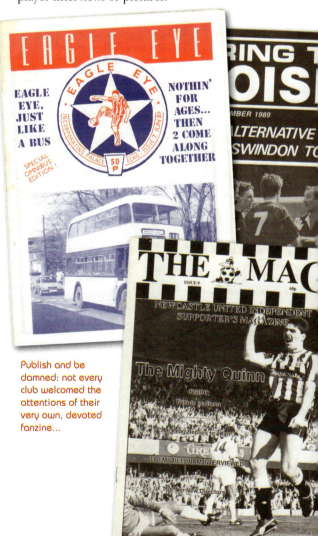

Publish and be damned: not every club welcomed the attentions of their very own, devoted fanzine...

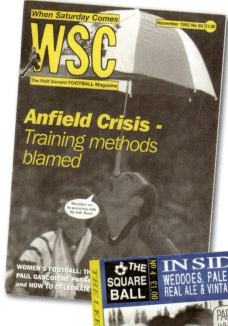

No such problem for the first wave of fanzine rebels , who offered an all-new diet of uncensored opinion cut with terrace humour, finally putting the majority view of 20,000 regulars above the handful of professionals and hired hands – the chairman, the players, the manager, the gentlemen of the press box – who were just passing through.

No matter if they were presented under headlines written using felt-pen, Letraset or John Bull Printing Outfit No. 7: here, for the very first time in print, were negative as well as

stories and arguments about everything from Subbuteo and the miners' strike to real ale and the Jesus and Mary Chain – complete with unashamed local bias and slang never before spelled out in print. Most important was a bedrock of unfakable shared memories and local obsessions that made the whole publication seem like double Dutch to oppo

> ## "When we started up there were nine fanzines in existence. A couple of years later there were 200. We're still going 23 years later, and there's only nine again!" Editor, The Fox

positive views on our beloved clubs and teams, jokes at our own expense, better jokes at our local rivals' expense, album and gig reviews, stories of away trips, pubs and pies... always pies.

Fanzine editors read other fanzines, together with the *NME*, *Viz* comic and music fanzines: they were never going to make the old guard's mistake of assuming football fans were only interested in football. In place of the previous pall of uniformity and agreement, here was a magnificently eccentric range of

fans, with their funny, wrong-coloured scarves and inflatable badgers.

And, somewhere along the way, we discovered it wasn't just the fans in our corner of our ground who felt the same way about all-seater stadiums and ID cards, about the wreckers who came to football to chuck bananas and seats on the pitch, and the wreckers who came bearing calculators. And pies.

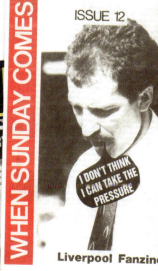

FIRST ROUND
WATNEY MANN CUP
SATURDAY, 1st AUGUST, 1970
Kick-Off: 3-00 p.m.

FERGIE'S DONS STORM EUROPE
It Could Never Happen Now

No one gave the Dons much hope back in March 1983 when a Bayern Munich side stocked with German internationals trotted out on to the Pittodrie pitch for the European Cup Winners' Cup quarter-final, second leg. Alex Ferguson's men – including the likes of Strachan, McLeish, Miller, Cooper and Rougvie – had won the Scottish Cup but hadn't yet repeated the act three times in four years. Yes, they'd earned a surprise 0-0 draw in Munich... but wouldn't that just make the Bavarians angry?

Aberdeen were given an Alp to climb when they went one behind on ten minutes – and yet another when Bayern renewed their lead on the hour. Even at 2-2, the Germans held away-goal

Days in Europa: a greater achievement than Man U's Champions League?

advantage – until Alex Ferguson threw in his sub, John Hewitt, at the deep end. The leggy young striker, just turned twenty, scampered on to a parried Strachan header and bundled in the winner with his very first touch.

In the semi, Aberdeen strolled past the now-defunct Belgian outfit Waterschei to face Real Madrid in the final in Gothenburg. A constant grey downpour made it seem a home from home for the Scots, whose fans sang them to 1-1 and into extra-time to the hot new tune of 'Here we go, here we go, here we go...'

Time for Fergie to work his 'Supersub' trick again: Hewitt came off the bench to dive in and head the clincher, launching into a star jump that has since been mimicked just the odd billion times in the Granite City.

Fergie had brought Europe to its knees with a whole team of home-country players – not a trick that's pulled off too often these days. And the all-conquering boss's special way of saying thanks to his talisman? He fined young John for daring to overtake him on a main road.

FIDDLING WITH THE RULES

It wasn't just Jimmy Hill on *Match of the Day* who was always pressing madcap plans for an offside zone, bigger goals and three points for a win. In the 1970s, every Tom, Dick and Harry had a Big Idea how to bring back goals into the game now that winning, and shutting up shop, was becoming increasingly important.

Watney-Mann, those noted brewers of fizzy beer, came up with a wizard wheeze to set the game back on fire, and decided to showcase their ad-mens' action plan in a special pre-season tournament. Featuring the two top-goalscoring teams from each of the four divisions, the 'action-packed' Watney Cup set off the 1970-71 season "dedicated to setting a fast pace, giving lots of action and providing more goals."

Fulham-Derby was the first game of what proved a hugely influential tournament, though not because the 'no draws' rule brought about extra time and a 3-5 final result: this was Britain's first ever corporate-sponsored football trophy. Out on the pitch, the inaugural Watney Cup was also notable for the first ever shoot-out in the British game (with Denis Law becoming the first ever player to miss).

Meanwhile, the Texaco Cup kicked off in the same season, featuring seemingly random clubs from England, Scotland and the Irish Republic. It was chiefly of interest because the FA allowed the offside rule to be amended, with a no-offside line painted across the pitch 25 yards from goal.

Not to be outdone, the Watney Cup was back again the following season with offside only in force inside the penalty

*The penalty system of deciding drawn gar

Caption comp: enter
our Grand Prize Quiz
and win Texaco Cup
Final tickets.

area. The final ended 4-4 between West Brom and Colchester, and then 4-3 on penalties to the sharp-shooting Baggies.

Apparently, the experiment created too many goals, too much fun for the FA bigwigs: the Watney Cup was scrapped after 1973, and the games played are sometimes even excluded from players' and clubs' records because of the sacrilegious rule fiddling.

FLICKING THE Vs

There's only one digit-based signal of discontent and defiance that carries the age-old stamp of British disapproval, and that's the two-fingered salute.

No, not the bunny-ears sign used by Winston Churchill at the end of the war. We mean the unambiguous sight of two fingers being wobbled vigorously in your direction, or in the direction of your hapless victim.

This most venerable sign of gleeful contempt has recently fallen on hard times thanks to the imported single-digit salute and the devilish double fingers beloved of rubbish rap fans, but perhaps now the time is ripe for a comeback. To this end, here's Cardiff wild man Robin Friday showing the nation's youth the way forward.

Having clashed early on with goalkeeper Milija Aleksic in the Bluebirds' vital 1977 relegation battle against Luton, Friday followed up rather high and very late. After a dressing down from the ref, he held out his hand in apology, but was snubbed.

Twenty seconds after the ensuing free-kick, the mercurial misfit had won back the ball, beaten three men, rounded Aleksic and knocked the ball into an empty net.

Once more, with feeling, Sir Robin?

Once more, with feeling, Sir Robin?

IT'S
WATNEYS' RULE
ABOUT NO
DRAWS!*

JP 1971
ST 7th

duced in the Watney Cup 1970.

THE FOOTBALL CARD ENGINE

Here's how to transform your humble pushbike into a revved-up, throbbing beast of a motorcycle, all too easy to mistake for a 750cc Norton Commando (provided you're only listening rather than looking).

All you need is:

1 – One giant pile of football cards;
2 – Two clothes pegs;
3 – An anti-social desire to terrorise your neighbours like those cool Hells Angels you've seen on *Nationwide*; and,
4 – A tragic disregard for your future financial security.

If you've got a teetering pile of cards, it naturally follows that you've got an even bigger pile of swaps, collected up over weeks of frustration while searching for the two or three you need for the set.

All you have to do is use the pegs to secure the cards on to your bike frame so they stick a little way into the spokes. Then push off, taking note of the unusual sensation of slight resistance as you wobble down the gutter, turning heads with a guttural, engine-like *Vrrrrrrrrrp.*

Use your swaps pile and a clothes peg to transform your pushbike into a revved-up, throbbing beast of a motorcycle.

When the cards become limp and spent, and the engine sound slightly less annoying to Mrs. Fenwick at number 34, simply replace with fresh, stiff swaps from your pile – manfully ignoring your elderly neighbour's warning that in one afternoon you might easily burn through £100's worth of future sought-after collectables at 21st-century prices.

Next: how to make a Victorian 'stamp snake' out of your granddad's priceless philatelic heirloom.

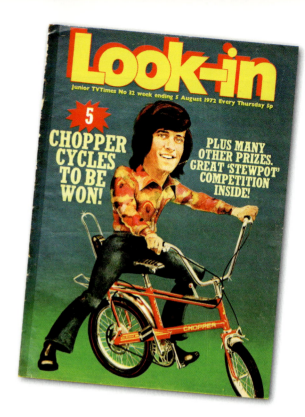

FOOTBALL LEAGUE REVIEW

By the start of the 1970s, the Football League was beginning to suspect that the future was theirs, all theirs, an impression based solidly on the growing stature of their midweek, floodlit League Cup experiment, and a steady rise in visibility relative to their old enemies at the FA.

Run from the back bedroom of secretary Alan Hardaker's Blackpool bungalow, the League was devoted to showing everyone what a big, happy family their 92-member club was. The *Football League Review* was a feelgood customer mag, given away free inside club programmes, where it bolstered many four- or eight-page lower-league efforts. However, the *FLR* was conspicuous in its absence from certain larger League grounds, where power brokers were already wary of growing League influence.

The *Review* was 5 pence 'when bought separately', which is to say never. It was full of behind-the-scenes peeks at the day-to-day running of all the League clubs, an article on the bootroom at Barrow being just as likely as

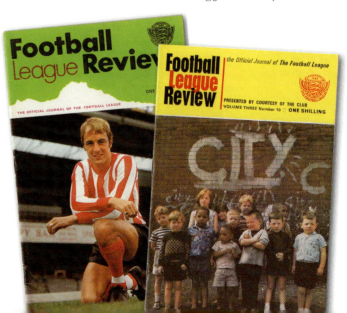

a visit to the Arsenal trophy room. Then and now, its allure was almost entirely down to staff photographer Peter Robinson, who spent whole seasons travelling around snapping mascots at Mansfield and tea-ladies in Tranmere, thinking up ever more unusual formations for his teamgroups.

"I was conscious that I was different when I talked with other photographers at games," he told *When Saturday Comes*. Robinson never missed an angle, an expression, an oddity or a location, showing more interest in football culture than the game itself. "I felt that you didn't just have to start photographing when the ref blew his whistle. I was interested in the whole build-up to the game."

Arguably the greatest football photographer of all, Robinson went on to work for FIFA, shooting World Cups right up to 1994, but then found himself unable to secure a Premier League photographer's licence. The FA told him he'd first need to shoot amateur football on parks and recreation grounds for a year. He remains frozen out, unwilling to attend a match with the usual modern restrictions on where he can point his lens.

"The way the football authorities see the game now is the way they want it reflected back to them," Robinson observes. "Fans in replica shirts with painted faces... this is the way football will be sold."

FOOTBALLERS' WIVES WHO AREN'T IN POP GROUPS

England's World Cup Finals campaign of 2006 was unusual not for the team's results but for the size of their entourage. The squad's luggage truck at Frankfurt Airport was weighed down not just by 23 kits, tracksuits and toilet bags, but by equipment belonging to a further 95 backroom staff and specialists, including chiropodists, masseurs, shrinks and warm-up/down/sideways coaches.

Then there were the additional two trucks needed to carry the portable wardrobes, multi-gyms, tanning paraphernalia and bling belonging to the players' wives and girlfriends – the newly coined WAGs. The girls had been invited along at their own insistence on grounds of equal rights and equal billing, backed up by their celebrity model co-workers within the camp.

As coach Sven had already leaked the news that he was quitting after the tournament, all pressure of expectation was lifted, and an end-of-term atmosphere descended on the grand international shopping expedition.

Everyone was a winner.

Thanks to Posh Spice and Cheryl Cole, England even got out of the group stage at the inter-squad karaoke.

Whatever happened to bewildered doe eyes, twinsets and beehives?

FOSSILISED FOOTBALL-CARD BUBBLE GUM

I had a funny turn the other week, sitting out on the patio.

For the first time in ages, I was Home Alone for the whole day, and as soon as I'd come around from a rare, lazy lie-in, I put into operation my audacious plan for a day off. A day *completely* off – no kids, no phone calls, no email, no internet – for the first time this century?

Now was my chance to set up my old record player and blast out some anti-social vinyl, or maybe I'd finally get around to sorting out our suitcase full of old photos. Still dazed by schoolday dreams, I made coffee and wandered into the garden in my dressing gown. Struggling to focus on the back page of the paper in the morning sun, I just inhaled the pungent newsprint. Bees buzzed. Church bells chimed.

When I woke up again, I plucked the yellowing, crinkly newspaper off my head, adapting slowly to the news of where I was... and when.

electrical connections inside my head.

I was whisked back directly to the sloping driveway of my infancy.

This was where I used to spend endless hours kicking a ball against the garage door, seeing the wide-open spaces of Wembley instead of paving slabs and privet hedge.

I remembered the very feeling of kicking and whistling here around the dawn of the Seventies, recalling my bittersweet yearning for the only decade I'd ever known, fearing the rumoured horrors of junior school and responsibility ahead. Once again, I could feel the 1970s looming unknown, the very numbers of the years running out of control into science-fiction territory, just like the Teenies today.

Bloody hell, I thought. Only seven, and I was at it even then.

Casting around for certainties, here was the patch of front lawn where we used to play *Voyage to the Bottom of the Sea*. Through the gap in the houses opposite, I could see the big old country house that stood for years in a perpetual state of demolition.

When Lesley and the kids arrived home that evening, they found me sitting on the lawn surrounded by piles of detritus from a whole afternoon's sniffing and licking. Cans, packets, bottles...

That's when I discovered how Richard Dreyfuss must have felt in *Close Encounters of the Third Kind*, when he sculpted a mystical mashed-potato mountain and tried convincing sceptical infants that it was the key to something big.

Close encounters of the collector card kind: next stop, mashed-potato mountains.

On a whim, I reached out and picked a fat, green leaf off the privet bush. For the first time in thirty years, I instinctively punctured the centre of a leaf with my thumb nail, raised it to my lips and blew.

My whistle made a disappointing *pthuh* – I was out of practice – but the bitter taste of chlorophyll, the squeaky raspberry sound, the smell of the leaf and the buzzing sensation in my lips all combined to trigger a million rusty

I'd spent the rest of the day trying in vain to suck back memories as visceral as my privet-leaf Wembley, but had found it a tough trick to pull off to order. Raw custard powder had proven powerful, as had vintage paperbacks with red edges, and children's medicine. Brasso. Playdoh. Nail polish remover. The cans were just for drinking, although lager is commonly used to forge routes back in time.

I was whisked back directly to the sloping driveway of my infancy, seeing the wide-open spaces of Wembley instead of paving slabs and privet hedge.

My greatest experimental hit was an Anglo Bubbly from the corner shop, which succeeded in momentarily depositing me outside another – Mr. Sherrard's on Fairfield Road. How sweet to taste again that sugary, artificial-pear flavour, identical to the thin, fossilised slab of bubble gum inside a packet of football cards.

All that was missing was the faint hint of cardboard imparted by contact with the bottom, gum-scarred card. And the cards, and the shop. But what about the park? And that old Saturday-afternoon feeling?

This was just the beginning...

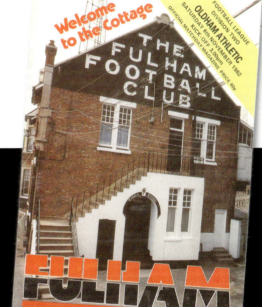

The Cottage: the only surviving free-standing pavilion at any senior British ground.

NASL BY THE THAMES

From the mid to late Seventies, Britain's top footballing superstars who were getting on a bit found a new way to earn a few quid. They all got summer jobs in the North American Soccer League. They showboated around in huge stadiums with retractable roofs and artificial turf.

But what to do during the proper football season when you don't quite fancy the rigours of a Football League Division One campaign?

Fulham provided the answer. Craven Cottage became a sort of NASL by the Thames for some of the world's best players who were going a bit curly at the edges. Bobby Moore was the first, leaving Upton Park for SW6. He was then joined by George Best and Rodney Marsh for the 1976-77 season. They dazzled the likes of Hereford with some sublime skill and Best surprised everyone, including himself, by turning up for all 42 league matches.

But somehow, the glorious has-been experiment didn't quite fit together. Fulham only avoided relegation to Division Three with one game to spare...

Best and Marsh: back from the boozer, 11.30am.

73

9

GARDEN GOALS

Ah, the memories inspired by this Garden Goals advert from 1974. Most of them bad. The country was in the grip of depression and three-day-week strife. £5.55 (inc. VAT) represented a month's grocery bills and a TV licence. It did not, in any way, represent 'Every Boy's Dream' of extra-strong galvanised steel tubing and rot-proof net. Not for me, anyway. The 65p carriage fee alone added up to more than three weeks' pocket money.

Out of dire necessity, I was forced to make my own goal out of garden canes and that green plastic netting that grows in sheds. In turn, I was Johan Cruyff, running backwards down the side of the lawn, then Robbie 'Rensenbrick' and on to Johnny Rep, letting rip a rocket shot; but every time I scored or hit the woodwork, the whole rickety mess of cane and net and string was gathered up and swept up into the rockery. No great problem, mind. I just spent the next ten minutes setting it all back up again, time and time again.

Then Mum came out of the house and she was actually crying. I'd destroyed every one of the big red velvety tulips she was growing for the Huncote Show, and it was no use either of us trying to stand them back up again or wipe away our tears.

If only I'd noticed the confident sub-heading in the ad: '10 DAYS MONEY-BACK OFFER'.

I could have enjoyed ten days' worth of "shooting and saving fun with Dad and envious pals," then claimed to have been only partially impressed with a net that could stop a ball, sent the whole rig back, and even reclaimed the Postal Order.

The clever things you think of after the event.

GENUINE SHOWBIZ FANS

Here's a quiz question for you, and a possible method of winning yourself a pint on Saturday night when your mates' thought processes are running at somewhere below 100 per cent ... when the conversation turns, inevitably, to football trivia.

The question is simple: what do the following ne'er-do-wells, chancers and respected celebrity types all have in common?

Bill Oddie	Goodie and noted twitcher
Shane Warne	Cricketer
Johnny Lee Miller	Sick Boy out of *Trainspotting*
Gary Numan	Futuristic pop hero
Nigella Lawson	TV chef
Vidal Sassoon	Hairdresser
Minnie Driver	Actress
Morten Harket	A-Ha
Father Ted	aka Dermot Morgan, RIP

Give up? Here's some more celebs with the same thing in common...

Jimmy White	Snooker star
Russell Grant	Astrologer
Dannii Minogue	Kylie's sister
Busta Rhymes	Rapper
Renee Zellwegger	Bridget Jones
Rodney Bewes	Likely Lad
Bryan Adams	Musician
Paul McGrath	Footballer
Roddy Doyle	Playwright

If you're ready to give in, here's some more clues to give the game away. How about John Motson, Michael Caine and Richard Attenborough? David Mellor and John Major? Raquel Welch out of *One Million Years BC*... wearing a big, furry blue bikini and a caveman-chic Micky Droy scarf?

It's hard to say why celebrities nowadays find it so hard to say,

"Nah, I'm not really that interested in football."

That's right, they're all Chelsea fans, taken straight from the exhaustive list of 172 notable public figures on the ever-alert The Shed website.

It's hard to say why celebrities nowadays find it so hard to say, "Nah, I'm not really that interested in football." Not that we're suggesting, of course, that Geri Halliwell hasn't been a Stamford Bridge regular since 1957...

So much for that that feeling of camaraderie when Eric Morecambe used to sneak in a mention of his precious Luton Town – a secret bond between a junior-school kid and a middle-aged man sitting up in bed with his comedy partner. And it used to be cool how Elton John would play Vicarage Road to raise money for a new striker. Comedian Eddie Large was always childishly chuffed to get in a mention of Man City; Jasper Carrott was a Brummie Blue through and through, and Mike Yarwood was a Stockport nut.

And that was just about that for celebrity football fans.

Let's count up for the sake of a scientific comparison: six.

Sixteen, if you count Ken Dodd and his Diddymen.

GIRL OF THE MATCH

Yeah, yeah, yeah. We all know about Jimmy Hill's busy time inventing modern football in the 1960s (see 'Coventry City – Sky Blue Revolution'). And in the following two decades he returned as chairman to continue his work, making Highfield Road the first all-seater stadium with the first electronic scoreboard; but let's not allow these lapses of judgment and taste eclipse the PR genius's role in developing the classic 1970s football programme.

Before the young go-getter started using his bi-weekly boss's column to whip up enthusiasm, programmes were just a teamsheet sandwiched in a folded sheet of adverts. But, before too long, *The Sky Blue* had become a nine- by five-inch, full-colour magazine for all the family, complete with player recipes, a crossword and a flimsily clad Sky Blue Bird on the back page.

In the interests of deflecting any accusation of male chauvinism, best mention that Tommy 'Mr. Magic' Hutchison's Quiche Lorraine is greatly improved by an extra five ounces of Cracker Barrel cheese.

GLORIOUS AMATEURISM

No higher ideal has ever suffered such a fall from grace. Within generations, the very notion of Glorious Amateurism has tumbled from laudable to laughable, from quintessentially British to pathetically outdated. But, as with so many chunks of our sporting heritage that were written or sold off in the late twentieth century, it's easy to overlook the positives of the Olympian ideal.

Even in the 1980s, a hundred years after the FA had grudgingly accepted professionalism, the stuffy old busybodies who ran the show in their spare time still secretly resented players making decent money out of the game. And, in a curious alignment across the ages, it's an attitude that survives today in a million barstool conversations that take place every weekend – the only time a modern man ever gets to use the word *obscene*.

Of course, no one's saying any preposterously skilled squad member should play for nothing; the question is whether his salary really needs to stretch to a country estate and a team-size jacuzzi full of Cristal Champagne, supermodels and security guards. It rankles when a brat makes four times more in a week than we do in a year. And they still fluff open goals. Sadly, it's driven a wedge between fans and heroes which never used to exist when we could look up to solid, grown-up players who commanded our love and respect.

The Amateur Cup: winning wasn't as important as maintaining decorum whilst taking part.

the agents and marketing men who still imagine they're vital to football. A global business driven by brands and celebrities, bankrolled by suckers and helpless addicts.

At the end of the day, we don't imagine there'll be too much of a kerfuffle. Even football industry executives were fans once, so they'll most likely do the decent thing and step down once they know they've been rumbled trying to make off with our game. In turn, the megalomaniac owners, the electronic billboard magnates and media barons will soon realise their evil game is up. Then it'll simply be a case of easing our heroes on to £20K a year – decent money for kicking a ball around – and asking a nice FA secretary with her hair in a bun to find out whatever *did* happen to Terry Hennessey.

Fans will soon step into the breach, cheerfully volunteering to press the button on the fixture-list computer and to make up the packed lunches for the national side's next coach trip abroad.

Like our old mates, the ousted FA fuddy-duddies, we'll get to carpet players for staying out late, for flicking the Vs or for gossing at each other.

And won't that be glorious?

GOAL! LOLLIES

Interesting concept. Rather than littering the floor outside your local Co-Op with your spent lolly stick, you take it home and "paint it to look like your favourite football star."

But what if you don't happen to be an artistic genius with an interest in micro-sculpture? And how can a lolly stick, no matter how well painted, be caught offside or take a goal kick, as promised? All is revealed in the sentence near the end, where the advertising copy becomes refreshingly honest: "It must all sound too good to be true. It is."

Oh well, maybe we should just put our trust in Lyons Maid and send them our 25p in any case. Best be quick, though: offer ends 30 December, 1978.

> "When you look at other sports, like golf, the players earn a lot more money without running around.
>
> I wish I had that little cart to take me to corner kicks."
>
> Thierry Henry

Low pay for players used to work very nicely, as a negligible wage bill meant admission prices could be kept to a minimum. Clubs didn't build up absurd debts. They had no reason to demolish the Popular Side to improve corporate banqueting facilities. There was no such thing as the Professional Foul, just the good, honest amateurish variety.

It was the influx of megabucks that brought with it the fly-by-night primadonnas, the scared-to-lose managers and spoiling coaches,

ALLAN CLARKE

Apply adhesive here only.

139

Completed 450 League appearances last season. Voted the
Players' "Player of the Year" as
well. Turned professional in
April 1961 and has Under-23 and
27 full caps. Defensive half-back
who made his initial appearance
v Swansea. Ht. 5ft. 11½in. Wt.
12.9.

NORMAN HUNTER

GOALHANGING

Track back? Defend from the front? Team game? Hmm, I don't think so.

How refreshing it would be to watch a Premier League coach attempt to communicate to a proper centre-forward the importance of spending a single second retreated any farther down the pitch than the halfway line.

A decent old-school forward could make it through a whole season without once facing away from goal, to which he would linger as closely as a toddler to his mum's skirts, and just as helplessly dependent for thrills and hugs.

What was that strange white blur in the penalty-box when the ball pinged in from the wing, arse-high at 70mph?

That was Allan Clarke. One touch. One-nil.

Track back? Defend from the front? Team game?
Hmm, I don't think so.

Sniffer would goalhang shamelessly for whole matches, plotting, eyes peeled for possible action, as monomaniacal as Romeo or Cyrano loitering by his target balcony.

Show the dog the rabbit, and he'd pounce.

A first-rate goalhanger – Lineker, before the busybody coaches got to him – would be disappointed to touch the ball at all if it were not to toe-poke it two yards into the net. Two or three touches per match would be his only contribution, like it or lump it.

Defend from the front? Is that what the coach's roly-poly arm signal means?

Yeah, right.

GOALIE GEAR

Just as the drummer is a noisy madman who chooses to hang around with musicians, so the goalie is to the football team.

At least it's easy to spot – and so to avoid – the modern goalie, thanks to his sponsored adoption of embarrassing extremes of grooming and behaviour. In the 1990s, he went in search of deals for ponytail-care products, or else ad space on his polished pate, and began to clown around all the more to help shift his replica multicoloured luminous jester suits.

The goalie is the one in the preposterous headgear, swinging or sitting on the crossbar. He's the seven-foot colossus with five-foot arms who doesn't have enough advantages at a corner. So he jumps and knees the centre-forward in the neck – and then complains that he's been illegally crowded.

The big, soft, selfish, overprotected, wobbly-kneed, fancy-dress letter-inner.

The goalie keeps his weird little comfort blanket and a pack of gum in that slightly insane flight bag of his... but have you ever seen the big, soft, selfish, overprotected, wobbly-kneed, fancy-dress letter-inner offer a bit to the centre-half?

Not since the 1980s, we'll warrant, when goalies were still salt-of-the-earth types, wearing nothing more unusual than an old green top with quilting on the elbows and chest, and gloves with little rubber nipples.

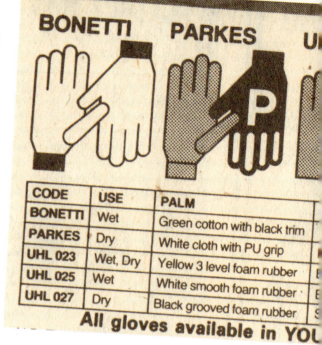

CODE	USE	PALM
BONETTI	Wet	Green cotton with black trim
PARKES	Dry	White cloth with PU grip
UHL 023	Wet, Dry	Yellow 3 level foam rubber
UHL 025	Wet	White smooth foam rubber
UHL 027	Dry	Black grooved foam rubber

All gloves available in YOU

GOALKEEPERS ARE DIFFERENT

Some people's lives can take the odd turn here and there, but only one person has a CV remotely like that of David Icke.

On leaving school, the Leicester lad signed up for Coventry City as a goalkeeper and then moved to Hereford before arthritis halted his career at the age of 21. Moving into journalism, Icke worked on the local Leicester paper and radio station through the Seventies, and spent the Eighties as part of BBC TV's sports presentation team. During this time, he gradually moved into politics, and became a spokesperson for the Green Party.

Then things got a bit odd.

He started to wear only turquoise, and informed the nation via the *Wogan* chat show that he was the Son of God. He then broke the news that we were ruled by reptilians from the constellation Draco. The Queen Mother, Hillary Clinton, Harold Wilson and many more prominent figures possessed hybrid DNA which allowed them to change from reptilian to human form if they consumed human blood.

Erm... okaaaay.

Icke's unique career progress can be neatly summed up by a selection from his many book titles:

It's a Tough Game, Son: The Real World of Professional Football (Piccolo, 1983).

Children of the Matrix: How an Interdimensional Race has Controlled the World for Thousands of Years – and Still Does (Bridge of Love, 2001).

PART EIGHT of BRIAN GLANVILLE'S latest novel, serialised only in GOAL. Ron Blake and Borough have made a promising start to the new season. The young goalkeeper has been in top form and now returns to play at Stamford Bridge, scene of his early days in football as a Chelsea fan. Can he make it a happy occasion?

Goalkeepers are different

E made another good start against Chelsea. This time, Jesse started on the left, but early in the game he went out on to the right, and I could see Chelsea were confused, you see a lot from goal. David Webb went with him, but Eddie McCreadie, the other back, didn't seem quite sure who to take, because we weren't using...

live at home. You know how old I was when I went away? Fourteen. That's how old. Good cooking. People who want the best for you. I've met your father and your mother; I like them."

I said, "I like them, and all; it isn't that." He said, "Well, what is it?" and I didn't know how to tell him; I said, "Well, for one thing, I'd like to be nearer the club." "Is that it?" he...

to be able to talk football all the time with somebody that really knew it, someone that was playing in your own side. I could honestly never get enough of that. At home, the old man always likes to discuss it, of course, but it couldn't be the same; not that he was ignorant or anything, but simply...

can learn them from," and as soon as I said it I felt sorry that I did, because he didn't mean no harm, old Mike. I realised that afterwards. It was simply his way. Everything was still...

The second half he minutes when we give time Asa Hart...

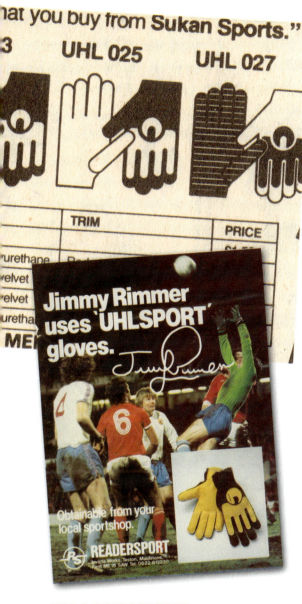

Jimmy Rimmer uses 'UHLSPORT' gloves.

Obtainable from your local sportshop.

READERSPORT
Invicta Works, Teston, Maidstone, Kent ME18 5AW Tel: 0622 812230

LEICESTER NEWS SERVICE
Telephone 50255

First with the local news on sport.
David Icke reports on city games, both at home and away.
Tune into Radio Leicester for David Icke's report on
95.1 VHF and 188 medium wave.

"...is those wooden stakes holding the rope around a cricket square."

"But won't the ball keep going on the cricket square?"

"That isn't a problem," I explained patiently, "because you're playing *inside* the cricket square. It's summer, right? And it's the only place to find that short, springy World Cup grass, like you're in Brazil or Argentina."

Gary's face clouded at the idea of something close to sacrilege, but he quickly came to his senses, realising that it's perfectly permissible to borrow equipment from a minority sport to help heighten the pleasures of the national game.

"But aren't the posts a bit far apart?"

Springy turf and handy posts can lend any cricket square a World Cup atmosphere.

"Not if you untie one from the other side of the square and move it across."

"Nah," Gary shook his head. "I'll tell you the best thing to use as goalposts: freshly planted saplings with a stake to hold them up – two of 'em, exactly the right distance apart."

Thirty minutes later we stole into the park around the back of Huncote vicarage. Gary had brought his ball to prove his point. He was still singing the praises of his perfect goalpost trees, one of which he admitted had suffered collateral damage over three or four busy seasons.

"It kept growing back, though," he excused himself. "I saw it a while back and it was all stunted, with eight little trunks growing up where we'd kept snapping them off with shots."

But time flies in the imaginary stadium of the mind, and Gary grew silent as we walked into the shadow of the vicarage wall.

You could still see how the multiple stems had once grown up out of the main trunk, but all that was left of the goalpost tree was a sorry stump, two feet across.

THE GOALPOST TREE
Despite our attendance at a meeting whose agenda covered the manifold trials of modern football, our attention was drawn out of the window and into the garden, where a sunny patch of lawn was made to look all inviting by a dwarf conifer and a prop holding up an empty clothesline.

"I'll tell you the best thing to use for goalposts," I said. "It's no use having two posts that aren't a pair. It's a distraction. And, worse than that, it's unrealistic."

"You mean the best thing to use for goalposts," Gary clarified, "that aren't goalposts."

"The best thing to use for goalposts is..."

"Jumpers are rubbish," he jumped in. "A goalpost has to be solid enough for rebounds, and a certain height."

published by Hamish Hamilton in the autumn

ten

suspended "...

The perfect goalpost tree: Ah yes, I remember it well...

79

GROOVERS
Extinct Football Species No. 4

It seems almost unfair that other footballers have to compete in the groover stakes with Frank Worthington, a man who habitually wore an 'ELVIS' belt buckle with his leather bell-bottoms without once drawing a word of ridicule. When Frank signed for Leicester City, it was the only occasion in the club's history that the traditional cheese-and-wine welcoming soirée was attended by more players' wives than players and officials. Fact. They just came to stare. Although the number of wives subsequently invited back to Frank's pad to sample the original Extended Play 'A Date with Elvis' has surely been exaggerated.

Nevin outmanoeuvred opponents with revolutionary logic and dribbles soundtracked by the Cocteau Twins' ethereal swirl.

Never, ever Joy Division's 'She's Lost Control Again'.

Reading's attitudinous legend Robin Friday preferred a snakeskin shirt to leather strides, and contemporary grooves to any retro Fifties scene. He was probably the only League footballer to spend the summer of 1974 in a Cornish hippie commune, or to then undertake a rigorous training programme based around LSD. Friday played his Led Zeppelin LPs loud, all night, in a flat painted black so the patterned wallpaper didn't distract him from his druggy hallucinations.

The ultimate rock 'n' roll footballer, Friday had MILD and BITTER tattooed beneath his nipples, reflecting the darker side to his notorious bingeing. Instead of aspiring to his rightful place as an England possible, he would strip naked in nightclubs or even in the team hotel, where he once launched a volley of snooker balls around the bar before scarpering in the buff to kidnap an equally confused swan.

We always thought the Cobblers' Brian Faulkes looked like a man who might have a few LPs with swirly covers in his record box, more positively promoting ideals of peace and love on the football field. Likewise Villa's teen flair sensation Brian Little, who modelled his helmet of hair on that of Ozzy Osbourne, but who had the good sense to avoid getting into rounds with Black Sabbath.

Not so, Friday. Retired at 25 because he was "fed up of people telling [him] what to do," he was, almost inevitably, dead by 38.

At the noisy DIY end of the Seventies, future England left-back Stuart Pearce was a regular on the West London punk scene, even showing up as one of the crowd furiously pogoing on the inner sleeve of the Lurkers' 'Fulham Fallout' LP. Indeed, he's still into the brash, boisterous melodies of the Lurkers, the Stranglers and Chelsea. When Psycho notched up an MBE in 1998 for his sterling services to English football, they also took into consideration a record collection brimming with pure danger.

Into the 1980s, when Pearce had moved on from pogoing for Wealdstone to big-

Stuart Pearce

league Coventry City, there was only one player who ever made it into the pages of the *NME*, and that was Pat Nevin, football's first and last art-school groover. Foppish of fringe and pasty enough to be taken for a smackhead in his all-black gear and moody raincoat, it's hard to imagine what young Pat chatted about with Doug Rougvie and Micky Droy on the team bus. Joy Division and Russian literature, if his interviews were anything to go by.

Pat was so sullen, he wouldn't have been out of place in an Echo & the Bunnymen video – one where they just walk around with cheekbones, looking like they might smash something up if they could be bothered. But, like so many of football's groovers, his love of music seemingly enabled him to play to a different beat out on the pitch, out of synch with the obvious moves and familiar shapes. He outmanoeuvred opponents with revolutionary logic and dribbles soundtracked by the Cocteau Twins' ethereal swirl. Never, ever Joy Division's 'She's Lost Control Again'.

Pat was so cool he went to modern art galleries. He even hung out with John Peel, and dared to face down his own fans for their racism and violent tendencies. A classic outsider, he brought fans together by demonstrating the absurdity of hating a player because he had the wrong hair, the wrong background, the wrong skin.

By the end of the 1980s it was still possible to find fans who regarded John Barnes as a brilliant, if unwelcome foreigner in an England shirt; but his emergence as a gold-chained, backward-capped, mirror-shaded gangsta rapper on 'Anfield Rap' must have melted many an icy heart. It was that rare combination of unself-conscious boogieing and not caring that he looked a bit of a knob that broke down my own prejudice, which was based on the fact that Liverpool always won everything. And that line about the crowd going bananas... never was a footballer so effortlessly cool in the deeply unpromising circumstances of an FA Cup Final song.

And then he nailed it again in Englandneworder's cracking 'World in Motion', a World Cup song that replaced jingoism with the delicious notion of sneakily singing 'E for England'. Even from Pat Nevin's perspective, this was supercool: a football single by Joy Division, minus Ian Curtis, plus MC Barnesy...

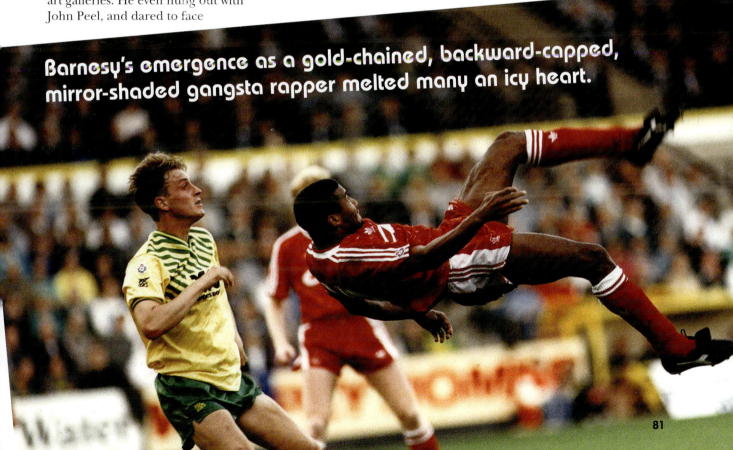

Barnesy's emergence as a gold-chained, backward-capped, mirror-shaded gangsta rapper melted many an icy heart.

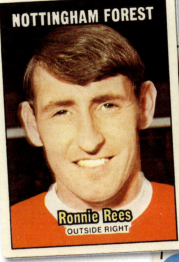

HALFWAY FLAGS

Whatever happened to halfway flags? One century they're there, minding their own business, thoughtfully flagging up the end of the halfway line... and the next century – maybe you haven't even noticed – all gone.

To find out, I contacted David Barber, the FA historian, a fan who has attended over 5,000 matches in his thirty-year tenure, and who knows absolutely everything about football. A useful, if underused, resource for people who don't.

I asked if he could shed any light on the disappearance of the mysteriously maligned flag, mentioning that I remembered seeing several circa 1987.

"I did some research into this a year or so ago," Mr. Barber replied. "I can remember that halfway flags weren't mentioned in the Laws until 1938.

"Crucially, the Law stated that they MAY be placed on the field, i.e. they weren't compulsory. I think they became unpopular because they obstructed, albeit slightly, the view from the dugouts."

No need to ask why the FA/PL didn't just tell the celebrity VIPs in the dugout to crane their necks a quarter of an inch.

Two Ronnies: one second on WBA's left wing, the next second on Forest's right.

HASTILY RECOLOURED KIT

There aren't many things in life that can cause man or boy as much alarm as a hastily recoloured kit on a football card or sticker.

For starters, there's the creeping sense of injustice as you see through the sticker company's little ruse – spotting the iffy, last-minute airbrushing and feeling soiled by the messy evidence of a crime.

Oh yes, it's a crime, all right. Cue righteous indignation at the perpetrators of the cheapskate sticker album, who simply couldn't be bothered to ask for a shot of Ian Wallace (Nottingham Forest) in his nice new kit, preferring instead simply to

colour in the old sky-blue shirt from the previous season's Ian Wallace (Coventry City). And witness how they compound their crime, trying in vain to cover their tracks with fake creases and shadows and spurious collar details. Caught red-handed.

But the filthiest trick in the sticker book has to be the unnatural horror of the head transplant.

First, an unsuspecting player is beheaded by the artist (or 'card sharp' in prison slang) who then sticks the offending appendage on to a perfect stranger's body in a disgraceful display of deceit and inappropriate forwardness.

The result of this unholy act: a Frankenstein's monster of a football card.

"I had the 1970 Mexico World Cup set. The Romanians had been photographed in black and white then coloured in. You'd open a packet and it would be one of the East Europeans and you'd scream... "The pictures were all from about 1962."

Mark E. Smith, The Fall

FRIENDLY FIRE

In English football, the 1979 scrap between Charlton's permed poaching partnership of Derek Hales and Mike Flanagan is probably the most famous incidence of fisticuffs between players nominally on the same side – all triggered when Hales strayed offside in a Cup match against non-League Maidstone, and Flanagan didn't approve. Also, we shouldn't forget Blackburn's Graeme Le Saux who, in a Judge Dredd-like case of instant justice dispensation, once broke his hand on team-mate David Batty's bonce.

In Scotland, however, this questionable tactic was elevated to new heights in 1994, just a couple of minutes into a pre-season friendly between Raith Rovers and Hearts.

That's how long it took the Jambos' twin centre-backs, Craig Levein and Graeme Hogg, to start exchanging less-than-constructive criticisms, which incited a two-handed shove from Hogg. Levein responded in kind, delivering a right hook with such ferocity that Hogg was knocked out, his nose broken – cue instant victory celebrations among whooping, wolf-whistling Rovers fans – before suffering the ignominy of being red-carded as he exited on a stretcher. Levein walked without waiting for the ref's verdict, condemning nine-man Jambos to a pointless humbling.

Only twelve matches into the season did Levein return, rejoining his old partner, who had been banned for ten. Cruel commentators later suggested the fondly remembered knockout punch figured high among Levein's qualifications for the job of Scotland manager.

TURNBULL'S TORNADOES

Eddie Turnbull was a member of Hibs' 'Famous Five', one of Scottish football's most influential forward lines. Tales abound of Turnbull, Ormond, Reilly, Johnstone and Smith's influence on Brazilian coaching during South American tours of the 1950s. And, as if that weren't enough mythmaking, Eddie Turnbull then returned for a second spell at Hibs, managing the club throughout their successful 1970s, with a side built around the solid defensive base of Pat Stanton, John Blackley and John Brownlie, with Arthur Duncan flying up the left wing.

Having limbered up by winning the Scottish League Cup and reaching the Scottish Cup Final in 1972, Hibs hit an all-time high on New Years' Day 1973 when they thrashed Hearts 7-0 at Tynecastle. Even finishing as League runners-up in 1974 and '75 didn't match the ecstasy of that day.

Our fans are the greatest, They cheer us each game, We're Turnbull's Tornadoes, Hibernian's the name...

The release of a local chart smash followed: 'Hibernian (Give Us a Goal)', twinned with a strangely familiar English folk song that was first borrowed by American slaves, then nicked in turn by John Lennon for 'Happy Xmas (War Is Over)'. Or 'Turnbull's Tornadoes', as it's known in Leith...

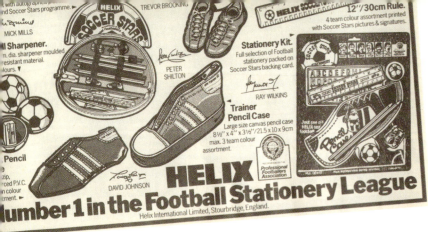

HELIX

What do you buy the Spurs fan who's got everything?

He's got White Hart Lane wallpaper on his desktop and black-and-white striped wallpaper on his office walls; he's got a Les Ferdinand 'Blue Peter Garden' screensaver; a 1981 Cup Final coffee mug and mouse mat, and a hollowed-out cockerel for an ashtray. He just recently snagged an original Martin Chivers Sliderama soccer projector from a car boot for 25p, which he keeps on his desk with his Amstrad computer and his original DIY-scrawled 'WE'LL TAKE MORE CARE OF YOU' pencil case devoted to Steve Archibald, full of Tottenham pens and pencils collected up over the years.

Few fans still own a signature-edition Justin Fashanu rubber.

But no one in their right mind has still got an authentic signature-edition Glenn Hoddle eraser, part of a whole range of Helix/PFA accessories in vogue thirty years ago...

HOME

It's already nine years since the last game was played at Filbert Street; eight years since they sent in the bulldozers, smashed it up and flattened our home to the ground.

Once, there was the North Stand, with its funny orange seats below executive boxes that hovered at crossbar height; the corrugated cowshed of the East Stand that backed on to the Burnmoor Street backyards; the steely Carling Stand that towered opposite, never even getting to see its tenth birthday; and, perhaps most poignantly of all, the Double Decker end with the Kop terraces skulking in the dark shadows beneath. The pitch, the floodlights, the scoreboard that never really worked properly. The famous inflatable 'Tent' that lay redundant for years, rolled up in front of the Kop. The whitewashed official gateway that guarded the north-west corner.

All gone.

Replaced by a hateful student accommodation block.

To be honest, even if it had been an architectural wonder to rival the Taj Mahal, I'd still think it was hateful. It's on our Filbert Street.

Even now, it's difficult to adjust to the fact that the place no longer exists, it having formed the backdrop to so much of my life. For all these years after its destruction I'd managed to ignore the place, passing no nearer than 200 yards when I walk to its successor to watch City's struggles. But eventually curiosity got the better of me, and one bright spring morning I decided to pay my final respects.

I parked up right next to Ground Zero amid the red-brick terraces and factory walls at the heart of Leicester's inexplicable Victorian nut quarter – Hazel, Walnut, Brazil… and Filbert Street.

Burnmoor Street looks the same as it ever did – although there's an almost indefinable something missing, apart from the crowds. A presence that isn't here, if that's possible. But the first real shock to the memory comes when you turn the corner: where the Double Decker used to loom, there's now just open sky and a tall wooden fence.

Looking through a gaping hole towards Filbert Street, there's a surprising expanse of wasteland pitch hidden away. Peering up the wing I try and place the exact spot where a scything tackle from enthusiastic young full-back Tommy Williams sent Norwich City's winger Jimmy Neighbour over the ad hoardings and into the front row of the East Stand. At least he fared better than Blackburn Rovers' Simon Garner, whose steaming progress down

I wore my best 'God, I'm sick of being hassled by the pigs but you won't make me lose my cool' expression...

and wondered what the Clash would say.

the wing was hilariously – you had to be there, and twelve – halted by a large snowball flush in the face.

Continuing on my way behind the ghost of the Kop, here is the spot where I first saw a fight between adults. Well, they were adults to me. In those days they were referred to as 'juveniles', a term now only used for young blackbirds and starlings. Even the term 'juvenile delinquents' has fallen out of usage. But that's pretty much what they were.

I remember lots of shouting, then punches and kicks being aimed and then long-haired men running past wearing bell-bottomed trousers and V-neck jumpers with stars on them. One had on well-polished brown Doc Marten boots, and a red silk scarf round his wrist with little white Liver Birds all over it.

So struck was I by this fleeing glam rock gladiator that I tried to assemble my own wardrobe to match, chasing my little brother up the garden with my royal blue 'Super Foxes' silk scarf.

Onwards, past what was once the turnstile for Pen 3 and is now a student's room full of iPods and laptops with WiFi and stuff like that. I recall a time when I was so bloody eager for my football fix that I'd get to the ground before the turnstiles opened at half-past one and lean against the wall reading my programme with the other early birds. I remember the grand feeling of self-importance the first time I warranted a search before handing over my £2 to get in. I wore my best 'God, I'm sick of being hassled by the pigs but you won't make me lose my cool' expression and wondered what the Clash would say.

85

Bentley's roof: top left behind trolley and terraces – once the finest free Filbo viewpoint.

WE APOLOGISE FOR ANY INCONVENIENCE CAUSED DURING THE CONSTRUCTION OF THE FIRST PHASE OF FILBERT VILLAGE.

The road now swings to the right and you're heading out towards the centre spot. Filbert Village may look like a big complex but it only occupies about a third of the old site. The rest is boarded up, hoarded away, awaiting further developments.

SHOULD YOU HAVE ANY CONCERNS PLEASE CONTACT THE MAIN ENTRANCE RECEPTION.

I realise I'm now walking near to what the tabloids dubbed 'The Tunnel of Hate' after we played Barnsley one night and the ref had an absolute shocker. Among the general vitriol and disapproval thrown at him was a more tangible plastic bottle, which bounced off his head. The tunnel was cordoned off by blue fencing after that, and no longer could we offer the players advice and encouragement as they came on and off the pitch. No longer could we try and touch them with our dangling scarves... or aim missiles at referees.

To my right is the home dugout where Jock

Approaching the south-west corner, Brazil Street turns into Lineker Road (a nice World Cup flavour to this corner) and we're now behind what was the Carling Stand, or pre-1993, the old Main Stand. Looking through the electric gates you can see into a forecourt. The back wall is roughly where balding ex-panel beater Gary Coatsworth was standing when he wellied the hardest shot anyone has ever seen past the Luton Town goalkeeper in 1994.

Around the corner, on the other side of a fence, I spot a survivor. A stretch of car park that used to lie right outside the players' entrance. To the developers, it's just another hectare of Tarmac at an inflated market price; but to me it's worth more than any number of gated apartment blocks.

Lineker never looked like a man who would have a street named after him. Maybe a large, willing greyhound, but never a street. Especially not a street right there, under his feet in the six-yard box.

Wallace and his assistant Ian MacFarlane would turn the air blue with Scottish profanities in the late Seventies and early Eighties. To my left is where I used to sit on the wall in the family enclosure. Where we gawped at Sheffield United's glamorous Argentinian Alex Sabella as he came to take a throw-in. Not everyone was so awestruck by this exotic pioneer. "Yer big Argie POOF!" someone shouted after him as he went on his way, legs unfeasibly tanned and shiny in the floodlights.

A few yards from there marks the spot beneath the Carling Stand, its occupants gasping with audible horror, where Alan Shearer booted Neil Lennon in the face before assuming the facial expression of a wronged angel in 1998. He wasn't banned for life because England had a friendly the following week. They even cut the tape of the incident out of *Match of the Day*.

Halfway across the pitch, thirty yards from goal, Alan Birchenall struck a bullet into the top left-hand corner past Leeds' David Harvey back in 1974. But now the road swings to the left to join up with Filbert Street. From here, through a break in the high board fencing on either side of the road, there's a better, more heartbreaking, view of the pitch.

I pace it out from the Filbert Street pavement, though the ghost of the back wall of the North Stand, through the orange seats, over the perimeter track and twelve yards and I reckon I'm standing on the penalty spot. The spot from which penalty-king Gary McAllister occasionally found the net in the late Eighties is now in the middle of the new access road, broken boarding on either side allowing access out into hallowed scrubland.

The north-east corner is now a concrete floor overgrown with shrubs, occupied only by a lonely shopping trolley. This was where the away fans used to be housed when segregation was first dreamed up in the Seventies, a riot of noise and activity compared to this desolate scene. Later, they gave this corner to the Supporters' Club, with standing at the back and seating at the front, and it was from right here in 1979 that I saw scrawny teenager Gary Lineker's debut against Oldham. At the time, he never looked like the kind of man who would have a street named after him – maybe a large, willing greyhound, but never a street. Especially not a street *right there*, under his feet in the six-yard box.

Back on Burnmoor Street, I head back to the car past a house that still shows signs of having at one time been converted into a turnstile block, the only physical reminder of the stadium that still survives – unless you count the house a few doors along which the Supporters' Club bought up for their HQ.

But today there's no one home.

Filbert Street was a far from perfect stadium, with two huge stands standing over two Fourth Division corrugated sheds, but it was a perfect fit for us and for Leicester. It was exactly half-decent. From the stands, you could look out over the city and you knew where you were.

At last, I realise what's missing from the atmosphere of the familiar terraced street. Swinging into the car, I look up automatically for a final glimpse of the great white floodlight pylons towering high into the sky over the rooftops.

Up the Filberts: if only they'd sited the main entrance on Brazil Street...

13

HOME INTERNATIONALS

How we used to thrill to the needle and colourful fan antics of the traditional England-Scotland head-to-head in the Home Internationals. How we relished the tantalising possibility of an upset against Wales or Northern Ireland. And how we made excuses when it actually happened.

Then, in 1984, a thinktank of self-appointed FA bigwigs took a look at the cluttered international fixture list alongside the record books and decided a hundred years was enough. In England's total of 266 games, Scotland had won 31, Wales 12 and Northern Ireland just six.

Time to bring on the serious drama of the Rous Cup, where the British Championship minnows were axed and replaced, first with the mighty Brazil, then with Colombia… and so to Chile.

Crossbar-snapping tam-o-shanter shenanigans aside, Scotland's greatest Home International moment came in 1967, when they took on the newly crowned World Champions at Wembley, winning a famous 3-2 victory and the proud mantle of 'Real' Champs of the World.

In an age when England's many friendly matches are dispensed as 'little favours' by bureaucrats and politicians, isn't it time to bring back the old oppo, chosen by history?

Crossbar-snapping tam-o-shanter shenanigans aside, Scotland's greatest moment came at Wembley in 1967, when a 3-2 victory earned them the mantle of

'Real' Champions of the World...

HOT SHOT HAMISH

Oh dear, we are living in serious times.

"I am surprised that this stereotype is being perpetuated in this day and age," complains Angus McNeil, SNP MP for the Western Isles. "The creators were living in more politically incorrect times."

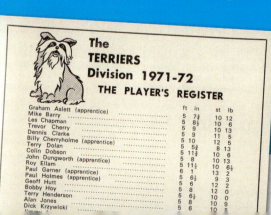

Willie MacDonald, the manager of Isle of Lewis side Back FC, is even more damning, telling the *Sunday Times*: "This will not raise a smile up here. A guy who has never seen a football and is going around with a sheep is absolutely ridiculous. Some things in it are horrific and this type of character has never existed on the islands."

McMutton the psychotic pet sheep: known for snapping cross baas.

Apparently, not everyone was as delighted as me to hear news of a *Hot Shot Hamish 2009 Annual*. I pre-ordered the reprinted strips sharpish, and had to wait months before I could start reacquainting myself with a boyhood hero, right from the very first frame...

"On a bleak, rain-swept, mist-enshrouded island in the lonely Hebrides... the Princes Park players spent six rain-sodden days. A training holiday!"

They soon bump into a huge, blonde, sheepskin- and kilt-toting Highlander by the name of Hamish Balfour. And within three frames he's tapped back a stray ball with such ferocity that it demolishes a stone wall.

That's how, back in August 1973, *Scorcher* comic set up the classic story of an innocent abroad in the big city, brightening the prospects of a lowly Scottish basement outfit. Fred Baker's still-funny scripts were brought to life by the stylish Argentinian illustrator Julio Schiaffino, who always pictured such teams playing in San Siro-sized stadiums.

Princes Park FC's path to glory was never smooth, with clashes between Hamish's boss Ian McWhacker, his permanently furious Daddie and psychotic 'wee pet sheep' McMutton; but there was usually a happy ending involving a snapped crossbar.

Hamish's place was sealed in the hearts of Princes Park fans the day he noticed a failing beam under a crowded stand, holding it up like a muscle-bulging Atlas to save the lives of, ahem, thousands of spectators.

And so: a big-hearted, humorous international role model. Not the kind of Highlander that Angus or Wullie would want to be associated with.

Huddersfield Town

PLAYBOY

"Bill Shankly said, 'Do you want to come and play for Liverpool?' I nodded at him, because it wasn't a difficult decision. And he added: '... because we need you.'

"They NEEDED me? Can you imagine the impact of that on a young player? It was fantastic."

Frank Worthington is reliving for us the time he almost signed for Liverpool, long the subject of fan and media conjecture. He'd signed the papers, done the TV interviews. It was all down to the medical. All perfect, except for the last test: Frank's blood pressure was high. Here's why.

"Now, I was a bit of a rascal at that time and I was living fast. I was having a good time on the pitch and a good time off it as well. I used to go

to the In-Time club in Leeds, very small and select. I used to see the dancing girl in a cage, have a drink, though I was never a big drinker, have a dance at the disco. Leeds has always had a very high standard of good-looking females and it was a brilliant place to go. It was a great time.

"I had a Ford Mustang at the time that had belonged to the Beatles manager," Franks sighs. "I had all these trappings of a potential England footballer, but perhaps it was a bit much at that age..."

FER ARK

The KC Stadium may boast a parkland setting, 25,586 seats in a trendily asymmetrical bowl, a 1,500-seat Sports Arena, two multi-use all-weather pitches and a community learning zone with a health & fitness suite – and it may *also* have hosted Hull's only two seasons in the top flight – but Tigers' fans of a certain age will still hanker for Boothferry Park. Football supporters are funny like that.

They do things differently in Hull, as indicated by the cream phone boxes and tiger-print football shirts. Boothferry Park took seventeen years to build due to shortfalls in finance and the outbreak of World War II, but it was just about ready to use by 1946. By the mid Sixties it was considered one of the best grounds outside the top flight, with its own train station, Boothferry Halt, behind the East Stand, an indoor sports hall and, unusually, six floodlight pylons, once the tallest in Europe.

But lack of success on the pitch saw falling gates, parlous finances and a crumbling ground, with the North Terrace surrendering territory to KwikSave. When the majority of letters on the illuminated sign failed to light up, the ground earned the nickname 'FER ARK'.

During seasons in the lower divisions, and several financial crises, a stadium like the KC and Premier League football would have seemed unattainable. Not for the first time, Hull thought differently.

The bigger they are: Boothferry Park's floodlight pylons were once Europe's tallest.

Tigers' fans of a certain age **still hanker for Boothferry Park.**

NEVER MIND MATE — READ ALL ABOUT IT IN TONIGHTS:— FOOTBALL "POST

IN FOR FREE

The chances of getting to watch even a quarter of a football match for free are now much reduced. There used to be hills in town centres, and gaps between stands; but these potential chinks in clubs' armour were plugged by the advent of corrugated steel stadiums built to the same design as any other warehouse on the featureless industrial park. Except without the roof, of course – just in case you happen to own a hot-air balloon.

It must have been around 200 years ago when Craven Cottage groundsmen reported to Fulham chairman Tommy Trinder that they'd found a gap in the club railings by the river in Bishop's Park.

"Leave it," he told them, explaining that the club might lose a couple of bob today, but they'd gain fans for life. "That's how I used to get in when I was a kid."

First game at Adams Park – and a free view in from this handy pile of builder's rubble.

IN THE BUFF

It was the same old faces every week waiting outside the newsagents, autumn, winter and spring – the old and the young. Just before 6.00pm the *Mercury* van would rumble into view, stopping just long enough for eager hands to help the driver unload his buff-coloured bale, and off down the road to the newsagents in the next village. Our booty would be hauled into the shop, the string snipped and the *Sports Mercury* distributed to those of us who couldn't rest until we'd read a report of a game that some of us had seen finish just eighty minutes ago (unless we were after confirmation of a result we'd just heard played out on the radio).

The *Buff* gave you the chance to settle down in a favourite armchair, to check the pools and peruse the results and league tables at your leisure. In the days before Sky News and even Ceefax, it was either this or wait for the arrival of the Sunday papers.

This ritual went on up and down the country for many decades. *Green 'Uns, Pink 'Uns, Blue 'Uns* and *Buffs*. Any colour as long as it wasn't white. Here was sports journalism at its most demanding, where reports were phoned in on the hoof, assumptions were made before the final whistle, and last-minute goals were any editor's nightmare. As the *Sports Argus* headline proclaimed on West Brom's 1968 FA Cup Final meeting with Everton: "IT'S EXTRA TIME..." (with a small white space hastily filled in with "then Astle scores.")

Gradually the need for a Saturday evening sports edition lessened and then disappeared altogether. The internet was one blow – suddenly you didn't need to be standing out on the street in January – but the killer was the spreading of fixtures over the weekend due to the demands of TV.

In 2005, Paul Robertson, editor of the Newcastle *Evening Chronicle* called time on the *Pink 'Un* after a run of 110 years. "Newcastle

Reports were phoned in on the hoof, assumptions were made before the final whistle, and last-minute goals were any editor's nightmare.

United had just ten 3 o'clock kick-offs in 21 games up to Christmas," he explained to *The Independent*.

One by one, the rest had to admit defeat and hold up their hands in surrender, in Liverpool and Manchester, Leicester and Coventry and Birmingham... although the Norwich *Pink 'Un* and Ipswich's *Green 'Un* are both websites now. If you can't beat 'em, join 'em.

INJURIES BEFORE CRUCIATES AND METATARSALS

An imaginative infant, I used to love the idea of being heroically injured out on the football pitch. At bedtime, I would only nod off to sleep after acting out, under the covers, a set-piece involving a slow-motion foul, my flying through the air and lying semi-conscious on the soft, warm, dimly floodlit turf (the realistic bit), while the crowd roared to draw the ref's attention to my squirming plight.

Everybody did this kind of thing, right?

The dislocated shoulder was a favourite, acted out hundreds of times after it was suffered, in real life, by Arsenal's Peter Simpson. Mick Jones and his FA Cup Final dislocated elbow was another injury which caught my imagination.

What a shame I'd moved on to fantasies of flying through space in a special lie-down UFO Interceptor – co-pilots with purple hair by now an optional attraction – by the time Bryan Robson began to provide so many alternatives to counting sheep.

No one in English football history has suffered as many World Cup-wrecking injuries as Robbo. His weekly catalogue of old-school sprains, abrasions, breaks, twists, fractures, dislocations, gashes and impactions could alter the whole nation's mood.

After three decades of minor injuries involving little reflected glory, I finally made a nostalgic breakthrough last Thursday, training on the Astroturf with Kibworth Tuesday.

It wasn't just the small crowd of impatient well-wishers that gathered round. It wasn't the painful kick I'd received on the top of my foot. But what a thrill when an off-duty GP explained the throbbing, and I finally discovered the whereabouts of my heroic metatarsal.

Under the covers I would act out a slow-motion foul, and lying semi-conscious on the soft, warm turf...

FIRST AID BOX

Accident waiting to happen: Robbo on a football pitch – temporarily.

93

INTERNATIONAL HONOURS

What an honour it must once have been to be selected to play for your country. Eleven men representing millions, walking out into a packed gladiatorial dustbowl on the other side of the world, doing your duty on behalf of your Queen. Ignoring the catcalls, the din of tinny trumpets, the damp handshake of the referee from a country that the skipper suspects may not have been on the right side in both World Wars. Singing the words of the National Anthem louder than the oppo mumble along to the rhumba rhythm of their tinpot dictator's self-penned song of praise...

That's how it always was in the comics, anyway.

Such was the clamour for international duty, League Representative XIs were also assembled to recognise the sterling work of players of character, testing to the limit their steel under fire.

None feigned injury, none made excuses, none cried, "club before country."

Inter-League Match

Secretary, J. H. Long

Irish League versus Football League of Ireland

EASTER MONDAY
3rd APRIL, 1961
KICK-OFF 3 P.M
CLIFTONVILLE
BELFAST

OFFICIAL

FINDUS
Chosen for England
ALAN BALL

6d

None feigned injury, none made excuses, none cried,

"club before country."

ITV SUNDAY AFTERNOONS

Today an old friend emailed me an mp3 file entitled 'Star'.

I instantly recognised the blaring, barely-in-control brass section of the *Star Soccer* theme tune and was transported back to a mid-Seventies Sunday afternoon at two o'clock.

Good old Hugh Johns: he commentated on Wolves in sheep's clothing.

The Sunday dinner that had taken Mum hours to cook was wolfed down in two minutes. Roast beef and Yorkshire puddings lay in my stomach, barely chewed, as I rushed to turn on the old black-and-white telly so that it would warm up in time for that blasting fanfare, played over a backdrop of one of the Midlands grounds, and the welcoming

South Midland baritone of commentator Hugh Johns – a dark-chestnut, favourite-uncle tone underscored with a hint of Naval-issue cigarettes.

There was little room for manoeuvre in the editing suite, back then. The main game, however incident-packed or dull, ran for fifteen minutes up to a half-time ad break, followed by another quarter of an hour for the second half.

Part three brought fifteen minutes of a game from another ITV region, maybe yours. Granada's Gerald Sinstadt was the voice of *Kick Off*; Tyne Tees was Kenneth Wolstenholme on *Shoot*, while LWT's *The Big Match* was fronted by Brian Moore...

After part four's brief highlights of another game – usually Norwich or Ipswich from

Anglia's *Match of the Week* with Gerry Harrison – and a round-up of results, the weekend seemed almost over.

Dozens of games went untelevised every weekend and that's why seeing your team was so special. With perhaps only two or three TV appearances in a lean year, the novelty never wore off.

Star Soccer's run, from 1968 to 1983, coincided with some great times for Midlands clubs. Derby, Forest and Villa all won the League title and the League Cup hardly ever left the region with Stoke, Villa (twice), Forest (twice), and Wolves (twice) all lifting the three-handled trophy. All the other Division One teams had smatterings of great players: Francis and Latchford (Birmingham), Hibbitt and Richards (Wolves), Greenhoff and

Hurst (Stoke), Cunningham and Regis (West Brom), Weller and Worthington (Leicester). Even down the leagues, Walsall had Alan Buckley and Notts County Don Masson.

The 1983-84 season saw the introduction of *Central Match Live*, and things would never be the same again. How we marvelled at those live televised matches, having previously been restricted to only three or four per year; but, of course, they only led to saturation coverage of more games than you could ever want to see.

Hugh Johns, the voice of Midlands football and a comforting constant across hundreds of Sunday afternoons, sadly passed on in 2007. No doubt which music would have given him a suitably stirring send-off.

The Sunday dinner that had taken Mum hours to cook was wolfed down in two minutes. I rushed to turn on the black-and-white telly, so it would

warm up in time for that blasting fanfare...

OSBORNE OVERWHELMED

A good indication of the FA Cup's prestige a few decades ago was its capacity for catapulting modest footballers into superstardom in the time it took to steer the ball past an onrushing keeper.

When Roger Osborne walked out of the Wembley tunnel for the 1978 FA Cup final which saw Ipswich Town playing the underdogs to Arsenal, he probably wasn't even the most famous person living in the Suffolk village of Otley (that honour would surely go to bird impersonator Percy Edwards). But his 77th-minute winner ensured that he was a household name by teatime.

Bobby Robson's side dominated their more fashionable opponents and had hit the woodwork three times before

David Geddis skinned Sammy Nelson down the right and hit over a hard, low cross which Willie Young could only block into Osborne's path. The midfielder made no mistake firing a left-footed shot past Pat Jennings and into the net, as David Coleman told the nation: "And Osborne, this member of a family of twelve, who've come in a special bus to watch the match, puts it away."

As another barometer of the Cup's prestige, Osborne was so overcome with joy at scoring a Cup Final goal that he emerged from the celebratory scrum looking distinctly shaky and was substituted after a spell of treatment, having momentarily blacked out.

These days, when one of the Big Two routinely lift the FA Cup, it's difficult to imagine anyone getting quite so excited.

Ipswich Town

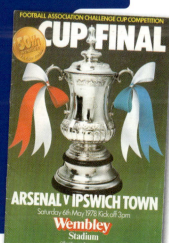

j

JAM JAR LIDS

Hartley's Strawberry Jam was already yummy enough, without them coming up with a further incentive for us to consume it even more greedily.

The introduction of footballers' faces to the lids during the 1971-72 season was marketing genius: Alan Ball, Gordon Banks, Colin Bell, George Best, Billy Bremner, Bobby Charlton, Ron Davies, Geoff Hurst, Jimmy Johnstone, Bobby Moore, Peter Osgood, Martin Peters. A stellar line-up of football stars; twelve jars' worth to collect. That was a lot of jam – and a major expense for parents watching every half a new pee – but we ploughed through it somehow.

A 'jam samwich' was one of the few culinary treats you could prepare without parental guidance, and the more you slapped between the slices the nearer you were to your next fantastic lid.

And if you were too full of Mother's Pride or Hovis for another sandwich but couldn't wait to get your hands on the lid with Colin Bell wearing his England tracksuit, you could always dip a spoon in and steal a couple more inches... nom nom nom.

THE JOCK-STRAP

I've never worn a jock-strap, and I'm not even sure what they're supposed to be for. Does *anyone* today still wear one? Are they officially a thing of the past, or maybe just confined to minority sports like rugby and sumo wrestling?

I've seen one on the changing-room floor a few times over the years, but have never liked to stare. I guess scrotal support is the idea, as a little cotton pouch with complicated leg straps surely wouldn't offer much protection against a free-kick in the plums.

The thing is, no one I play football with wears a jock-strap, either, although I can't help thinking some of us might have done if we'd been playing as adults thirty years ago. Without beating about the bush, could it be that genitalia has shrunk since the Seventies, rendering our tackle no longer worth supporting or protecting?

Maybe pants are tighter today, making extra jock-strap support unnecessary.

But I wear boxers.

THE JOKER IN THE PACK
Extinct Football Species No. 5

They don't really have dressing-room jokers any more, beyond the player who dishes out the most 'stick' about the apprentices' pitiful wage packets.

Whatever else slips away, Gazza will never lose his honorary title of the game's greatest practical joker. This is the man who, on the spur of the moment, borrowed the brand-new £250,000 Middlesbrough team bus to nip down the bookies and crashed into a wall, causing a £20,000 dent; who cheekily waved a dropped yellow card at the ref when he was playing for Rangers, suffering a booking as a result of the official's sense-of-humour bypass.

Like all dedicated jokers, Gazza could be painstaking in his preparations, offering to pay for his mate Jimmy 'Five Bellies' Gardner to

Young Player of the Year 1987-88 – in the last of Gazza's three seasons with Newcastle.

Gazza hopped out of his taxi and persuaded a workman to let him **'have a gur'** on his pneumatic drill.

THE JOKER

JOSSY'S GIANTS

Football's just a branch of science, right? Were you one of the 6.3 million viewers who sat glued to *Jossy's Giants* back in the Eighties, making it the most successful TV kids' drama of all time?

It was Cambridge historian and hyperactive Voice of Darts, Sid Waddell, who wrote the series about a kids' team – "swapping your homework for footwork, kicking the ball until it's dark." And when we asked him about the show, he let on that it was all based on a true story.

"When my son Daniel was nine he played for Churwell Lions, for a team run by Sonny Sweeney," Sid told us. "Sonny looks like a Scottish clan chief but only 5' 6" high; pale hair and wild blue eyes. He'd captained Scotland as a fifteen-year-old, but he came here to Leeds and couldn't make the first team thanks to Bremner.

"Sonny dressed the goalie in corporation bin liners and Sellotaped him in. He was teaching these kids catenaccio when they were seven, using ludo pieces and a Christmas cake Santa Claus on a ouija board!"

Not only that, the real-life Giants are still in business. "He's got 160 seven- to sixteen-year-olds playing for Churwell. Sonny's ambition is to take them to play in the Maracana, but the best we've done so far is Germany and a trip to play a Glasgow borstal!"

Joswell 'Jossy' Blair: ex-pro contender, now boss of the Glipton Giants.

fly out to Lazio for a visit, then booking him on to a tortuous series of flights, sending him zigzagging halfway round the world.

Best now remember Paul Gascoigne when his larger-than-life talent matched the scale and innocent glee of his pranks.

Let's hold on to the image of Gazza stopping his taxi in the middle of a busy London street, and hopping out to persuade a workman to let him 'have a gur' on his pneumatic drill, spending twenty minutes happily destroying the pavement. And what about the time he booted a ball out of the training ground, quickly volunteering to hop over the hedge to fetch it. Gazza went missing. Only 24 hours later did he re-emerge through the hedge with the ball, straight faced, as if nothing had happened.

JUMBLE SALE STADIUMS

They don't build stands like this any more.
Proper stands, that looked like grim
Victorian factories. Stands that stood awkwardly
across the corner of the pitch, with nothing
whatsoever to do with the rest of the stadium,
and grimy glass sides that prevented fans in

many of its 2,000 seats from seeing the far
penalty box. Stands that looked like they were
falling apart, but in fact had large sections of
pitched roof purposely left out so as to allow
punters on the back rows to see the opposite
touchline. Stands built on stilts over fans

cowering underneath on shadowy terraces.
Work on Chelsea's North Stand began in 1939 but it wasn't finished until after the war. At the end of the Swinging Sixties, they decided its glowering mood didn't fit in with the King's Road's new-fangled boutiques and groovy bistrotheques. They used the Safety of Sports Grounds Act as a flimsy excuse, and demolished the grim, satanic garden shed after less than thirty years of use; but it lives on in the nightmares of Football Supporters Association officers and Health & Safety jobsworths.

Cuckoo Lane's scoreboard stand: from the same jumble-sale as Derby's old exec boxes.

Farewell also to Oxford United's Manor Ground, which somehow managed to fit at least nine assorted stands and terraces around the pitch, most of which looked like the shoebox efforts we improvised for our Subbuteo ground.

Never again will we wander down the quaintly tree-lined alley behind the Cuckoo Lane End, or wonder what the original plan was for the Osler Road side, which ended up with no less than three jerry-built stands jostling for position.

Could Hudson, Worthington or Bowles jump over a Mini?

Duncan McKenzie could!

JUMPING OVER MINIS

"I was only sixteen at the time. It was one of those things that kids do," explained Duncan McKenzie to *Leeds United Monthly*.

Well, I don't remember doing it, do you?

McKenzie, born in Grimsby in 1950, played his football when maverick talents were not in short supply; but could Hudson, Worthington or Bowles jump over a Mini?

McKenzie could, and he did so before a game at Elland Road, just to prove it.

He could also throw a golf ball the length of a football pitch, another impressive if ultimately useless achievement.

Having made his name at Nottingham Forest, McKenzie was Brian Clough's first signing as short-lived manager of Leeds. Supporters of Anderlecht, Everton, Chelsea and Blackburn also enjoyed his talents in brief but brilliant helpings. Everton fans still talk about him nutmegging Tommy Smith in a Maine Road semi-final against Liverpool. The Anfield Iron's verdict was: "The best place for Duncan McKenzie is in a circus."

I'd buy a ticket for that.

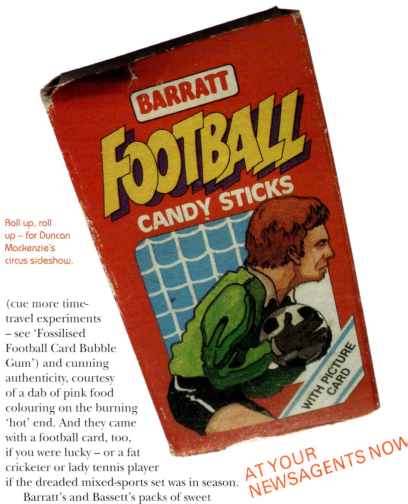

JUNIOR FAGS

Just because you hadn't yet stumbled into double figures by 1970, that was no excuse for not joining the rest of humanity and nurturing a healthy nicotine addiction, using all the props and substitute substances contributed by forward-thinking grown-ups.

Junior school kids across the nation were duly provided with bubble pipes, and soon struggled to put a foot on the floor of a morning without lighting up and blowing a roomful of Fairy Liquid bubbles to clear their heads. The liquorice pipe was sprinkled with rock-hard sugar balls, but still tasted like earwax. Not a patch on a plastic wallet full of apparently authentic pipe tobacco, which only on further inspection turned out to be desiccated coconut, dyed brown for its sins. And then there were the joke cigarettes from the novelty rack at Modern Toys: how wicked it felt to puff talcum powder from the end of a cardboard tube.

Sweet cigarettes, however, were clearly the best option for L-plate smokers, both in terms of their unique, chalky-sweet flavour

(cue more time-travel experiments – see 'Fossilised Football Card Bubble Gum') and cunning authenticity, courtesy of a dab of pink food colouring on the burning 'hot' end. And they came with a football card, too, if you were lucky – or a fat cricketer or lady tennis player if the dreaded mixed-sports set was in season.

Barratt's and Bassett's packs of sweet cigarettes were a throwback to the cigarette cards that had died out in the war; but we never realised that at the time. We were too busy posing manfully with our sugary cig dangling from our lips, fooling absolutely everybody.

Along with the fag ads in the *Football League Review* – always proffered invitingly in a perfect pyramid from a full packet – sweetie cigarettes made me yearn for a future snug bar filled with smoke and laughter, where fellow smokers in polo necks would drink warm pints of beer and talk in leathery catchphrases.

We were too busy posing manfully with our sugary cig dangling from our lips, **fooling absolutely everybody.**

"Player's: Part of the British Scene."

"Worthington 'E': for the Sporting Men of the Midlands."

"The Size, the Taste, the Style. A Big, Satisfying, Born Leader of a Cigarette – 29p with coupons."

Soon there would be no more sitting out in the car park with crisps and a Vimto, listening to Johnny Walker's Top 30 rundown. Soon I would learn not to shudder at the seawater taste of lemonade shandy, and I'd stride right into the sun-striped gloom of the adult world. I'd pull up a bar stool next to a girl smoking alone, and quite possibly challenge her to a game of dommies.

THE KAYS CATALOGUE

Imagine a method of getting pictures of thousands of highly desirable items right under the nose of a shopper, without them having to leave the comfort of their own sofa. Cooyer, eh? The Kays Catalogue of Autumn/Winter 1982 was like a fat, glossy printout of the internet. It offered punters of all ages a tantalising glimpse of the good life in a 1,004-page cornucopia of goods we wanted but couldn't afford – so just as well everything was available on the tick.

Okay, it might have ended up adding 50p to the price, but 'Britain's favourite catalogue' ensured your mum got your six-function Sekonda LCD alarm watch *right now*, in plenty of time for Christmas. You wouldn't want to miss out on a watch that could magically play a tune to wake you up in the middle of double biology, or your daily union meeting. Especially if it was 'The Yellow Rose of Texas'.

Re-entering this world of 1982 frozen in aspic, the clothes and everything electrical appear strikingly pricey for thirty years ago, primarily because they were either hot new tech (Sanyo Personal Micro Stereo Cassette

I'm into CB: What's your handle, good buddy?

It was a tough choice on the all-action pyjama front: a red-belt polyester-cotton kung fu kimono, or
an authentic Admiral England kit sleepsuit?

Player, £99.95 or 38 weeks at £2.65) or manufactured in Britain, where workers were traditionally paid for their skilled labour.

Ideal's Electronic Detective game is just such a chunk of cutting-edge clutter, "The ultimate in 'Who done it?' games, where one to four players combine human deduction with advanced computer logic to solve 130,000 different murder mysteries." That was more than *The Professionals*, *Hart to Hart*, the Metropolitan Police and *Magnum, PI* combined. No wonder it was £31.99, or twenty weeks of shelling out £1.60.

The Kevin Keegan-branded Grandstand Football Game also catches the eye, primarily because it looks better than our Kick-the-Goal Soccer. It's a little hand-held football pitch with lights to show you where the ball is supposed to be. "Two skill levels, records each goal scored. 'Ball in Net' display. Simulated footballer figures, full action sound effects and referee's whistle."

Nice touch, Kev, chucking in the whistle. Maybe you had to be there. Yours for £19.99, or twenty weeks at £1.34.

What a tough choice you were faced with on the all-action pyjama front: do you go with a red-belt polyester-cotton kung fu kimono, or get Mum to dig deeper for an authentic-looking Admiral England kit sleepsuit? The Admiral top looks almost too good for the bedroom, like it might double up as a football jersey for up the park. But what if people notice you're wearing your jimjams, and take the piss? Best stick with the Bruce Lee option.

Strange how, even decades after the catalogue was superseded by Spring/Summer 1983, you

The Kays Catalogue of Autumn/Winter 1982 was like
a fat, glossy printout of the entire internet.

fall into just the same mental traps – picturing yourself wearing a swanky manager-style car coat, and the reception it would invite down the pub; gazing longingly at the rows of little knobs on the CB set, dreaming of being able to talk direct to a lorry driver trundling up the A1 – slowly but surely losing your grip on reality.

There's no chance Mum will ever pay out six quid for pyjamas as long as Woolies knock out a stripy two-pack for half the price.

And thirty quid for a computer game? Dream on.

Best wait for the far-distant 2010s, when you'll be able to flick through your antique shopping catalogue and snap up all the goodies for pennies via eBay. Like the Anglo Bubbly, the old ground pilgrimage and the recreation of Eighties feuds at 'Masters' six-a-side tournaments, the Kays Catalogue certainly takes you back.

TO-DAY'S TOP SOCCER READING VALUE!

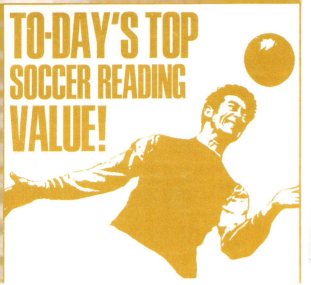

KEEPY UPPY

The law of going up the reccie states: "Should there be six or more players available, they shall be divided into teams accordingly on a pitch size determined by the two captains. Should there be five, then they shall play cuppies – two teams of two kicking into one goal, taking turns as goalkeeper. And should there be three or under, they shall play keepy-uppy."

It takes two minutes to understand the rules of keepy-uppy and a lifetime to get past fifty.

The ball cannot touch the ground and should be constantly propelled upwards by feet, knees, thigh, chest or head.

One summer we did virtually nothing else and managed a glorious 72.

Here we see rare images from the grand Leeds United Keepy-Uppy Tournament of 1971.

Left to right: Terry Cooper manages a well balanced 27; Johnny Giles a rather stiff 19; Terry Hibbitt an erratic nine. Keep practising lads…

KICK-THE-GOAL SOCCER

Fashioned in beige and orange plastic to match the wallpaper, and featuring the kind of stunning graphics that showed up on the very first digital watches, this instantly addictive Japanese computer game seemed like a dream come true in 1979.

What you had to do was Use the Buttons to Control the Direction and Movement of the Ball-Carrier, starting each play from exactly the same position, and trying to weave your way through the seven oppo players who swarmed like flies over their patchy pixel pitch. Only ten years earlier man had flown to the moon using only one billion gallons of kerosene, a large tin can and a computer chip no more powerful than the one powering the Bambino; now the same technology was used merely to confound the opposition goalie by Kicking a Banana Shoot.

For the first time ever, it seemed cool not to play football or even go outside, but to stay in and close the curtains so the little overhead views of your virtual, wriggling players grew brighter and more exciting. This was science fiction. The real world of grass and mud and sky began to seem a dim second best.

Big in Japan: 'Maneuver Your Ball-Carrier to Successfully Score a Goal."

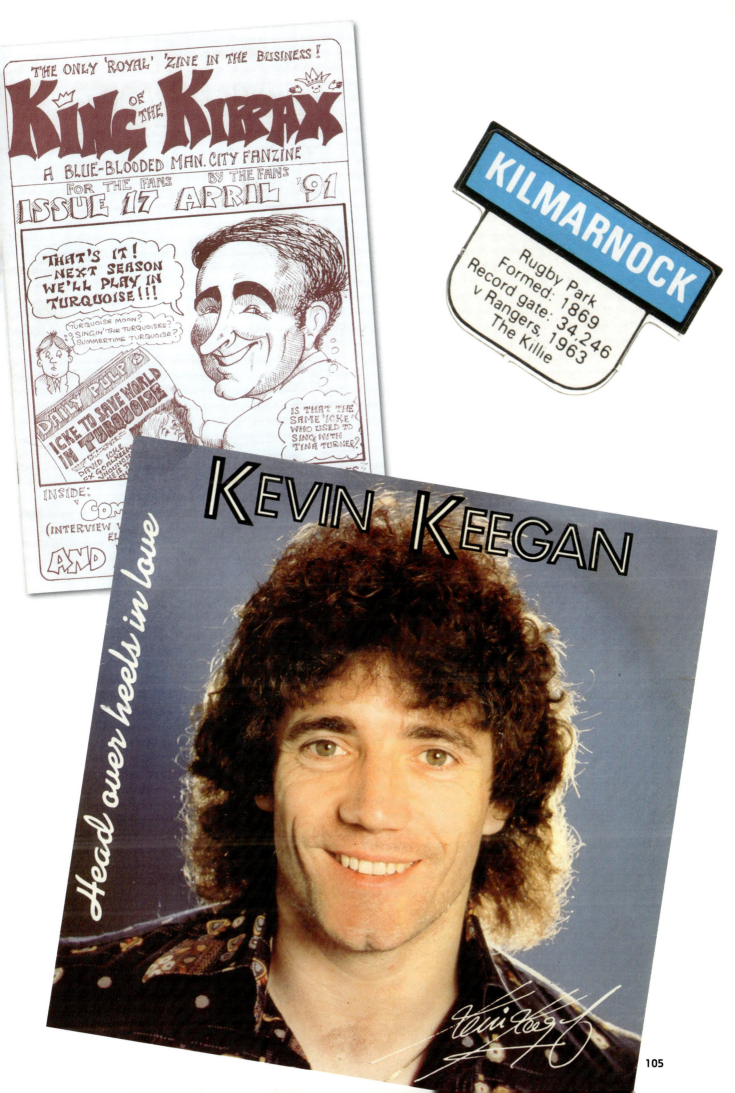

THE LANDLADY

When a promising kid was signed up by a professional club, often being uprooted from home for the first time, there was never any question of the youngster running off the rails in the big city.

A tried-and-tested system was in place to provide apprentices with good, basic accommodation and a hearty diet; also, to ensure they were up in time for training and in bed before the pubs shut. The lads were given free rein once their bootroom duties were over, although subtle checks were in place to ensure they didn't spend too much of their modest apprentice's wage on booze and fags, or too much of their free time in the company of the wrong kind (which is to say, any kind) of young lady.

The name of this multi-functional system was 'the landlady' – long replaced with a 5-star hotel suite, a personal minder, a club taxi on 24-hour call, loneliness, temptation and delusions of grandeur, all on a limitless budget.

Ooh, I can tell you if she'd had that El-Hadji Diouf in her digs, she'd have given him a thick ear for putting his elbows on the tea table. But she'd have forgiven him with a mumsy cuddle when she took him up his cocoa, and that would have made all the difference.

"Could you kindly set the table, Mr. Hernandez? It's kippers for tea tonight – your favourite. And then you and Mr. Smalling can come through into my parlour for a nice game of cribbage, for matchsticks."

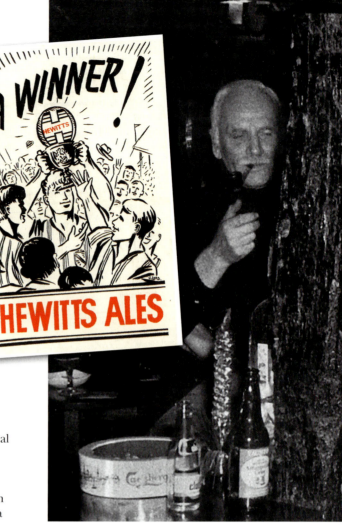

Full English: Eat up your fried bread now, it's full of energy.

THE LANDLORD

Acting on a tip-off direct from Upminster, I tapped 'Pub 1960s' into YouTube and at last paid a visit to my childhood-fantasy laughter-filled snug bar of the past, which I hadn't realised I'd told so many people about.

What an unexpected pleasure, joining not just Bobby Moore and Martin Peters but a couple of delightful young ladies for a Saturday night sherbet.

Mooro: "Tina's not the best darts player in the world, but she enjoys a game while she's waiting for me."

Me: "Gah, just my luck – she's only hitched to the England skipper."

Mooro: "After the match we often meet our wives for a quiet drink in the local. It's a nice, friendly place, and it's great to get together for an evening out."

Voiceover: "Like Mr. and Mrs. Bobby Moore, Look In at the Local!"

Ironically, now I've successfully made it to manhood and can set foot inside a pub, I'm beginning to yearn for a Cortina in a country-pub car park, a bottle of Vimto sucked through a straw and 'Seasons in the Sun' at number one.

If you know where to look, there are still a few pubs that haven't been converted into empty restaurants, although no first-class footballer would be seen dead in a boozer today. Not exclusive or expensive enough.

One for the road: Same again all round, on the house... and time for a sing-song.

In a whitewashed country boozer, an ex pro could hold court nightly, staging historical re-enactments and talking tactics with the chicken-in-a-basket condiments.

But it isn't the current crop of stars that I miss, it's their predecessors.

It was an unwritten rule of football for nigh on a century; it was a cliché, an affectionate in-joke and a source of unparalleled joy for fans whenever a professional footballer hung up his boots and became a pub landlord.

When players fell off the end of their career aged 36, too slow even for showboating down the leagues, their junkie knees not worth another season of pain and humiliation, full-time bar-leaning was the fading hero's traditional progression.

In a whitewashed country boozer, an ex-pro could settle down to the easy life, holding court nightly to an honoured inner circle of village regulars. On Friday and Saturday nights, fans would flock in and he would move on to full-blown historical re-enactments, even talking tactics with the chicken-in-a-basket condiments.

It was easy running a pub. Cleaning out the pipes, doing the orders, seeing to the food, serving behind the bar, cleaning glasses and wiping tables was like an extension of housework for the little lady. Organising Bank Holiday outings to the races – that was the important

business that only the landlord could handle.

But not every ex-footballer was born to run a boozer.

Bobby Moore ran Tipples in Bethnal Green, Shamps in Lower Clapton and Sweethearts in South Woodham Ferrers. He also rebranded the Black Bull in Stratford as Mooro's, but it burned down the night before its big launch. Meanwhile, all he'd ever wanted to do – the greatest reader of the game in English football – was to stay within the fold as a coach or manager. But that's where our World Cup-winning skipper's CV counted against him.

Asking for a transfer to Spurs in June 1966 and 1970 had burned Bobby's bridges at West Ham; he was an East End boy, which led certain organisations to view him with suspicion; his multiple business dealings were questioned; a few individuals even gave credence to the laughable theft charge cooked up as a distraction from the 1970 World Cup.

And so here's to Bobby, and what might have been.

107

LEAGUE LADDERS

During the long summer, when the nation became obsessed with cricket, and football knew its place and dared not intrude, the football magazines needed to make sure that we all returned to the fold in August – and they tempted us back with brightly coloured pieces of cardboard.

It was the old-school shoot-'em-up comics of the 1960s, *Lion* and *Valiant*, that first tried to entice football kids with these beginning-of-the-season 'free gifts', but they're more popularly associated with *Shoot!* and *Scorcher*, the all-new, all-football publications that tapped a burgeoning market around the dawn of the Seventies. The league ladder era extended into the Eighties, with *Roy of the Rovers*.

The ladders would be gifted to us first, followed by the team tabs week on week until we were raring to go by the time of the Big Kick-off. Using the *Sports Final* paper as a template we would then undertake the fiddly, time-consuming task of putting each club in its appropriate slot in the scheme of things.

In the days before computers, even before Teletext, the appeal of being able to stare at

the league table was considerable. But, after the third or fourth week, updating your league ladders became a bit too much like hard work.

Once the boredom set in, you could play God in a parallel universe by taking Liverpool out of the top spot and relegating them to the Fourth Division, Rochdale proudly taking their place. Or you could put Rangers and Celtic in the English First Division, just to see what it looked like. Ultimately, you could just shuffle them all up and put them in as they fell creating your own, wildly unlikely, version of the Football League. Look... Swansea in the First Division, and Burnley in the Fourth!

Several years after I left home, my mother exhibited her devotion to her eldest son when she poked something across the table to me over Sunday dinner.

"Is that anything important? It nearly went up the vac."

It was a team tab, black with yellow writing. It was 'EAST FIFE'.

Was it important? Well, sort of.

THE 'LEAGUE LINER' DISCO TRAIN

Specially commissioned by the well-meaning Football League, the *League Liner* express train was used to whisk lucky fans to away fixtures throughout the first half of the Seventies. Three-hundred Burnley fans were the first to sample the delights of the on-board discotheque, the games room and TV lounge with footy on tape – and then the honour was shared around the supporters of every League club.

The buffet car was Champers class, and on-board variety entertainment was often laid on, featuring a comedian, singers and a high-kicking disco dance troupe.

The only down side: the main event of Stockport-Shrewsbury could seem somewhat tame in comparison.

THE LEAGUE OF NINETY-TWO

For 104 years, the Football League was run as a collective – or, if that brings to mind Russian peasants working million-acre farms, you might prefer to think of it as an economic cartel, or as an influential interest group, more like the Masons.

As the sole suppliers of first-class football, the 92 clubs had a lot in common. It paid them to work together to nurture crops of new players, to arrange money-making matches with one another, and to provide mutual support. Big and small, the clubs worked *in league* – sharing the crumbs from the giant clubs' tables to help sustain football's sleeping dwarves.

Just one problem. Apart from the Football League historically running the game, the game was also run historically – you'll sense a potential for conflict – by the Football Association.

As early as 1988, the top ten clubs had threatened to form a breakaway Super League. The FA publicly considered the threat to excommunicate the rebels, setting all their dealings, fixtures and players outside international football law... and the split didn't happen.

Then in 1992 the whole First Division mutinied from the Football League in order to wrest control of the ballooning TV money pouring into the game. So did they FA clamp down? Or did they play along, hoping to retain power while taking over their old rivals' role, even inviting the Premier League to share their Soho Square office space?

The League was crippled; but how did things work out for the FA? We noticed their name was dropped from the Premier League in 2007...

"Apart from onfield discipline, it has backed out of regulating completely," ex-FA chairman Lord Triesman told a Parliamentary select committee investigating English football, adding that game's governance in 2011 was "thoroughly unsatisfactory."

"The decisions that really decide what is going to go on in English football are taken by the Premier League. But I have always thought that football is one sport," he declared tardily. "The interests have got to reach from Old Trafford right through to football played by kids organised in parks. You can't have just one interest dominating it."

Show a leg, there ..

Two dancers from the Talk of the Midlands and compere Ricky Disoni entertain the fans on the luxury League liner train which took 300 people in style to the away game at ...

FOOTBALL LEAGUE

DIVISION 1	DIVISION 2
ARSENAL	ASTON VILLA
BURNLEY	BIRMINGHAM CITY
CHELSEA	BLACKBURN ROVERS
COVENTRY CITY	BLACKPOOL
CRYSTAL PALACE	BOLTON WANDERERS
DERBY COUNTY	BRISTOL CITY
EVERTON	CARDIFF CITY
IPSWICH TOWN	CARLISLE UNITED
LEEDS UNITED	CHARLTON ATHLETIC
LIVERPOOL	HUDDERSFIELD TOWN
MANCHESTER CITY	HULL CITY
MANCHESTER UNITED	LEICESTER CITY
NEWCASTLE UNITED	MIDDLESBROUGH
NOTTINGHAM FOREST	MILLWALL
SHEFFIELD WEDNESDAY	NORWICH
...MPTON	OXFORD U...
...KE CITY	PORTSMO...
...ERLAND	PRESTON NORTH
...ENHAM ...SPUR	QUEEN'S RANGE...
...ES ...ROMWICH	SHEFF UNIT...
	SWINDON

BIRDS EYE

4 Beefburgers

Play "Spot the Ball" and join Leeds United.

LEAGUE CHAMPIONS 73–74

Leeds United

100 PER CENT BEEF

"Th'maght loook the same but th'doon't taaste the same," reasoned the serious-faced little Yorkshire kid when his brother came up with a scheme that involved eating cheap beefburgers instead of Birds Eye, all so that t'Mam would then be able to save enough money to buy them groovy Leeds United tracksuits.

No chance. Even though Leeds were the biggest club in the country at the time this junior philosopher wasn't going to eat inferior burgers.

Cue voiceover as the advert ends: "Birds Eye Beefburgers — somehow, other beefburgers just don't taste the same."

My problem was just the opposite. Persuading my mum to buy Birds Eye beefburgers instead of a cheap alternative, just so I could get hold of the 'Spot the Ball' form on the back of the packet, and go in for the most fantastic prize imaginable.

Fifty lucky winners of the first prize would "meet the Leeds team at their hotel for lunch; go on the players' coach to the match; a guided tour of the club's facilities; then reserved seats for the match with tea afterwards in the player's lounge..."

At LEEDS! The LEAGUE CHAMPIONS!

Irrespective of club loyalties, it seemed like a trip to Nirvana for any ten-year-old of the time. There were even 600 runners-up prizes of soccer watches, tracksuits and practice balls. You just couldn't lose.

Having successfully persuaded Mum of the merits of quality over economy in beef products, I carefully studied the Spot the Ball photo and agonised over where to place my fateful single cross.

I carefully cut out the packet emblazoned with Billy Bremner, Joe Jordan, Peter Lorimer and the rest, and scraped together the coppers for a first-class stamp. I addressed my envelope to 408 Sydenham Road, Croydon CR0 2EA in my neatest handwriting, and ran to the post-box to ensure I beat the closing date of 31 August, 1974.

And then I waited.

I waited and waited and waited.

I waited on the bottom step in the hall and stared at the letter-box, willing a congratulatory letter to drop on the doormat.

"We are pleased to be able to tell you... please be at the Holiday Inn at... no need to bring any lunch, but an autograph book and a camera would be a good idea...

please note that Leeds United AFC cannot be held responsible..." and so on. The fine print would be of more interest to Dad than me.

I waited for that letter. And waited. And waited.

I'm still waiting.

I'll settle for a practice ball.

THE TENT

It was delivered to Filbert Street in February 1971, costing £5,000, weighing 24 hundredweight and covering 90,000 square feet. Officially known as a polysphere, to everyone in Leicester it was simply 'The Tent'.

At the first sign of snow or ice it would be rolled out of the trench at the foot of the Spion Kop where it lived, and inflated with hot-air blowers. Fully pumped up, the unique curiosity was roomy enough for players to train underneath, which made for surreal photos and even a *Blue Peter* feature.

In those days only a select few clubs had under-soil heating, and what a smug luxury it was to watch *Tiswas* of a wintry Saturday morning safe in the knowledge that our match was one of a handful that was definitely on.

As an unexpected bonus, the TV companies cottoned on and often rushed to Filbo when their scheduled game was called off. However, this backfired against Birmingham in December 1976: the game went ahead in such bone-chilling conditions that the pitch froze after The Tent was folded away. Trevor Francis, Kenny Burns and

co. wore rubber-soled trainers and won 6-2 against City skating around in normal studs... and the cameras caught every humiliating moment.

By the winter of 1978-79, when a terrible blizzard caused a collapse and all the expense of a new Tent, City's directors began to wonder why no other club had adopted their all-weather miracle. Hmm: something to do with the running costs, the huge effort required to clear the terraces and surrounding streets of snow and ice, and the relatively high crowds for fixtures rearranged in April...

And so The Tent was phased out – though thankfully only after a truly iconic moment in January 1979, when the weather had wiped out all but four FA Cup Third Round ties. Second Division Leicester were 1-0 up against First Division Norwich – with Keith Weller wearing a pair of ladies white woollen tights to protect his arthritis from the cold (not because his wife had found them in the car, as Frank Worthington had suggested!).

Keith raced down the right wing and danced around two defenders before beating Kevin Keelan at his near post. A sublime moment... all thanks to The Tent.

LEICESTER HOME

FOX FAVOURITES

KEITH WELLER

All-weather training under plastic. If only they'd thought of growing tomatoes as a sideline...

So why did no other club adopt City's surreal, Blue Peter-pleasing, all-weather miracle?

LINIMENT

Ahhhhhhhhh – I love the smell of liniment in the morning.

Unfortunately, both medical and sporting science have taken supposed leaps forward in recent years, so there's no such thing any more.

Players now simply warm up properly instead of trying to save two minutes by smothering stinky, deep-heat goo all over themselves. In fact, liniment might even be banned on Health & Safety grounds, if a £50 million player has ever made my schoolboy

error of applying a good handful of Vick/Ralgex-style instant fire to his legs, and then going for a wee.

But here's good news for liniment addicts of the old school.

Bath City's Twerton Park has a reputation as one of the most tumbledown legacies of pre-war football anywhere in Britain. Bristol Rovers were exiled there for ten years up until 1996, and away fans didn't all revel in the heartwarming timewarp facilities, although they're certifiably up to non-League standards.

For this reason alone, security is not tight at Twerton. Drop by of a weekday morning, present a semi-credible story ("I'm doing research... for a book?") to Bert the caretaker and, for a small token, he will surreptitiously usher any liniment-headed chancer through the hallowed Players & Officials entrance.

Ironically titled, the changing rooms at Twerton Park have not changed one iota since the week they were installed by local chippies in 1935.

Although not a drop of liniment has been splashed on a rosy thigh since the Eighties, the wooden floorboards, the wooden benches and locker doors, the very soul of the place is suffused with the unmistakable smell of eternal youth. With a tight hamstring.

Health Warning: After applying 'Instant Fire' to afflicted muscles, players should exercise extreme caution in their lavatorial arrangements.

Liverpool

CHAMPAGNE MAGNUM

It's difficult to explain just how great Liverpool were in the Seventies and Eighties, especially to kids who might simply see them as a club near the top of the Premier League's second quartile.

You could start with the eye-boggling row of numbers that represents the silverware amassed: League Championship 1972-73, 75-76, 76-77, 78-79, 79-80, 81-82, 82-83, 83-84, 85-86, 87-88; European Cup 1977, 1978, 1981, 1984; UEFA Cup 1973, 1976; FA Cup 1974, 1986, 1989...

But the stats alone don't portray the awesome sight of Liverpool at Anfield, attacking the Kop with all the insistence of waves crashing on the shore. For a furiously back-pedalling Wolves or Spurs or Norwich, you knew it was only a matter of time. It wasn't if the Reds would score, but when.

As for how and why, Liverpool's overpowering period of success was at least partly due to their magnificent line-up of moustaches.

What bare-lipped opposition wouldn't feel a little bit intimidated by such a manly array of facial furniture: Bruce Grobbelaar's 'Fu Manchu'; Mark Lawrenson's 'Sergeant Pepper'; Graeme Souness's 'Magnum', Terry McDermott's 'McDermott'.

Backed up by Ian Rush, John Aldridge, Alan Kennedy, Jimmy Case, David Johnson, and with Steve Heighway's 'Mexican Bandit' on the bench, they had a yard-and-a-half of bristles between them in a team look that could have been planned to steal trophies.

So come on, all you current crop. If you want to return to the top of Division One and get your hands back on tinplate, you know what you don't have to do..

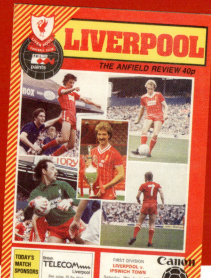

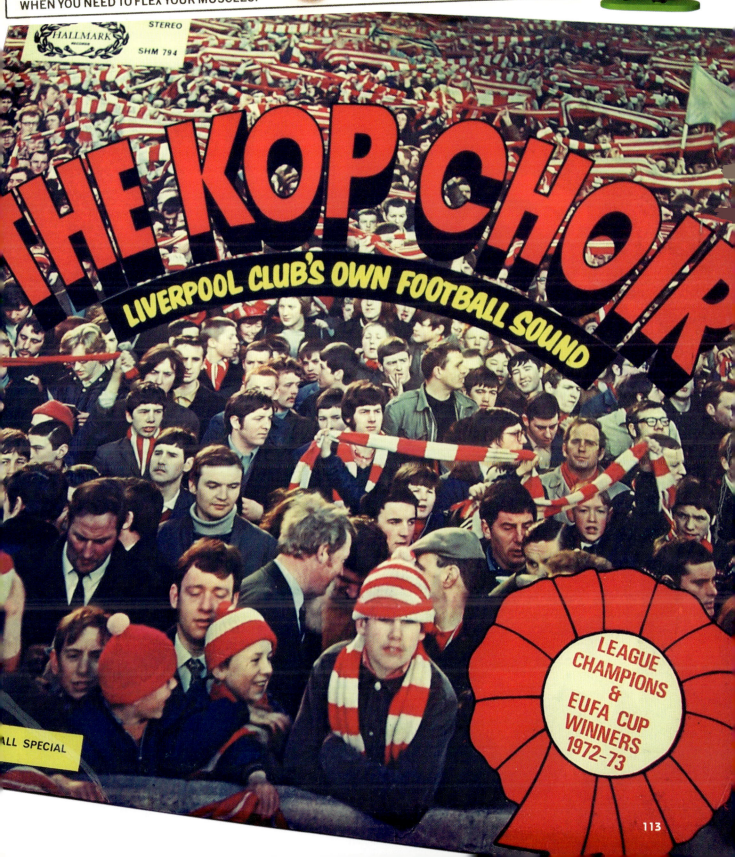

LOOK AT ME

One of the side products of football kit design, from the game's Victorian roots right through to the 1980s, was its ability to level out differences of class, style and status. Pull on a football top and a pair of boots and it was impossible to tell whether Monday morning would find you in a miner's helmet or a banker's bowler.

Fozzy's checklist: Headband, check; short shorts, check; permy mullet and beard, check...

Up until 1923, when numbers were first introduced to football shirts, a player was identifiable solely by his size ("Watch the big lad up front") or hair colour ("He's a tricky dribbler, that ginger-knob"). Thereafter, a football team consisted of little more than numbers between 1 and 11 ("Name and number, player. I'm booking you for ungentlemanly attempts to garner attention.")

As the modern era approached, effective anonymity didn't sit happily with the game's growing number of fancy Dans, big-time Charlies, would-be rock stars and underwear models. The pressure to allow names on shirts soon became a squealy insistence but, even then, players kept fighting to overcome the ego-crushing handicap of having to wear the same shirt as their mates – with understandably varied results.

Black boots became stripy boots and eventually white boots, which begat pink and silver and metallic lilac boots. Look at me. Look at me. Look at me.

Hair became hairstyles: perms, crops, mullets, crew cuts. Whole teams dyed their hair platinum blond, others all grew comedy moustaches; big beards, sideboards, afros, goatees, pony-tails, love patches, braids, patterns carved in stubble.

Then there were headbands, Alice bands, scrunchies, combs. Sock tags, wristbands, Lycra cycling shorts, nose plasters, gloves, under armour, undershirts scrawled with personal messages, protective spectacles. Rings, medallions, St. Cristophers, piercings, ostentatious sticking plasters covering up jewellery...

Look at me. Look at me. Over here, in the snood.

I'm number 99 because it's my lucky number. Look at me.

LOST IN SPACE

It's February 1979, a time of great transition at Filbert Street.

Jock Wallace has taken the reins of a broken carriage and is desperately trying to keep it on the road. Leicester have won only five games all season, and face the threat of relegation to Division Three for the first time in their history.

The familiar old faces of the Jimmy Bloomfield era are departing one by one – Keith Weller has just crossed the Atlantic to join the New England Tea Men – to be replaced by kids barely out of school: Andy Peake, Dave Buchanan, Gary Lineker. The vulnerability of the teenagers is underlined by the freezing cold. There are goose-pimples on their lily-white knees and they clutch their shirt cuffs to keep out the bitter cold. The worst winter in years sees hundreds of games postponed across the country. Not at Leicester though, because we've got The Tent (see 'Leicester City – The Tent'), which brings the *Match of the Day* cameras rolling into town.

Orient are the visitors, in their distinctive red shirts with white 'braces', boasting exotic-sounding players with names like Banjo and Chiedozie. And, just to remind City supporters of better times, Jimmy Bloomfield is their manager.

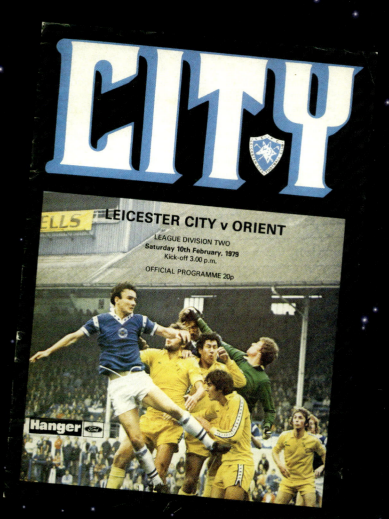

On the way home, the BBC broadcast vans reminded us that we could look forward to
watching a classic match all over again...

City concede an early goal to the Londoners and there are groans around the ground. Not another home defeat. Already Sheffield United, Notts County, Charlton and West Ham have helped themselves to two points from Filbert Street. One more defeat and this collection of youngsters and veterans (and not much in-between) will be done for, even with Jock Wallace at the helm...

But wait. This game is about to explode, and a turning point in the season be reached. The 12,000 who have braved the wintry conditions look on in wonder at City's gutsy response.

Five goals fly past the stout figure of John Jackson in the O's goal. A long-range effort from Bobby Smith; a Buchanan header; a determined nod through a crowded penalty area from Larry May. In the second half, Tommy Williams nets from close in, and Mark Goodwin chips the advancing keeper. For Orient, Chiedozie scores twice, and the more domestic-sounding Kitchen once, all resulting in a thrilling 5-3 win for City.

On the way home, the BBC broadcast vans outside the Main Stand reminded us that we could look forward to watching a classic match

all over again. City on *Match of the Day* was a rare treat, and I could picture Jimmy Hill's beaming, chinny smile as he promised the viewers "a feast of goals from Filbert Street."

I was bursting with pride at the thought of the whole country watching Jock's young braves; but, but to our huge disappointment, it was never to happen.

Something, somewhere, had gone wrong. The transmission had been beamed back to London, but due to a technical fault it was never received. Not a second of it. Ever since, we've only been able to relive our moment of glory in memories and photos.

Meanwhile, 32 years later, the Beeb's lost City-Orient transmission will still be travelling across the universe at a speed of 186,000 miles per second, so maybe someone* will be able to enjoy Larry May's header again... but not on this planet.

Someone 32 light years, or approximately 185 trillion miles, away. Get in there! 3-1!

Leicester-Orient: eight-goal explosion alert

115

LOWER-LEAGUE SIGNINGS

These days you'll seldom find a top club taking a punt on a lower-league signing. There are few potential stars left to be discovered as the Premier League scouting systems are as tight and effective as a purse seine tuna-fishing net: hardly anything of value can slip through the holes. In the modern game you're more likely to see players travelling in the opposite direction, sent out on loan from bloated top-flight squads to small-town lower-league clubs, just to get a game.

A few decades back, however, any chief scout worth his trilby knew how to sniff out a bargain from the Third or Fourth Division... or even lower than that.

Of all these football sages, Geoff Twentyman, chief scout at Liverpool, had perhaps the best track record, recommending the signing of Kevin Keegan and Ray Clemence from Scunthorpe United; John Toshack from Cardiff City; University of Warwick student Steve Heighway, playing for Skelmersdale United; Northampton Town's Phil Neal; Alan Hansen from Partick Thistle, and Chester's Ian Rush. The Reds paid £200,000 for Rush, or £578 for each of his 346 goals, and also made £500,000 profit from farming him out to Juventus for a season.

It would often pay a big club to make a smaller club 'an offer they couldn't refuse' for a small-town hero. Bradford Park Avenue couldn't turn down £34,000 for Kevin Hector when Derby came knocking, although the future Rams legend would have been cheap at twice the price.

Fifty-six goals in 135 appearances was enough to bring Plymouth's Paul Mariner to Ipswich Town's attention, and he was soon on his way to Portman Road for £220,000. Such deals kept the League in a healthy state of symbiosis: Argyle gained financial buoyancy; Ipswich gained Mariner the goal machine, who himself gained medals and England caps. Everyone was a winner.

Another man with a £220,000 price-tag was Crewe Alexandra's David Platt, who signed for Aston Villa in 1988, scored fifty goals for the Villans and then moved to Bari for £5.5

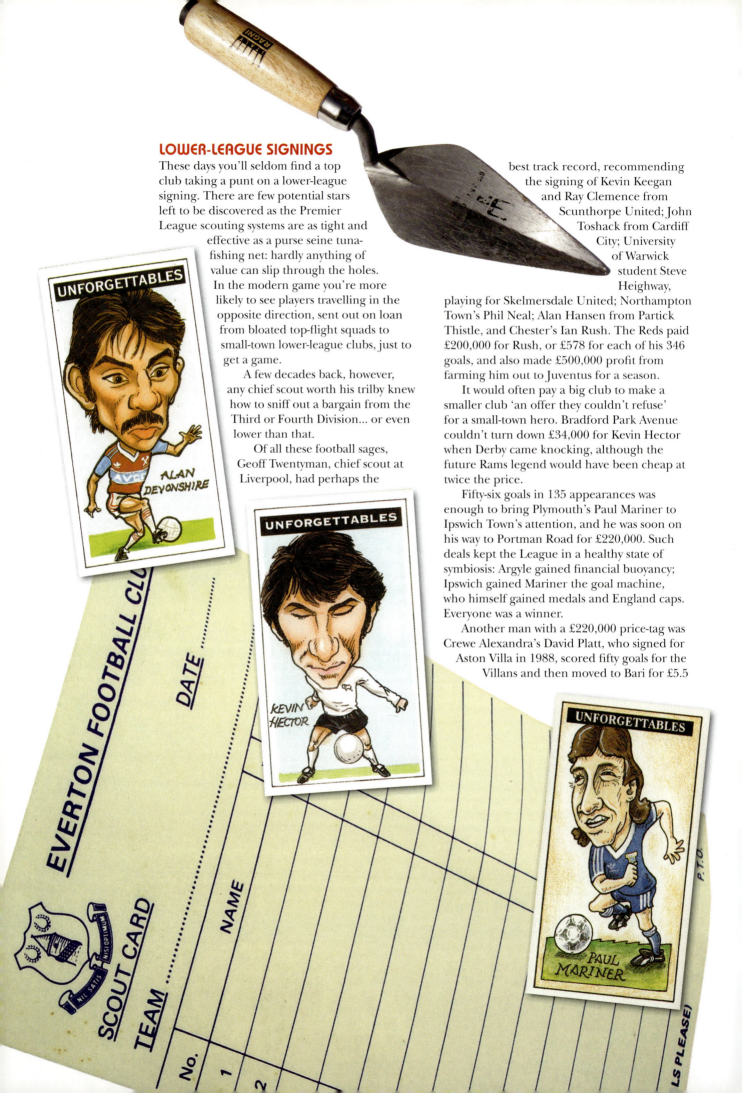

UNFORGETTABLES

ALAN DEVONSHIRE

UNFORGETTABLES

KEVIN HECTOR

UNFORGETTABLES

PAUL MARINER

EVERTON FOOTBALL CLUB

DATE

SCOUT CARD

TEAM

NAME

No.

1

2

P.T.O.

LS PLEASE)

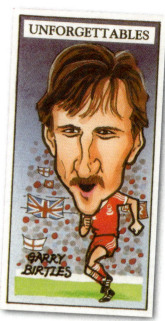

DAVID PLATT

GARRY BIRTLES

Birtles: from Long Eaton United to Nottingham Forest for a cool £2,000.

million. The value of a good scout, eh?

The London area could always provide rich pickings if you could spot the non-League twenty-somethings who hadn't been through the sausage machine of a pro apprenticeship as a teenager.

West Brom scout Ronnie Allen was so impressed by Isthmian League Hayes FC's striker that he offered to pay the £5,000 asking price out of his own pocket when faced with a sceptical Albion board. They eventually agreed to cough up, and electrician and semi-pro footballer Cyrille Regis signed in May 1977.

Coventry City had to stump up a little more for another sparky when Bobby Gould was impressed by Wealdstone left-back Stuart Pearce. The Sky Blues parted with £30,000 to secure Psycho's signature, but two years later he moved to Forest in a deal worth ten times that.

But the greatest lower-league bargains were quite literally secured in exchange for goods rather than cash. Crystal Palace cannily persuaded Greenwich Borough to part with their promising 22-year-old plasterer-*cum*-striker for a set of training weights. Ian Wright's next move, six years later, cost Arsenal £2,500,000.

It was a steal of the same magnitude as Watford's swap deal with Sudbury Court, a few years earlier in 1981. The signature of John Barnes had set back Graham Taylor's Hornets just one set of first-team kit. Six years later they sold him on to Liverpool for £900,000.

The Reds never had to shell out like that when Geoff Twentyman was on the case.

Any chief scout worth his trilby could sniff out
a basement bargain from the Fourth Division

THE FUTURISTIC MASTERPLAN

Hatters fans must have experienced all kinds of nostalgic thrills in 2003 when a wildly ambitious, apparently barking plan for the future was floated by the club's property-developer chairman, John Gurney.

The vision was based around a 50-75,000-capacity stadium built over the M1's Junction 10 spur road. At first glance, right down to the Teflon roof held up by air pressure, it was strikingly similar to property-developer chairman David Kohler's Nineties dream of a Space Age 'Kohlerdome'... except Gurney had also thrown in a surrounding Formula 1 race track, where he hoped to stage the British Grand Prix.

Unfortunately, the strategy didn't make 'London Luton FC' "the largest (in financial terms) club in Europe", but instead left them in administration when Gurney's reign ended just two months after he'd bought the club for £4.00.

Back in the late Eighties, under the five-year chairmanship of notorious

Thatcherite MP David Evans, fans weren't only forced to endure the sight of Millwall hoolies dismantling their stand, but also a revolutionary political response that included a members-only identity-card scheme, a sweeping ban on all away supporters, conversion to an all-seater stadium and the installation of a plastic pitch.

Even in 1982, the club's owners had been sorely tempted by a move to Milton Keynes, and the promise of playing in a futuristic 'super-stadium' as the 'MK Hatters'.

And at no point did any of these schemers think to ask what the fans thought: thanks, but no thanks.

Luton Town

WE SHALL NOT BE MOVED! NO to Milton Keynes! SUPPORTERS OF LUTON TOWN F.C.

LUTON TOWN

MAGAZINE SHIN PADS

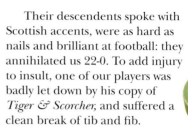

Our junior-school football coach wasn't one for the new, namby-pamby ways of the mid Seventies. Shin pads were part of the malaise: might as well wrap us up in cotton wool and put us in a box on the mantelpiece as let us stuff big-girl's-blouse shin guards down our socks.

Here was a man who would give us a bollocking for closing our eyes when heading a ball (a ball which didn't even weigh two stone and have laces in it, like it did in his day). According to Coach, players only ever got injured because they'd bottled out of a 50-50 challenge. No one ever got hurt steaming fearlessly into a tackle.

Their descendents spoke with Scottish accents, were as hard as nails and brilliant at football: they annihilated us 22-0. To add injury to insult, one of our players was badly let down by his copy of *Tiger & Scorcher,* and suffered a clean break of tib and fib.

Coach's philosophy on shin pads was also shattered. By the next game we all had a new pair.

THE MAGIC SPONGE

Don't go all soft and warm: that's the heartfelt warning from old-school Oldham physio Jimmy McGregor, aimed at the revisionists in his profession who are controversially given to filling their magic bucket with warm water on chilly days, as a sop to airy-fairy types.

"It's known as the magic sponge because of the shock treatment it gives to injured players," McGregor put his case passionately to the *Football League Review,* just forty years before we threw it into our cutting-edge forum for football debate. "It can only do its work if the water is ice cold."

Safety first: for local derbies, trade up to a couple of copies of War and Peace.

I felt like putting my hand up and saying, "Dave Mackay" – well-known super-hard man and leg-break victim – but I didn't dare.

In the face of several parents' concerns, Coach came up with what must have been, for him, a nauseating compromise. We'd be allowed to wear magazines down our socks for competitive games – just as good as shin pads and nowhere near as expensive. This worked in league matches, where we played local school teams that were just as timid as us, but came unstuck when we visited Corby in the cup.

Corby may be in Northamptonshire, but it's actually part of Scotland. When Glasgow-based Stewarts & Lloyds set up a steelworks there in the 1920s, during a decline in the Clyde Valley steel industry, workers poured down in their tens of thousands, many making the 300-plus-mile journey by foot.

As if to emphasise his opinion, Jimmy launched into a bullet-point tirade:

- A cold sponge revives a dazed player;
- A cold sponge takes away the immediate pain from a bruising;
- A cold sponge lessens the inflammation;
- A cold sponge numbs the damage done by sprains and abrasions, and
- A cold sponge can check blood flow.

Only then did we notice which edition of the *FLR* we'd been cribbing from, realising that the physio had been dousing his lads in iced water in the frozen midst of January 1968.

"Hot water might be comforting to a lad lying on hard turf on a freezing day," McGregor barked. "But it does him no good."

It's probably best if we don't get in touch with Oldham Athletic to try and track Jimmy down, to find out what he thinks of those big modern canisters of pain-killing spray. At least, not without first applying a liberal squirt in our earholes.

"The magic sponge's
shock treatment
only works if the water is ice cold."
Oldham physio, Jimmy McGregor

THE MANAGERESS

It was back in 1989 that fitness coach, feminist and friend of the chairman's family Gabriella Benson became manager of her local Second Division team, Everpool United. Or was it Glipton Giants? Barnstoneworth, or something.

It came as a massive blow for feminism which, although strictly just-pretend, ignited a million considered feasibility arguments in snug bars across the country.

"Women wouldn't command enough respect to be a boss."

"She wouldn't last a minute."

"They don't understand the game."

"'Ere, I wouldn't mind playing under that Cherie Lunghi, though but."

It's almost as if *The Manageress* alerted top-shelf publisher David Sullivan to the multi-faceted skills of womankind, inspiring him to install young Karren Brady as chief exec of Birmingham City – an incredibly brave and successful decision which won the budget blue-movie producer many startled admirers.

The Manageress was a groundbreaking stereotype-smasher of a series, which just happened to star one of *FHM*'s 100 Sexiest Women on the Planet as boss of… Girlchester City? Queen's Park Hydrangeas?

So how come no one can remember the name of the club Chezza so expertly helmed?

Quite Interestingly, the producers were careful never to mention the team by name, always referring to them as 'us' or 'we' or 'them' or 'useless males' – which enabled them to tackle the issues of rampant sexism and racism, corruption and stimulant abuse without ending up in court.

We wonder if it's OK to recall the series was filmed at Reading's Elm Park…

FOOTIE
THE FOOTBALL FANZINE WITH BITE
August 1990 £1.00

EXCLUSIVE
THE MANAGERESS SPEAKS!

ARRIVEDERCI ROMA
beautiful moments from *Italia '90*

MY TEAM: CHARLIE REID
of The Proclaimers

CARTOON CAPERS
with Stain & Grievous

RIMINI:
the truth about the deportations

Top Eighties boss Gabriella Benson: but which team did she manage?

Fixtures :

FOOTBALL LEAGU[E]

Aug.	19	Notts County .....
	23	Newcastle United
	26	Crystal Palace ....
Sept.	2	Fulham ....
	9	Burnley ....
	16	Bristol Rovers ...
	23	Sheffield United ..
	30	Sunderland ......
Oct.	7	Millwall ....
	14	Oldham Athletic .
	21	Stoke City ....
	28	Brighton & Hove
Nov.	4	Preston North En[d]
	11	Notts County ....
	18	Crystal Palace ....
	21	Fulham ....
	25	Leicester City .....
Dec.	2	Cambridge United
	9	Wrexham ....
	16	Charlton Athletic
	26	Orient ....
	30	Blackburn Rovers
Jan.	20	Bristol Rovers ...
Feb.	10	Sunderland ....
	24	Oldham Athletic .
	26	Luton Town ......
Mar.	3	Stoke City ....
	10	Brighton & Hove
	17	Preston North En[d]
	24	Newcastle United
	31	Leicester City ....
Apr.	2	Sheffield United ..
	7	Cambridge United
	9	Luton Town ......
	14	Orient ....
	16	Cardiff City ......
	21	Charlton Athletic
	24	Burnley ....
	28	Wrexham ....
May	5	Blackburn Rovers
	11	Cardiff City ......
	14	Millwall ....

	P	W
Brighton & Hove A.	35	19
Crystal Palace	34	14
Stoke City	35	16
Sunderland	34	17
West Ham United	32	15
Notts County	32	13
Orient	35	14
Fulham	33	12
Burnley	31	12
Preston North End	33	9
Cambridge United	34	9
Leicester City	33	9
Charlton Athletic	35	10
Bristol Rovers	32	11
Newcastle United	31	13
Luton Town	33	11

Manchester City

INFLATABLES

The latter half of the 1988-89 season saw perhaps the last fan-driven, organically grown football craze sweep across the country.

Unlike most supporter-inspired movements, the origin of the inflatables craze isn't lost in the mists of time or open to debate, but can be pinned down to one man and one date.

Frank Newton, co-founder of the trailblazing *Blue Print* fanzine, took a giant inflatable banana to the Manchester City v. Plymouth Argyle game on 15 August, 1987. His matchday accessory went down well with fellow City fans. Christened 'Imre Banana' after striker Imre Varadi, it travelled home and away all season, in an ever-growing crop of pneumatic fruit.

After a few months the banana craze reached that tipping point where it changed from a joke among friends to a phenomenon that gripped thousands of the club's fans. Then the craze spread further afield, firstly through the Second Division, as City's opponents became infected, and then throughout the League as a variegated vinyl madness gripped the nation.

One visitor to Maine Road recalls: "There were 4,000 of us in the Platt Lane Stand with various inflatables including a Champagne bottle, a plane, a family of tennis

racquets, several dinosaurs, a skeleton and hundreds of balloons... but we were soon outdone when the home side came on: literally thousands of bananas were held up as one. Even the Man City players had them. It was an incredible, hilarious sight!"

Another supporter admitted: "I was very impressed by the Man City fans' efforts, so I bought a blow-up Tyrannosaurus Rex. In our corner of the East Stand there was a killer whale, a giant cigarette with 'No Smoking' written on it, a banana and a crocodile."

A giant cigarette, a killer whale, a Tyrannosaurus Rex...

And then, just as quickly as they had arrived, the inflatables disappeared, all but gone by the start of the 1989-90 season. A bit of a problem for any club souvenir shop who had ordered hundreds of specially commissioned inflatable whatevers, and a lesson to big business to keep their noses out.

PUMP IT UP
Rampant inflation grips the nation...

Manchester City	Bananas
Stoke City	Pink Panthers
West Ham	Hammers
Grimsby Town	Harry the Haddock
Norwich City	Canaries
Bury	Black puddings
Blackpool	Towers
Oldham	Dogs

Big Banana

LIFE BEFORE PRAWN SANDWICHES

"Away from home our fans are fantastic, I'd call them the hardcore fans. But at home they have a few drinks and probably the prawn sandwiches, and they don't realise what's going on out on the pitch. I don't think some of the people who come to Old Trafford can spell 'football', never mind understand it."
– Roy Keane

Roy Keane's studs-up, thigh-high challenge on the 'corporates' may have struck a chord with the common fan and entered the football lexicon but, even for Keano, the challenge had come in rather late.

Bubbles, a star writer on a weekend trip back to his grimy home town and his estranged wife. Liza Minnelli made her screen bow in the film (as the love interest); ditto Bobby Charlton and Denis Law (playing themselves out on the pitch).

Bubbles takes his boy to Old Trafford to see United v. Chelsea; but after arriving in a Rolls Royce Silver Shadow, he isn't going to rough it in the Stretford End. The glass of their

Watching football through glass seemed so bizarre in 1967, it featured in an Albert Finney film.

As far back as the mid Sixties, the grand plan for the development of Old Trafford had included football's first glazed, private hospitality boxes, to cater for the better-heeled match-goer. When the United Road Stand was completed in the summer of 1965, the architects had then inspired the United board with their recent work at Castle Irwell racecourse, and got the go-ahead to include a row of 55 five-seater boxes tucked under the state-of-the-art cantilevered roof. For £250 a season, you could enhance your enjoyment of the match with central heating, TV and a telephone; food and drinks were served non-stop, and crowd noise was piped up from below into the sealed Dress Circle.

The idea of watching football through glass was so bizarre in 1967 that it was used as a plot device in Albert Finney's directorial debut, *Charlie Bubbles*, written by fellow Salfordian superstar Shelagh 'A Taste of Honey' Delaney. Finney himself played

private box becomes a metaphor for the divide between working-class England and the newly wealthy. The son, disappointed at missing out on the big match atmosphere and his father not showing any interest in the game, slips away and takes himself home.

Not everyone had such an unsatisfactory time in the aquarium as Jack Bubbles. Executive boxes and corporate facilities soon caught on, and now you'd struggle to find a club in the Football Conference North that didn't offer their match-ball sponsor a comfortable chair, an unrestricted view and yes, maybe even a prawn sandwich.

Oh, Manchester. So much to answer for.

THE MANUAL ACTION REPLAY

Back in the days when TV audiences were still dazzled by the technology involved in screening an action replay five minutes after an incident had occurred, along came this cheeky new version of an old trick which put replay power firmly in the hands of the fans.

Fact is, there was no simple scan or search facility on a massive reel of crinkly, flyaway film – and don't forget you needed not one but two expensive cameras pointing at the match if one of them was going to be unspooled and rewound laboriously to hunt for a goal.

It was just as quick, and far less palaver, to provide every fan with a personal flick-book of the goal, the next day.

You can keep your new-fangled video-cassette recorder with its confusing system of 'record' and 'rewind' and 'play'. If it ain't bust, don't fix it, we say. Best stick with this decent, reliable technology, as tested out by a million little stick men jumping up and down in the corner of the nation's jumbo jotters.

Flick to kick: Ronnie strikes from 30 yards in the thick Hereford mud.

MEN ONLY

It wasn't just children who became obsessed with hoarding away random pocket-sized items emblazoned with the name of their team, or collecting the whole set of anything once they were safely in possession of numbers 17 and 426. A whole world of grown-up collectables arrived on the market as soon as the nascent football industry realised men are just slightly larger versions of boys: all they needed was the excuse of a little footballer or a badge stamped on an end-of-line, impractical or downright shoddy article, and they'd soon start gathering them about their person.

Birmingham City's Beau Brummie Comb in Case cost 5p in the new money, both grooming accessory and sheath being hand tooled in luxurious blue plastic and stamped with the all-important cartoon bulldog. Available only through the club shop, these dog combs were 100 per cent official merchandise – although precious little hoo-hah was made of that fact at the time.

Licensing rights on football club names and copyright on nicknames and player images were rarely enforced or leveraged until the Eighties. The clubs mentioned on millions of rosettes, scarves and fringed lampshades enjoyed no direct cash benefit from such tributes: before terms such as 'customer' and 'churn rate' began to appear in the football industry lexicon, they were only too chuffed to think that anyone cared.

The only slight design fault with the Tottenham Player Key-Ring of the late Sixties was down to the fact that he'd started life as a useless little statuette that sold like very cool cakes. Duly recycled, it briefly became the height of North London fashion to chuck your Tottenham Player into the fruit bowl at the swinging wife-swap fondu party. He was certainly a conversation starter, even when tossed casually on the bar; problems only arose when you came to put the bulbous six-inch toy away in your trouser pocket.

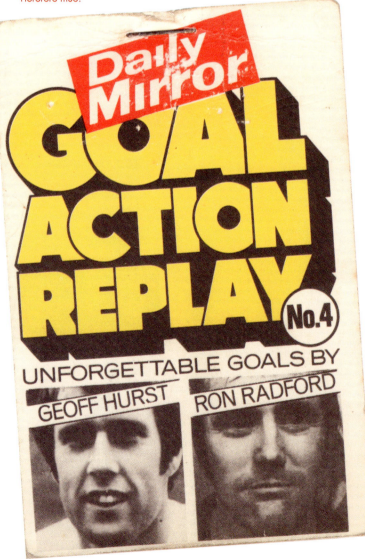

Stealing a march on most clubs, the early market leaders in men-only stocking-fillers were Spurs' great local rivals. As early as 1952, Arsenal had assembled a wide range of man-friendly goodies, available at 'enrolment sites' on match days or by post from the Honorary Secretary. Is it just us, or does 29 shillings and sixpence (£1.47½ in today's money) seem a bit steep for a silver-wired, silk-embroidered blazer badge? Surely, that must have been a king's ransom, fifty years ago? Interesting to note that the chromium-plated car badge actually went down in price over twenty years, knocked down from 25 bob in 1952 (£1.25) to just £1.00 plus 4 pence postage and packing in 1972.

The blazer badge takes me back to the Christmas a well-meaning auntie bought me one as a 'little extra' to my jigsaw or selection box. I never knew they were so pricey; but even if I had, it wouldn't have solved the sticky problem of what to do with the thing while I remained resolutely blazerless. Eventually, I homed in on the side of the airing cupboard in my bedroom, where the expensive glue behind the badge's peel-off backing proved to be the most powerful adhesive known to man. Many a happy hour, I spent, tugging and levering, only ever dislodging frontal fluff. I bet my quality furry fox badge is still there to this day, unless it's since tipped some house-proud DIYer over the edge into buying a flame-thrower or demolishing the whole cupboard.

Superior Glass Ash-tray (Rubber base). Price £2.50, plus 13p. postage. Box Cuff-links, Red with Gold cannon, 70p, plus 4p. postage. Team-mate carpet slippers (Red and White) sizes 7–10, Price £1.23, sizes 2–5 £1.25, 13p. postage in each case. Every pair of slippers includes free indoor football. Price £1.17, sizes 11–1,

SOME OF THE SPECIAL ITEMS IN THE GUNNERS SHOP

Table Lamp £1.50 + 25p. package and postage. Car Badge £1.00, + 4p. package and postage. Shoulder Bag (Canvas) £1.25, + 15p. package and postage.

12

On the subject of sheer class, let's bring back the real leather season ticket slipcase, so our trousers aren't cheapened by the touch of paper. Let's bring back club-badge cuff-links and beret badges as the perfect accompaniments to our proudly badged blazers and Superior Glass Ashtrays (with rubber base).

And who, in all honesty, doesn't feel a very real need for a pair of smart football boot-style slippers in their own club colours? Arsenal's enviable red-and-white Team-Mate Carpet Slippers (£1.17, £1.23 or £1.25, plus 13p P&P) must once have sold by the lorryload, especially when kids of all ages got to hear about the 'free indoor football included with every pair'.

MIDDLESBROUGH
FOGGON

MIDDLESBROUGH
HICKTON

football

Middlesbrough

CHAMPS AT LAST

What a relief, when Middlesbrough broke their century-long trophy duck, lifting the Worthington Cup in Cardiff in 2004. Since then, they've gone on to confound even their own expectations, storming through to the final of the UEFA Cup in 2006; but Boro fans aren't the type to let a little success go to their heads.

In fact, in a strange way, they still cherish memories of the wilderness years, and the extremely minor victories they used to claim as relatively important ones. And who can blame them?

At the end of the Nineties, Boro came so close, so many times. They made it to Wembley twice in 1997, losing out to Leicester in the League Cup and then to Chelsea in the FA Cup final – only to return the very next season and once again lose to Chelsea, in the League Cup final.

Before then, they didn't even come close, which puts into perspective Boro's hunger for silverware back in 1974, when 'Charlton's Champions' (of the Second Division) lined up for a team group behind a mighty silver cup – which on closer inspection turned out to be the Northern Intermediate Cup, a youth team competition for Northern League clubs.

Fans can now also laugh about their entirely incidental Anglo-Scottish Cup 'triumph' of 1976, when Boro defeated those fearsome Highland warriors, Fulham, over two legs, without even scoring a goal.

It was Teesside legend Les Strong's own-goal that gifted Boro the Cup, which was then unfortunately lost the next season. That's 'lost' as in 'mislaid'. But the precious memories will never disappear down the back of the sofa.

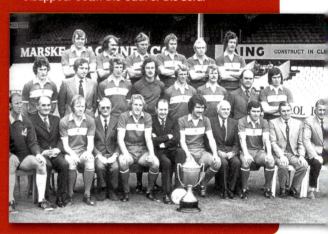

Millwall

ONLY A GAME?

When it became all too clear to Millwall and Ireland up-and-downer Eamon Dunphy that his career was finally winding down, he set about writing a 'Diary of a Professional Footballer' about his final season at Cold Blow Lane.

Published by Kestrel Books in 1976, *Only a Game?* put its author firmly on the path to a second career in the media. The book changed football writing – and the way fans think of pros – forever. Here's why:

"I'm sitting in the stand, wanting them to lose, but unable to show it," Dunphy admitted. "Because there are people around, I've got to pretend to want them to win. I can't jump up in the air when Sheffield score. Which I want to do. And when Millwall score I'm sick, but I have to jump up in the air. And

there is this terrible conflict all the time. And it is the same for everybody who is dropped."

It makes for an uncomfortable, eye-opening read, and not just for Millwall fans.

"You are always pleased when they have been beaten, because it means you are a candidate again. You are sick for the lads, of course, but your predominant emotion is delight."

It's blank, brutal and, above all, honest.

Vital reading. Except perhaps for the Lions' clueless star kid, Gordon Hill…

Only a Game?
Eamon Dunphy
THE DIARY OF A PROFESSIONAL FOOTBALLER

A revised edition of the classic book, with a new introduction by Eamon Dunphy

Edited by Peter Ball

MIRRORCARD

★ 34 MILLWALL

STAR SOCCER SIDES
SERIES OF 100
Buy the *Mirror* regularly to complete your series

Back row (l. to r.): Brown (B.), Burnett, Mackie, King, Dorney and Bolland.
Centre row (l. to r.): Holmes, Brown (S.), Coxhill, Jacks and Neil.
Front row (l. to r.): Bridges, Possee, Cripps, Dunphy and Allder.

MIND THE GAP

Pity the poor old modern pro, who must occasionally feel like a talented younger brother brought up by cantankerous parents in the shadow of a favourite elder son.

"Look at me, Dad. I've got football skills that weren't dreamed of back in the 1990s, and I've got a girlfriend who models fake all-over tan."

"Ah, you wouldn't have caught *Our Bobby* earning your kind of obscene money. I don't know, with your diamonds stuck all over your mobile phone and your little nicks cut out of your eyebrows."

"But Dad, I've been voted into the UK's Top 50 Eligible Celebrities by readers of *Eligible Celebrities* magazine."

"You know *Our Bobby* could down a gallon and then do a hundred press-ups on the bar? He was a proper head-turner was *Our Bobby*, especially when he put his teeth in..."

Fact is, today's pro can never compete with the players of even ten years ago precisely *because* he's so wealthy and talented, so polite and well turned out.

You wouldn't have caught Joe Jordan spending £50,000 on a pearl-white set of Gangsta gnashers. Joe had his four front teeth kicked out in a Leeds United reserve-team game: all the better to terrorise any unfortunate sod going up against him for a header, when he earned the horror-flick nickname of 'Jaws' without once resorting to cannibalism.

Back in the day, Joe was the star of a Heineken ad, where a pint of lager 'refreshed the parts other beers cannot reach'. Joe's teeth grew back, temporarily, while fresh graffiti outside Elland Road claimed: 'Joe Jordan kicks the parts other beers cannot reach'.

Once he'd slipped out his false front teeth, Joe had nothing left to lose. Stripped for action, he stood outside any real-world concerns such as the desire to find a mate, or to eat an apple.

Compare and contrast with, ooh, let's say Ashley Cole...

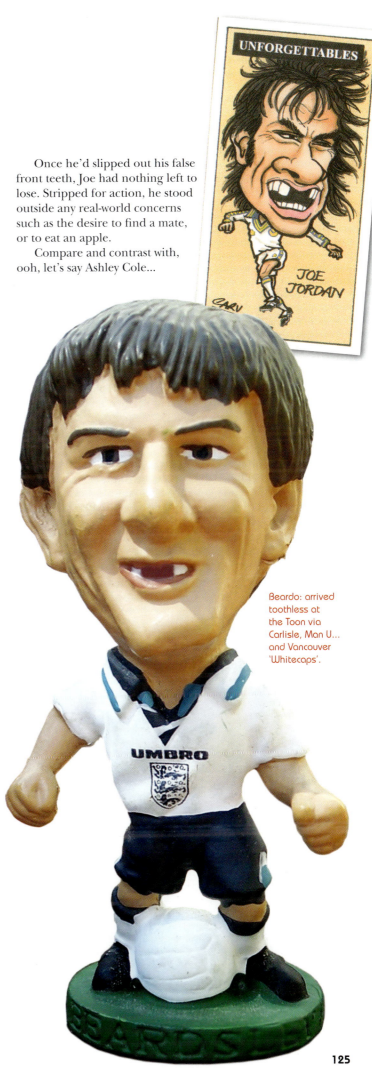

Beardo: arrived toothless at the Toon via Carlisle, Man U... and Vancouver 'Whitecaps'.

"There they were, all six-footers wi' Ambre Solaire suntans, Colgate smiles and slick-backed hair. And there's us lot — midgets. Ah've got nae teeth, Bobby Lennox hasnae any, and old Ronnie Simpson's got the full monty, nae teeth top an' bottom. The Italians are staring doon at us an' we're grinnin' back up at 'em wi' oor great gumsy grins. We must've looked like somethin' oot o' the circus."
Celtic's Jimmy Johnstone remembers the 1967 European Cup Final.

125

MODEL PROFESSIONALS

Footballers have moved up – or at least a quarter of an inch forward – in the world, having strived for decades to leave behind their traditional station in life, the sports pages.

Tucked away for a century amid the transfer tittle-tattle, football reports and scores, they were for too long discriminated against, unable to express their true personalities when coverage was concentrated on football.

When you're busy building a brand, it's far more valuable to appear in the gossip pages for being seen out with an underwear model on a date fixed up by your agent. Back pages are passé. Better to push for a feature, so you can show a tame snapper around your chrome-and-leather gaff and drop the name of the underwear model that your agent told you to mention.

But for taking your brand awareness to *a whole nother level*, it's priceless if you can claw your way into the news pages. Like when you finally get to meet the underwear model, and you snap when a pap pushes a camera in your face, and you're forced to teach him a lesson about privacy.

Even so, the crowning achievement for any footballer is to make the final ascension to the fashion pages. That's where your football royalty is to be found: your Crouchies, your Ljungbergs, your Lamps. Swimwear, barwear and awardswear

Mud was synonymous with football, a crucial factor in its tactics, skills and disciplines.

"I suppose you would say trendy, but not in a way-out sort of way": George on 45, flogging his Tyne Tex jackets and anoraks.

are where the top dollar lies. Oily abs, booted and suited, a nice cravat. Leave the sportswear to the losers with nothing but boot contracts to their names.

The new generation of model pros all agree: *Rrrespect* is due to old-school England pin-up Geoff 'Puffer' Hurst for showing the way forward. Check out the greatest moment in his entire career, modelling his smart new Pac-a-Mac (or 'Puffer jacket') with the help of the hunky World Cup 70 posse.

MUD

Mud used to be as central to the game of football as the ball itself. Placed on a freshly repainted centre-spot. By the Man in the Middle. At Central Park, Cowdenbeath...

Mud was synonymous with football, a crucial factor in its tactics, skills and disciplines. We played in mud and paid to watch better players struggle to overcome mud – their control, balance and ability to dive and tackle like demons all dependent on mud.

From the terraces, football smelled of mud. On big occasions, we sneaked on to the pitch

England's World Cup team wear

BARACUTA
MEXICAN
CONTAINING
TERYLENE

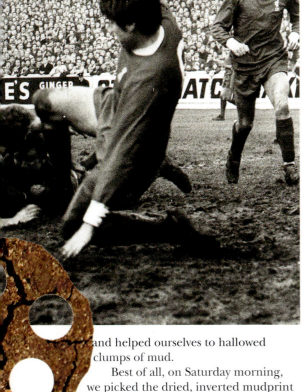

"Which goalkeeper has the biggest pair of hands in the First Division?"

If you didn't already know the answer was Pat Jennings, then you'd have an understandably burning need to find out.

Next, a sucker-punch one-two. I was still chortling at the 'Football Funnies' chosen by Manchester United's Stewart Houston when I was made to gasp by Kevin Keegan revealing how he'd been beaten up by officials at Belgrade airport, smashing some attractive Bulgarian pottery he'd bought for his family.

Unsettled, it was several minutes before I could properly 'Focus On' Paul Gilchrist of Southampton (Miscellaneous Likes: motor racing, oil painting, music); nod sagely at 'Bob Wilson Was Wrong to Retire' by Alan Ball; relax 'At Home With' John Radford of Arsenal and his Dutch wife Engel; marvel at John Greig's assertion that 'Rangers Can Win the Title Next Season', and gaze in awe at Man City's grinning Colin Bell on the back cover.

It's difficult to explain now how a photo could be so prized, Blu-Tacked instantly up on your wall, but in the days of black newsprint papers and monochrome TV, the eight colour pages in *Shoot!* were like oases in a grey desert.

For five years my collection grew, filling several boxes, until 1979 when my head was finally turned by an attractive newcomer called *Match Weekly*.

I'm sorry I dropped you, *Shoot!*, and I'm even sorrier that we now live in a world where kids can't leg it down to the newsagents to eagerly pore over the latest issue.

and helped ourselves to hallowed clumps of mud.

Best of all, on Saturday morning, we picked the dried, inverted mudprint out of our studs – a perfect, stud-holed fossil record of last weekend's 6-0 defeat – tossed it on the changing-room floor and started all over again, temporarily clean and full of hope for what the mud might bring.

MY FIRST SHOOT!

Just like Bobby Goldsboro, my first time was on a hot afternoon, the last day of June (more or less), although I can't recall whether or not the sun was a demon...

Allowed one comic a week, I'd already graduated from the entry-level *Beano* to *Scorcher*, but not until the summer of 1974, while immersed in the West Germany World Cup, did I consider myself man enough to step up to *Shoot!*

Eight pence was the price of admission, and I was soon in beyond the full-colour cover of Billy Bremner playing for Scotland against Brazil.

Now I could absorb an article by Bobby Moore; could puzzle over the fiendish problems posed in 'You Are the Ref'; study up-close World Cup action featuring Australia, Scotland, Holland, Zaire, DDR and Yugoslavia; pore over stats on the previous nine Finals; shed sympathetic tears over Bremner's article on Scotland's brave exit, and realise there were people just like me all over the country, courtesy of the 'Goal Lines' letters page and 'Ask the Expert' readers' queries.

NASL

It was obvious to every kid in England in the second half of the Seventies: the North American Soccer League was the future – a festival of fun with relaxed offside rules and shoot-outs, not to mention cheerleaders and players with Captain Kirk beer guts dressed like Evel Knievel.

It was almost impossible to imagine the thrill of Pelé, Bobby Moore and Franz Beckenbauer lining up together for the same New York Cosmos team, or other back-from-the-dead stars such as Rodney Marsh (Tampa Bay Rowdies), George Best and Johan Cruyff (LA Aztecs) continuing their legendary scoring runs on pitches of lime-green carpet set in towering Space Age kickerdomes.

In America, they played perky organ music when the home team were in possession, and doomy chords when the baddies had the ball. In America they scored six points for a win, not a chiselling two – plus a point per goal scored up to a maximum of three. For a short time, I personally considered the New England Tea Men franchise as one of my Top 10 teams,

inspired by a picture of the team taking to the pitch in a vintage fire engine, and Keith Weller's frontier spirit.

Without doubt, the NASL hard sell worked just fine over here – it was just unfortunate for the PR men that America was over there, and we were left with nothing to buy, nothing to watch, nothing to barbecue at half-time. As for the self-styled 'fannies' who briefly packed 80,000-capacity soccerbowls to watch survivors from *Escape To Victory* huff and puff, the novelty of the lucrative exhibition circuit understandably soon wore off.

By 1979, the 'All-American Issue' of the Marshall Cavendish *Football Handbook* ('in 63 weekly parts!') already had a very tired feel to it, with Rodney Marsh finally deciding to call it a day and a grotesquely paunchy, bearded Gerd

> In America, they played perky organ music when the home team were in possession, and doomy chords when the baddies had the ball.

Müller setting the tone. Even more chilling was one image of a player wearing a tight coffee- and chocolate-coloured shirt with gull-wing collars, numbers everywhere but on the back, a badge the size of a dinner plate and 'Buffalo Bill-style fringes'. He played for 'the now-defunct Caribous of Colorado'.

Many theories have been put forward to try and explain why football just doesn't work in the States, but few have been as memorable as that of conservative American economist Stephen Moore.

"Soccer is a sport for bureaucrats, socialists and overbearing mothers," he argued in the patriotic *National Review*, late last century. "After watching the first two soccer games of my six-year-old son, I finally understand why Europeans riot at soccer matches. For the same reason inmates riot in prisons: sheer boredom. Soccer at any level is about as scintillating as ninety minutes of Court TV. No other activity in life requires so much effort for so little reward."

Moore's spewing argument spiralled, via sexual confusion and a drain on talent 'from sports that really matter', to a grand theory. Roughly translating: if the primary object of a capitalist economy is to produce the maximum output for the least possible amount of exertion, then football – which involves huge volumes of effort without any appreciable result – is nothing but an indolent terrorist of a game.

As "the least offensive-minded game ever invented," he concluded, soccer represents "the Marxist concept of the labor theory of value applied to sports – which may explain why socialist nations dominate in the World Cup."

All rubbish, of course; but then so was much of the action at each of this century's World Cup Finals, where we've come to expect and accept skill and creativity to be cancelled out by a dive, a ref, a negative tactic, a marketing gimmick.

I don't know why, but every game I watch these days I'm haunted by that line about "so much effort for so little reward."

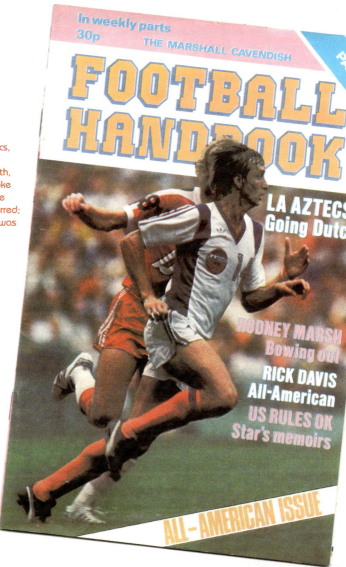

RIP LA Aztecs, 1974-81: Tommy Smith, Charlie Cooke and George Best co-starred; Elton John was co-owner.

FOOTBALL HANDBOOK

In weekly parts
30p
THE MARSHALL CAVENDISH
PAR

LA AZTECS Going Dutch

RODNEY MARSH Bowing out

RICK DAVIS All-American

US RULES OK Star's memoirs

ALL-AMERICAN ISSUE

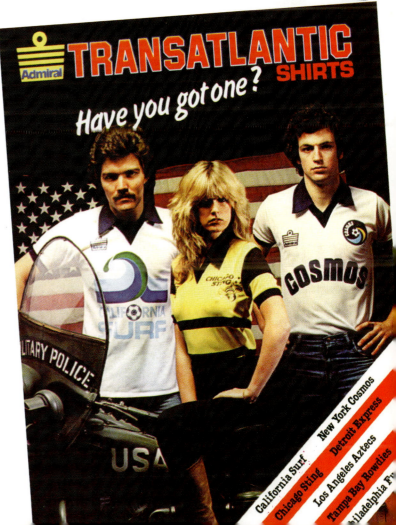

Admiral **TRANSATLANTIC SHIRTS**

Have you got one?

California Surf
Chicago Sting
Los Angeles Aztecs
Tampa Bay Rowdies
New York Cosmos
Detroit Express
Philadelphia Fu

```
      city megastore
      LCFC, Walkers Stadium
       Filbert Way
     Leicester, LE2 7FL
      0844 815 6000 option 3
    Open: Monday - Saturday 9am - 5pm
    Sundays    10am - 2pm


         18 December 2009


     Served by BLESSING

  4550 WHITE LETTER A        1    1.00
  4553 WHITE LETTER D        1    1.00
  4557 WHITE LETTER H        1    1.00
  4562 WHITE LETTER M        2    2.00
  4563 WHITE LETTER N        1    1.00
  4564 WHITE LETTER O        1    4.00
  4577 WHITE NUMBER 1        1   10.00
  59120 CALENDAR 2010
         5% DISC
  Discount                       -1.35
   59201 MUG THREE CRESTS    1    5.00
   59999 SHIRT PRINTING      1    0.00
   60088 GK SHIRT HM 09/1    1   27.00
  Discount                        1.35
         5% DISC

  Total Items           £53.00
         5% DISC
  Discount                   2.10

  Total Items           £50.90

  CARD                      £50.90
```

Club Headquarters :

The Bridge Hotel,
Castle Square
Newcastle upon Tyne,
Telephone 27780
Club Meetings held
every Tuesday at 7.30 p.m.

NAMELESS SHIRTS

Last year I visited the Club Shop to buy a shirt for my little lad, turning a festive blind eye to the absurdity of paying £29.99 for a child-size plastic shirt when I could have bought ten superior garments on the market for the same total price.

The real trouble began when I got his name applied to the back of the shirt. I was feeling pretty pleased with myself at having avoided the usual problem of sticking on a star player's name, as they tend to disappear as soon as they score in consecutive matches, leaving you with a useless shirt and an awkward social pressure to waste another thirty quid. Then I discovered that each iron-on letter in our longer-than-average surname cost a pound to be pressed into place – except for the Ms, which cost two quid each.

"Why do the Ms cost two quid each," I felt I had to ask the question.

"Because they're bigger than the other letters."

"But an 'M' isn't twice as big as an 'N' or a 'P', is it?" I argued. "Do you charge 50p for an 'I'? And what about my number '1'. If an '8' or a '0' is two quid, then I want my '1' for a quid, right?"

Sometimes it's almost as if they're deliberately testing the limits of our unconditional love.

THE GREAT STADIUM HOAX

St. James' Park hasn't always been the towering cathedral to Geordie ambition that we know today. In the mid Seventies it was an abandoned building site up one end, with the big, open Gallowgate terrace at the other and a couple of fairly modest-sized stands... but surely it wasn't bad enough to be airbrushed out of existence?

In retrospect, the club programme probably wasn't the most effective organ for the club to use in an attempt to convince the world that St. James's was an ultra-modern hyperstadium. Everyone who read the programme did so at the ground itself. They only had to look around to question the club's rather wishful representation.

The 1975-76 FKS *Soccer Stars* sticker album provided a more realistic chance of impressing the nation's kids. The Newcastle players had their backgrounds removed and the sweeping, multi-layered stands from some anonymous Spanish stadium substituted in.

Newcastle United

NEWCASTLE UNITED
ST JAMES' PARK
NEWCASTLE UPON TYNE NE1 4ST
Telephone Newcastle (0632) 28361
Telegrams Football, Newcastle
24 Hours Information Service 611571

Here's Tommy Gibb backed by Costa del Sol high-rises and sun-baked terraces.

Hang on... that ain't Newcastle!

Alan Kennedy, badly cut out and plonked in front of an impressive triple decker and giant scoreboard.

Glen Keeley, hovering above a 60,000 seater megabowl.

Next season: 'Newcastle in Space'...

'S CLUB

FICE

' Street
n Tyne,
IF

atch days

nings
p.m.

NEWSPAPER PROGRAMMES

"Welcome to your new-look *Miller*, your newspaper/programme which takes the place of the traditional club programme. Your new-look *Miller* will be bigger and better than the old-style programme and will contain lots, lots more..."

Four page turns (and nineteen adverts) later, you were all done, having partaken of very thin gruel indeed. It left you wondering quite what the old-look, smaller, worser Miller must have been like.

The late Seventies and early Eighties saw something of a trend for newspaper programmes, with Rotherham United, Tranmere Rovers and Shrewsbury Town among the clubs who signed up to publishers Sportscene and their hot new format.

It was bad news for fans, who needed more elbow room on the terraces for their half-time read, and also for those of us who liked our prog collection of homes and aways neatly arranged in a box. This unnatural, unwieldy combination of two media had to be folded twice to fit in with the normal-sized ones. They got raggedy at the edges, turned sepia at the first hint of sunlight and then got brittle and started to fall apart. They were hardly in mint condition when you handed over your 20p, never mind when you got them home from the game. Enough to tip your average programme collector with OCD right over the edge.

Previously, there had only ever been *The Ram*, Derby's tabloid-sized programme to, er, ram into your prog box. This newsprint groundbreaker persisted for around a decade, its lively red-top touches and unique appearance winning a place in fans' hearts, if not their back pockets.

But, ultimately, the newspaper programme idea failed to catch fire (unlike many of the programmes, which formed terrace bonfires and are now in short supply). Derby abandoned the format in 1983, reconforming to the norm.

The new-look, bigger, better, lots, lots more *Miller* lasted just one season: Rotherham fans were probably quietly relieved.

Four pages later, you were left wondering what the **old-look, smaller, worser programme** *must have been like...*

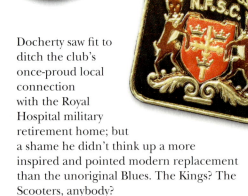

Never mind the Pensioners: Up the Kings, the Scooters... the Swingers?

NICKNAMES UNSUITABLE FOR A MODERN, GO-AHEAD CLUB

Pensioners, Heathens and Glaziers, Filberts and Foresters. Citizens, Throstles... even Biscuiteers.

You can picture the new breed of 1970s executive commercial manager, in their pin-striped suits with wide lapels, shaking their heads in amused disbelief. These antiquated nicknames might have served clubs back in the olden days, but they would never do for a forward-looking outfit with scarves and mugs to shift.

Take the Glaziers, for instance. Suitable enough for a team that started life in Sydenham Hill in the shadow of the great Crystal Palace; but Palace (the club) had moved home in 1915 and the Palace (the great glass exhibition hall) had burned down in 1936. When Malcolm Allison arrived at Selhurst Park in 1973 he quickly changed the club's nickname to the Benfica-inspired Eagles, with an according rethink of the club badge. The only surprise is that Mal's 'cosmopolitan' changes stuck around longer than he did.

It's hard to imagine Roman Abramovich's Chelsea empire still trundling along with its traditional, unathletic nickname of the Pensioners. Just as well Sixties boss Tommy

Docherty saw fit to ditch the club's once-proud local connection with the Royal Hospital military retirement home; but a shame he didn't think up a more inspired and pointed modern replacement than the unoriginal Blues. The Kings? The Scooters, anybody?

Leicester City had been known as The Filberts for nearly sixty years, ever since the club had evolved out of Leicester Fosse after World War I (well, at least it was a cooler nickname than the Fossils). It lasted until a mid-Seventies makeover, which generated a new club motto – 'If It Ain't Bust, Fix It' – and redubbed them the Foxes, in line with the club badge and the county's hunting tradition.

Even so, despite the marketing men's best efforts, it's one thing to design a new cartoon fox for the programme, and quite another getting the supporters to call the club anything other than 'Citeh'.

Witness a more recent attempted rebrand in Manchester, all too briefly the home of the Laser Blues...

Norwich City

BAYERN MUNICH AWAY

It was Norwich City's first and, to date, only European campaign, earned by virtue of an impressive third-place finish in the inaugural Premier League competition. After an easy First Round UEFA Cup win over Vitesse Arnhem, they were handed a Second Round date with mighty Bayern Munich; but if they were expected to enter the Olympiastadion in the role of sacrificial virgins, then Mike Walker's boys had other ideas.

A perception arose among Walker's staff and squad that their hosts were affording them less than total respect. A Bayern director had been overheard expressing the wish to meet Tenerife in the next round, and Norwich had been described by a newspaper as 'a rural town where mustard is made'. Although that sleight was largely true, it wound the Canaries' spring just a little tighter.

Mike Walker was illogically optimistic about his team's chances, marking out defender Matthäus as Bayern's weak link. Lothar Matthäus, that was: Germany's captain and FIFA World Player of the Year... but Walker was spot on.

After twelve minutes, a comically back-pedalling Matthäus headed a ball

straight up into the air, and it fell beautifully for Jeremy Goss to volley home from twenty yards. The evening took an even more surreal turn in the 29th minute when Mark Bowen nodded in a second. "This is almost fantasy football!" yelled Motty.

Although the Germans pulled a goal back, a 1-1 draw at Carrow Road saw Norwich into Round Three, though sadly they couldn't repeat the trick against Inter Milan.

But that night in Munich, they really cut the mustard – and Norwich go down in history as the only English club ever to have won amid the glassy peaks of Bayern's futuristic, soon-to-be obsolete and bulldozed Olympic Stadium.

THE ONE MILLION POUND MAN

The record transfer fee paid to a British club nudged gradually upwards during the 1970s. Martin Peters commanded a £200,000 price-tag when he switched from West Ham to Spurs at the dawn of the decade. Alan Ball's transfer from Everton to Arsenal saw the record rise by £20,000. Then Bob Latchford's 1974 move from Birmingham to Everton saw a jump to £350,000, and that wasn't topped until 1977 when Hamburg paid Liverpool £500,000 for Kevin Keegan. Two years later, West Brom paid Middlesbrough £516,000 for David Mills, but any theories about a glass ceiling were shattered one month later when League Champions Nottingham Forest outrageously doubled the outlay, breaking the £1 million barrier to secure the signature of Birmingham City's Trevor Francis.

Brian Clough arrived at a packed press conference in a casual red PVC top, twiddling a squash racket in his hand, implying that he was engaged merely in a tiresome bit of admin. But, at the time, the cheque he wrote was a jaw-dropper, and surely heralded the end of the game as we knew it.

How could any one player be worth a million pounds?

We got the answer three months later in the 1979 European Cup Final at Munich's Olympiastadion. Playing in his first ever European game, Francis scored the only goal against Malmö FF, a far-post diving header connecting with a fantastic John Robertson cross from the left.

Just two years earlier Forest had scraped promotion to Division One in third place... now they were the Champions of Europe. Worth a million quid? Every penny, young man.

Worth a million quid?
Every penny, young man.

NUMBERS 1-11

For the second season of 'Premiership' football in 1993-94, the game's new masters introduced an Americanised squad numbering system ranging from 1 to 99. It helped assuage the egos of the vast numbers of players signed by newly rich clubs, only to sit on the bench or to play in Littlewoods Cup ties against Fourth Division oppo. They might be number 39, but that didn't necessarily mean they were in the third team; it signified that they were potentially a linchpin in the boss's rotation system.

It made the old 1-to-11 system seem ingenious in retrospect, as this had told everyone at a glance who was playing in each position, while enabling any fan to quickly identify an unknown player in the programme.

The unfamilar number 11 for the visitors this afternoon? Ah yes, of course: that will be former Burnley danger man Steve Kindon. It won't be too long before Steve is flying down the left wing.

And centre-forward for the Rams? Let's see: number 9 is... Phil Gee. Born Pelsall, according

Notts County

THE OLD SCHOOL BOSS

Now that the average tenure of a Division One manager is less than two seasons, the very idea of any boss sticking with the same club for twenty years seems almost ludicrous. If the club stands still or goes down, he's sacked; any measure of success means he gets head-hunted and moves on. Simple.

And yet Jimmy Sirrel led Notts County from Division Four to Division One over two spells in charge, and still commanded the full respect of the board and the love of the fans – no burned bridges, no 'Judas' banners – when he returned for a third period at Meadow Lane, his long service finally spanning the years 1969-87.

The ex-Celtic winger and Royal Navy conscript was a hard man, "throwing jugs of tea" and "players against the wall"; but the Scot is equally remembered for his schoolboy chuckle, and a willingness to talk football with endless enthusiasm.

When Jimmy Sirrel died, aged 86 in 2008, countless fans recalled being ushered inside the ground as penniless kids, told to "help the groundsman" and then disappear on to the terraces. But what also emerged was a picture surprising to outsiders: of an innovator, a football thinker to rival – or, in fact, share technical notes with – his old friend Alex Ferguson, who he met on a Lilleshall coaching course in the Seventies. Not every fan recognises Sirrel's role behind one of England's first youth academies.

"The best team always wins and the rest is only gossip"
– Jimmy Sirrel

"Everything in life has improved," Sirrel gruffly observed. "Everything, whether it be the telephones, aeroplanes, motor-cars. So why should football go backwards?"

Present circumstances excepted, obviously...

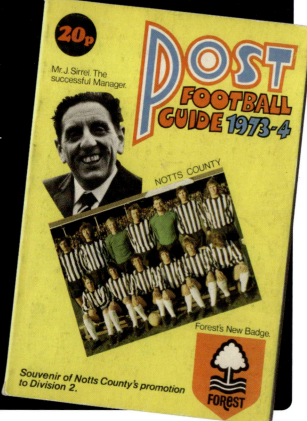

20p

Mr. J. Sirrel. The successful Manager.

POST FOOTBALL GUIDE 1973-4

NOTTS COUNTY

Forest's New Badge.

Souvenir of Notts County's promotion to Division 2.

FOREST

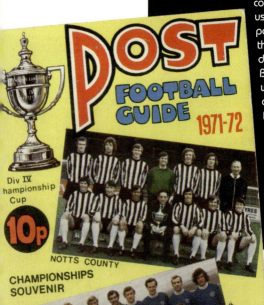

POST FOOTBALL GUIDE 1971-72

Div IV hampionship Cup

10p

NOTTS COUNTY

CHAMPIONSHIPS SOUVENIR

to his Pen Picture. Fifteen goals in 1986-87. Sonic the Hedgehog tattoo.

Eleven players, eleven shirts. Eleven numbers, 1 to 11, goalie through to outside-left.

Apologists may argue that the other 1993 addition of players' names to their shirts made up for losing the clarity and structure of 1 to 11; but it was just another Americanisation, another ego boost, another few quid on the price of a replica shirt.

The likely first eleven of any visiting side used to be known days, if not weeks, in advance of any match, and it was only ever necessary to make the odd Biro amendment to the teamsheet, and enter in the sub's name. Thereby robbing yourself of 90 per cent of its future eBay value.

Maybe big, meaningless numbers aren't so stupid, after all.

"I might be number 39, but I'm no third-teamer.

I'm a linchpin in the boss's rotation system."

It wasn't just the mouth-watering team line-up, drawn out in positions on the centre pages or listed neatly on the back page, that went missing from the programme. The grid of players running alongside the fixtures and results also went to pot, no longer providing an instant visual map of the season. Now the names of fifty players head the columns, boosted up in importance over the little numbered club shirts, the sprawling grid is a meaningless bodge.

Back in the day, fans used to buy a programme primarily to find out the teams, and as a souvenir of the match. Strange to think that the day's star billing is no longer among the mass of information provided by the matchday magazine – and that, even in retrospect, there's zero indication of who actually played.

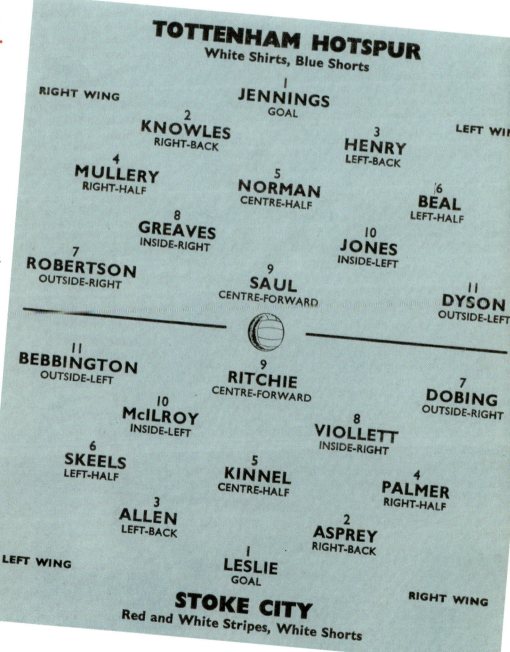

TOTTENHAM HOTSPUR
White Shirts, Blue Shorts

RIGHT WING

1 JENNINGS GOAL

2 KNOWLES RIGHT-BACK

3 HENRY LEFT-BACK — LEFT WIN

4 MULLERY RIGHT-HALF

5 NORMAN CENTRE-HALF

6 BEAL LEFT-HALF

8 GREAVES INSIDE-RIGHT

10 JONES INSIDE-LEFT

7 ROBERTSON OUTSIDE-RIGHT

9 SAUL CENTRE-FORWARD

11 DYSON OUTSIDE-LEFT

11 BEBBINGTON OUTSIDE-LEFT

9 RITCHIE CENTRE-FORWARD

7 DOBING OUTSIDE-RIGHT

10 McILROY INSIDE-LEFT

8 VIOLLETT INSIDE-RIGHT

6 SKEELS LEFT-HALF

5 KINNEL CENTRE-HALF

4 PALMER RIGHT-HALF

3 ALLEN LEFT-BACK

2 ASPREY RIGHT-BACK

LEFT WING

1 LESLIE GOAL

RIGHT WING

STOKE CITY
Red and White Stripes, White Shorts

THE OBSERVER'S BOOK OF FOOTBALL

I'm nothing if not a creature of habit and, even at primary school, Library Time always saw me heading for exactly the same shelf. There was a little block of books with the same shade of off-white spines. *The Observer's Book* series covered an enormous range of topics.

1 Birds
8 Dogs
24 Pond Life
29 Flags
31 Sea & Seashore
36 Churches
45 Zoo Animals...

But I was only ever interested in...

47 Association Football.

I would reach for that well-thumbed (by me) volume, and at a dinky five and three-quarter inches tall it was my *Little Book of Calm*.

Albert Sewell had compiled a straightforward pocket book of facts and figures – a guide to each of the Football League clubs, including 'colour plates' of their shirts, along with a history of the game and its various competitions.

This was the educational coalface where I toiled to learn the name of every ground, the colour of every strip, the size of every capacity, and every nickname of the ninety-two.

Good old Albert had even put their phone numbers in, which seemed to grow longer according to the size of the club. Liverpool: 051 263 2361; Crewe: 3014.

There was also a colour plate devoted to Goalkeepers' Colours which showed that any old goalie could take their pick from royal blue, scarlet, white or green, but yellow was far more exclusive, reserved – somehow heartbreakingly, from today's perspective – for 'Internationals Only'.

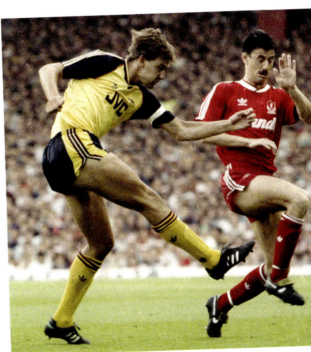

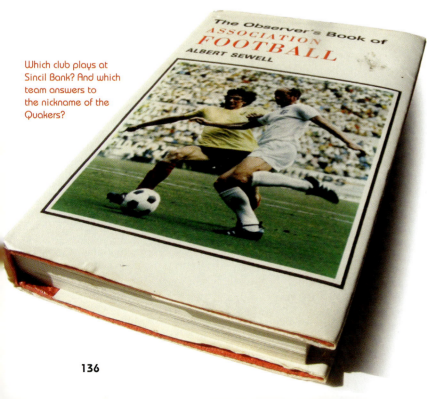

Which club plays at Sincil Bank? And which team answers to the nickname of the Quakers?

ONE-CLUB PLAYERS
Extinct Football Species No.6

Tony Adams, Arsenal; Ray Mathias, Tranmere; Paul McStay Celtic. The One-Club Footballer isn't quite extinct, but the end is in sight.

John McDermott, Grimsby; Willie Miller, Aberdeen; Keith Stevens, Millwall. There are surprisingly few on the official list...

Brian Stubbs, Notts County; Stuart Taylor, Bristol Rovers; John Trollope, Swindon... where a decade's service is required to qualify...

Ian Twitchin, Torquay; Joe Wark, Motherwell; Mark Weatherly, Gillingham... and even if you've been on loan

136

elsewhere for just a week, you're no longer a one-club player.

Dane Whitehouse, Sheffield United; Jimmy Armfield, Blackpool; Brian Labone, Everton. The players who never trousered a cut of a transfer fee are few and far between.

Paul Sturrock and Maurice Malpas, Dundee United; Ronnie Boyce and Trevor Brooking, West Ham; Nick Holmes and Matt Le Tissier, Southampton. And so many others blew it in the final straight, drawn in by a couple of winding-down seasons at Brighton or Hereford.

Tony Parkes, Blackburn; Keith Peacock, Charlton; Steve Powell, Derby; Paul Lake, Manchester City; Ron Atkinson, Oxford; Kenny Jackett, Watford; Marvin Johnson, Luton; Alan Knight, Portsmouth.

to represent Kansas City Spurs in a promotional NASL 'mini-league'. The talented, laddish, MG-driving Knowles, who liked to backchat referees, was not a likely convert, but he returned to the Black Country a fully paid-up Jehovah's Witness.

His conversion was as complete as it had been sudden. Eight games into the 1969-70 season Knowles gave up struggling to reconcile his football and his religion and hung up his boots. Forever. He swapped his old gold Wolves shirt for a dark suit and tie, to pound the pavements and knock on doors in the name of the Lord.

God's Footballer: Have you heard the good news?

Laddish, MG-driving Knowles returned home
a fully paid-up Jehovah's Witness.

There's one small enclave left in the North West – Jamie Carragher and Steven Gerrard at Liverpool; Ryan Giggs, Paul Scholes and Gary Neville at Manchester United – and, in an era when clubs loan out their youngsters to all and sundry, they will probably be the last.

Hang on, who's this? Peter Knowles, Wolves, 1962 to 1982...

Team-mate Frank Munro told *The Guardian*: "We all thought he'd be back in six weeks or eight weeks and we laughed it off. After about a year or so we realised he wasn't coming back." But still, as testament to Knowles' talent, a long succession of hopeful Wolves managers kept him under contract until 1982.

Even forty years on, Knowles claimed never to have regretted ending his career at the age of 23; but by this time folk-rocker Billy Bragg had joined the many fans wondering 'what if?, penning 'God's Footballer' about a player who hears celestial voices above the raucous sound of the Molineux crowd...

OTHER AVENUES
Extinct Football Species No.7

It's taken as a given that if you're good enough to make a living from playing football, then playing football is what you'll do until you become injured or too old.

Peter Knowles was plenty good enough. He made his debut for Wolves aged eighteen in 1964 and gradually established himself as the club's most talented player, winning England Under-23 honours.

Then, in the summer of '69, Wolves visited the United States

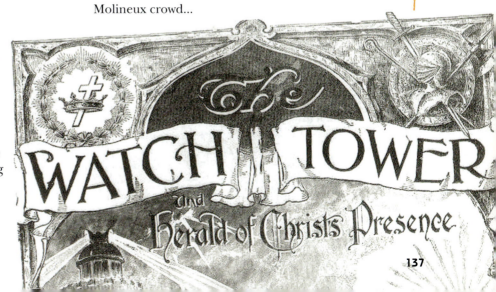

OVERSIZE THIRD-WORLD STAMPS WITH PLAYERS IN MADE-UP KIT

They were the jewels in the crown of my Stanley Gibbons *Adventurer Stamp Album*, a slim but bulging hardback book full of crinkly pages and sticky scraps of paper, with a picture of a Papua-New Guinean tribesman on the cover. You could tell they were a class apart from the dingy little oblongs collected up from boring countries like France and Egypt, because they were big and bright, commemorating one of the more recent World Cups. They featured all-action images of footballers who didn't just sport red or blue tops but exciting chevrons, hoops and stars.

My barnstorming third-world football stamps were four times the size of the commemorative issues launched on *Blue Peter*, and ten times more colourful than those boring pink or blue ones with the Queen's head that you were forced to lick hundreds of times every Christmas.

My favourite World Cup whoppers from Republique Togolaise boasted players in

bright sashes, chevrons and stars.

Some even came in little blocks, breaking all the accepted rules by joining on to different stamps in the same set. And yet more mystery: many of my football stamps were in too perfect condition to have been used postally, but curiously still bore neat little postmarks.

They were the talk of the neighbourhood, my six 1970 World Cup whoppers from the hilarious-sounding *Republique Togolaise*, which filled up the page for the stamps of Togo, Tonga and Trinidad & Tobago all on their own.

Their philatelic magic shone out as brightly as the players' pink and green sashes under my plastic magnifying glass.

MONGOLIA

FOOTBALL WORLD CHAMPIONSHIP
OF JUNIORS IN USSR ★ 1985

МОНГОЛ ШУУДАН

ໄປສະນີລາວ
POSTES LAO

COUPE MONDIALE DE FOOTBALL
SAN FRANCISCO '94

1991

330k

PE FOOTBALL
82

500F

DU NIGER

FOOTBALL WORLD CHAMPIONSHIP 1966   ENGLAND

60₮

2

MONGOLIA МОНГОЛ ШУУДАН

PENRHYN

WORLD CUP CHAMPIONSHIP

ESPANA 82

PENRHYN   PENRHYN   PENRHYN
NORTHERN   NORTHERN   NORTHERN
COOK ISLANDS   COOK ISLANDS   COOK ISLANDS

PENRHYN   PENRHYN   PENRHYN
NORTHERN   NORTHERN   NORTHERN
COOK ISLANDS   COOK ISLANDS   COOK ISLANDS

PENRHYN   PENRHYN   PENRHYN
NORTHERN   NORTHERN   NORTHERN
COOK ISLANDS   COOK ISLANDS   COOK ISLANDS

NORTHERN · COOK ISLANDS

WORLD CUP FOOTBALL

WORLD CUP FOOTBALL CHAMPIONSHIP · MUNICH · 7 · JULY · 1974

WM 74
OCEANIA
Australia
New Zealand

25c

COOK ISLANDS

Oceania

COOK ISLANDS

WM 74

$1

COOK ISLANDS

MUNICH · 7 · JULY · 1974

Dave was right. It seemed that *everyone* had a copy of the *Football 78* album in their school bag, along with a pile of swaps held in place with a laggy band. Even people who didn't like football. Even girls.

Our new favourite thing was twice as hefty as its predecessor, weighing in at a fat 64 pages; each club spread over two pages instead of one, and in total there were 525 stickers to collect. Panini's major new selling point was that these 'stickers' were actually sticky, not just pieces of paper that required the use of glue. Unable to afford a Pritt stick, my experiments with flour and water had produced messy results in previous years. But now you could swap your stickers – "Got, got, got, got... NOT GOT!" – and seal them immediately in their allotted square.

Swap yer: four Ian Butterworths, Kevin Steggles and Paul Brush for a Newcastle shiny...

PANINI

Benito and Giuseppe Panini began manufacturing their *figurine* (Italian for stickers) in Modena in 1961. It took another seventeen years for them to arrive in our school playground, but when they did the impact was huge.

For years we'd been content with our *Wonderful World of Soccer Stars* albums made by FKS, but when Panini's Football 78 hit the newsagents, they were blown out of the water.

In an inspired marketing move the album was given away free with *Shoot!* magazine (what young football fan would be able to resist the urge to fill all those empty spaces?) with a foreword written by its editor, David Gregory: "Every so often the soccer scene is set alight by a brilliant new talent – a player with the exceptional ability that sets him apart from the rest... a similar thing periodically happens in the world of football publishing – a presentation that is novel, superior to its competitors, and which is certain to capture the imagination of the avid supporter."

The stickers themselves were beautifully designed, clear head-and-shoulders shots with a club badge and a St. George or St. Andrews flag because, yes, the Scots had been included too. Clydebank's Billy McColl got to have his own sticker, and the English Second Division was also covered with a team group and badge for each previously ignored team.

Ah, those badges. There was a heartbeat jump when you ripped open your packet and saw a gold foil badge nestling among the half-dozen stickers...

Panini reigned for a good fifteen years, never straying far from their '78 blueprint, producing a series of highly collectable and well-loved albums until they, in turn, were replaced by Merlin around the time the Premier League was launched and the licensing fees leapt up.

It's good to see the company is still thriving around the world, producing thousands of sets of stickers annually for European football leagues and minority sports such as Barbie, ice-hockey and Harry Potter. Crikey, they even do the Scottish Prem: let's all move to Cowdenbeath.

141

PARKLIFE

Oadby Town's third-team goalie cast an anxious backward glance as he heard my plastic 'club names' football spinning once again up the back of his goal net; but he needn't have worried. I already had years of experience of kicking into the wrong side of the goal – still do. Even if you hit the ball harder than intended, the weight of the ball pushes the net down, so the crossbar works as a natural stop, and prevents the ball flying up and over into the goalmouth.

"Just don't kick it up the net when the ball's at this end," the goalie warned me, sounding surprisingly terse considering that he wouldn't be running to fetch any misplaced cannonballs that afternoon.

As if he needed to tell me in the first place, given the number of times he'd said the exact same thing to me or Tat or Nidge on all those other brilliant-grey Saturday afternoons when Dad hadn't taken me to the proper football, or when City were away.

"You hear me?"

Thumbs up. No problem. I am, after all, the only fan in his personal Kop.

I try a tricky chip from an angle, heading right for the top corner. The ball slitters over the corner of the net – no fancy stanctions here – and out along the goal-line. Nearly on the pitch, but technically well within our contract.

Now for a Penalty Prize competition, like on *Football Focus*. And as there's no goalie to beat on this side of the net, it's important to get the ball right in the corner, so there's no doubt he wouldn't have stood a chance.

1-0. 2-0. 3-0. Easy.

Give this one a bit extra.

The ball flies a little high for a perfect penalty, but it could still go in.

Refocusing my eyes for the first time beyond the imaginary diving goalie, I notice the oppo are on the attack.

My ball sails straight over the bar and lands plop in the mud, so momentarily there are two balls bogged down in the box – until the real ball ricochets away, and an oppo player boots my ball miles toward the far touchline.

Avoiding the goalie's glare, I trot off to fetch it.

It's nearly half-time – time for Vimto and football cards from Mr. Sherrard's shop.

He'll have forgotten by the second-half.

PLAYERS
PLEASE REMOVE YOUR BOOTS
BEFORE ENTERING THE BUILDING
Thank you

Hard liners: Stockbridge lay down the law, cramping the style of Petersfield Town.

NO BALL GAMES IN THE GOALMOUTH

NO CYCLING ON THE PITCH

NO GOLF PRACTICE

By Order

PET SCOTTISH SECOND DIVISION TEAMS

Cowdenbeath. Stenhousemuir. East Fife 5, Forfar 4...

Incanted like the shipping forecast's barely imaginable expanses of sea – Hebrides, Bailey, Fair Isle – the names of the clubs locked forever in the icy mud of the Scottish basement divisions have always triggered in me a curious yearning when they're recited on a wintry Saturday evening's *Sports Report*.

Why curious? Because when I was first afflicted I'd never even been to Scotland, let alone Cowdenbeath. If nostalgia is a longing to return to the apparent safety and innocence of the past, then I shouldn't be longing for a magical return to see the Blue Brazil. I understand how this confusion between place and time arises, and how it's possible to end up longing for a disappeared football ground when what I really miss is the simplicity of being twelve; but I've never even found out whether Cowdenbeath – unlike Raith and St. Johnstone and Borussia – is a real place.

So why the yearning? The only available facts in the national press told me the average attendance in the Scottish Second Division was 200 or so souls, and I was under no illusion that the standard of football at Central Park or Ochilview Park was likely to be any better than the weather – especially once I'd discovered that stormy waves regularly deluge the terraces at Arbroath's seaside Gayfield Park. But where other than in Scottish Division Two could you watch a game of football at a ground with a hedge running down one side? Or shout for the Bully Wee?

In truth, I was drawn by the Scottish clubs' promise of a miniature, secret, parallel world of football. An escape into adventure. However, from the day 25 years ago when I fell in love with a girl from Hawick (and eagerly checked the map for the nearest League club) my sole romantic interest in the Scottish nether reaches has lay with my

incomparable Queen of the South.

In real life, inconvenient large hills mean no one has ever taken the long and winding road from Hawick to Dumfries for football, with Hibs or Hearts the preferred option behind the local rugby. And so a pilgrimage to Palmerston Park remains but a treasured intention, the Doonhamers my pet Scottish Second Division team in name alone.

You might argue that it's random. It's patronising. It's trainspotting. Twisted nostalgia running haywire. But it's still a thousand times more meaningful than any British kid wearing a Barcelona shirt with MESSI on the back.

"Promotion Is Our Ultimate Goal."
Stenhousemuir (10th Place)

"We Hope For An Upturn In Fortunes."
Cowdenbeath (11th)

"We Look Forward To A Big Improvement."
Albion Rovers (12th)

"We Look Forward To An Exciting New Era."
Berwick Rangers (13th)

"We Must Adopt A Positive Approach."
Stranraer (14th)

Clydesdale Bank Scottish Football League Review, Season 1988-89

Stenhousemuir: not to be confused with East Stirlingshire, who hail from Falkirk but play in Stenhousemuir... or Stirling Albion.

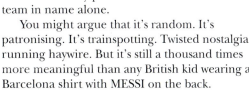

Forfar Athletic
(Colours — Sky Blue with Navy and White Vertical Stripe)

DAVE McWILLIAMS	1
BILLY BENNETT	
JIM CAMERON	2
KEN BROWN	
ALEX BRASH	4
ALEX RAE	5
ARCHIE KNOX	6
BILLY GALLACHER	7
IAN REID	8
JIM HENRY	9
JOHN CLARK	10
	11

Subs — Atholl Henderson, Henry Hall

East Fife
(Colours — Gold with B Facings)

ALAN BLAIR
RON McIVOR
BILLY GILLIES
DAVE CLARKE
COLIN METHVEN
WILLIE WEDDERBURN
RAB CAIRNS
JIM GEORGE
JOHN DICKSON
KEN MACKIE
JOHNNY GIBSON

Subs — Willie Herd and John Huskie

REFEREE — D. A. MURDOCH (Bothwell)

— J. G. GLASS (Dundee) W. PATTERSON (Kirkcaldy)

FORTHCOMING HOME MATCHES
Berwick Rangers (Scottish Cup, 2nd round) — Next
January, 1979. 3 p.m.
Stranraer, Saturday, 20th January

WAY GAMES

THE PETER BARNES FOOTBALL TRAINER

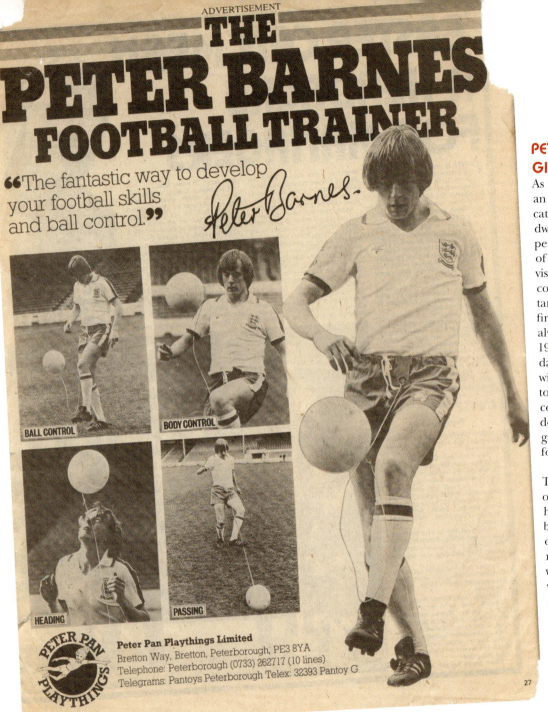

"The fantastic way to develop your football skills and ball control."

Peter Barnes.

BALL CONTROL

BODY CONTROL

HEADING

PASSING

Peter Pan Playthings Limited
Bretton Way, Bretton, Peterborough, PE3 8YA
Telephone: Peterborough (0733) 262717 (10 lines)
Telegrams: Pantoys Peterborough Telex: 32393 Pantoy G

27

PETROL STATION GIVEAWAYS

As the world spirals towards an all-encompassing and catastrophic war over dwindling oil supplies, the petrol station can be a bit of a depressing place to visit – especially when it costs the same to fill your tank as it did to buy your first car. But this hasn't always been the case. In 1971, for instance, your dad would tip you the wink when he was about to take his mustard-coloured Ford Cortina down to the nearest Esso garage: this was a mission for man and boy.

While the likes of Texaco and Shell seemed obsessed with making huge amounts of money by flogging us the world's overflowing natural resources, good old Esso were only concerned with making sure that small boys had plenty of great football stuff to collect. First, there were World Cup coins, then 'Squelchers', a series of little booklets so named because the info contained in them was enough to squelch any argument. There were FA Cup Winners coins, and the Top Team Collection of Photo-Discs built a squad of Britain's best players... but best of all was the literally titled 'Esso Collection of Football Club Badges'.

Esso even provided a splendid fold-out presentation card to stick them in and, frankly, if there was anything more exciting happening in 1971 – with all due retrospective respect to decimalisation and the troubles in Northern Ireland – then I didn't notice. It wasn't just

Any questions on the PBFT? A crack team of ten still await your calls at Peter Pan Playthings...

PETER BARNES FOOTBALL TRAINER

My mate Chris was the proud owner of a Peter Barnes Football Trainer back in 1978. He gave us a full demo up the recreation ground one Saturday morning, but we decided that the ball provided was too light for a satisfying full-blooded volley. We substituted in a leather ball, ingeniously tied the elastic to the pump adaptor, and let play commence.

This modified set-up didn't prove to be "The fantastic way to develop your football skills and ball control." It was, in fact, "The fantastic way to get a football smack in your plums and then get your shorts ripped off."

Good job there were no girls up the reccie, that day.

144

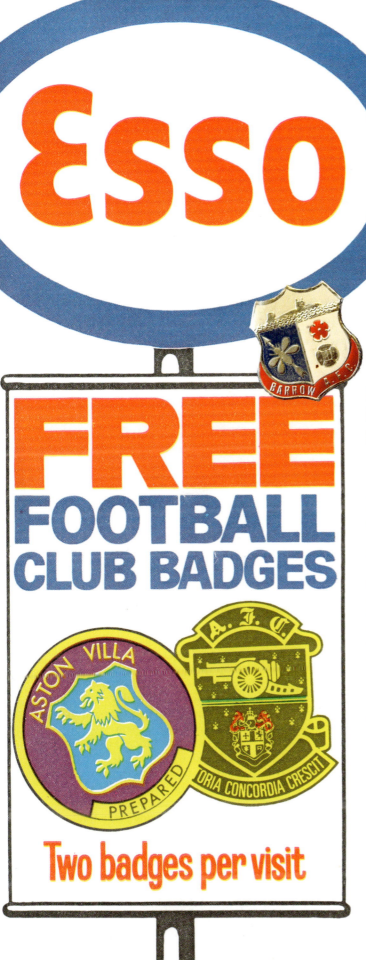

ESSO

FREE FOOTBALL CLUB BADGES

Two badges per visit

If there was anything more exciting happening in 1971 – with all due respect to decimalisation –

then I didn't notice.

the 20p blackmail job for the 'Starter Pack' of 26 otherwise unobtainable badges that made the heart beat faster. The little foil badges were irresistible. Everyone was collecting them.

When the garage man came out to fill up Dad's car, he'd first check the oil and water levels. My job was to grab him some tissue to wipe the dipstick with – and then we'd be handed the small but exciting envelope that contained our two free badges.

Sitting in the front seat, unencumbered by a seat-belt, I'd savour it for a moment, trying to guess which of the 76 featured clubs' crests were hidden inside, and then I'd tear it open...

Ayr United and Orient. Both bloody swaps.

145

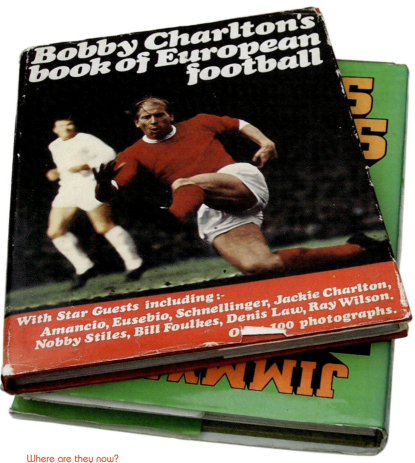

Where are they now?
Players called Bobby
and Nobby and Bill...

PLAYERS CALLED BOBBY AND JIMMY

Dave Beckham. Bobby Fowler. Jimmy Redknapp.
What might have been...

There can be no doubt in the mind of any fan of a certain age as to why the England football team are no longer capable of competing at the very highest level.

It's because we never could, and indeed never did. 1966 was nothing but a historical blip: England caught everybody else napping, and took full advantage in our one tiny window of opportunity. As soon as the rest of the world brought in the same negative tactics and the necessary enforcers, we haven't been able to compete in terms of skill, fitness, schooled technique, natural flair or devoted professionalism.

We're joking, of course.

The single factor that has really held us back from taking our natural place as world champions is the modern players' curse of either being given – or more often electing to convert to – first names that couldn't possibly belong to a footballer.

Robert Moore. James Greaves. Norbert Stiles. Doomed from the start, that lot would have been.

In our ongoing, desperate search for a way to win, the players need to take a leaf out of Harry Redknapp's book. He's the most successful English manager in the modern game, and he doesn't go around calling himself Harold, does he? It's obvious what he had in mind when he named his firstborn Jim – and it wasn't upward mobility.

Jackie Wilshere. Micky Richards. Gary Barry. Jackie Tel.

Now there's the core of a side that sounds like winners.

PLAYERS LIVING ON YOUR STREET
It Could Never Happen Now

Even now, it's impossible for most of us to imagine the heart-racing excitement of having Dennis Rofe living opposite your house in the late Seventies.

And, as luck would have it, there's now no need, because Ian Long can remember exactly how it felt to a nine-year-old resident of Church View, Narborough, to look out of his front window and see the real-life Cockney star of last night's *Match of the Day* mowing and edging his lawn.

"It was surreal," says Ian. "Sightings were limited, mostly involving me springing to my dad's side if he ever fell into conversation with Dennis in the street. I would silently try and will my dad to ask him for a free season ticket, or invite me to be mascot, or get me a shirt or a match ball, but the conversation never took the desired turn."

When Ian wasn't playing football in the street (hoping that Dennis was watching from a window, and picking up the phone to a scout) a popular pastime on his street was poddy 123. This was a variation on hide-and-seek where the seeker was based at a 'poddy post', counting to a hundred before going in search of the others, hoping to find and incarcerate them. Meanwhile, if anyone managed to reach the poddy post, then a triumphant cry of "PODDY 123!" could free all the prisoners and condemn the seeker to another turn. Got it?

"One day a game of poddy was in full swing," Ian tells us, "and my friend Andy and I needed somewhere new to hide. We saw that Dennis's garage door was open, so we slipped in and crouched down behind his grey Capri with its classy black vinyl roof. A great hiding place. Except the side door opened and in walked Dennis, demanding to know: ''Ere, what are you two doing?'

"I thought, 'I'll never play football in the county again after Dennis has finished with me', and with knocking knees we stutteringly

On Liverpool's Scotland Road, Shanks gives a team-talk to local kids before they play an Everton street team.

FOX FAVOURITES

DENNIS ROFE

explained that we were playing poddy and were very, very sorry and would never do it again.

"Dennis walked to the front of the garage and peered up the road. 'Is that the poddy post?' he asked, pointing at the distant 'Church View' sign. 'Yes,' we gulped, with visions of him booting us up there like a goal-line clearance. But to our amazement he went to his car door and said: 'Get in.' We both hopped in the passenger side and crouched down out of sight

while the best uncapped left-back in the country drove out of his garage and cruised up the street, stopping at the poddy post. We leapt out, gleefully shouting, 'Poddy 123!'

"Dennis was a true hero," Ian says, momentarily returning to the present day. "Not only did he play for City, but he also remembered what it was like to be a kid."

THE PLUCKY GIANTKILLER
It Could Never Happen Now

Remember when the Southern League no-hopers of Hereford United took on the might of First Division Newcastle, and managed a draw away from home? Three times postponed, the replay in the Edgar Street mud looked all over when Malcolm Macdonald scored with eight minutes to go. Never mind 'the great leveller': how many Cup ties from last season caused the names of the equalising scorer and the extra-time game-clincher to be seared into the national consciousness like Ron 'Goal of the Season' Radford and Ricky George, who sparked an ebullient invasion of parka-clad kids?

And what about three years later in 1975 when Wimbledon beat Burnley to become the first non-League club in a century to taste victory on a First Division ground? Next up was Leeds at Leeds – when Leeds were Leeds – and the champions engineered an iffy penalty with seven to go. Step up heroic beardie, Dickie Guy,

to bat out Peter Lorimer's bullet, only to be beaten by a cruel deflection in the replay.

The last time a non-League Dave toppled a Division One Goliath was 1989, when plucky Conference Sutton saw off Coventry City, who had lifted the trophy just two seasons before. So what chance of an upset now when a Premier League shark takes on a sub-basement tiddler?

For starters, the tie is always transferred to the away ground to enable the paupers to wring the maximum out of their one-off payday.

The vast, echoing surroundings only serve to unnerve the underdogs. They're on a hiding to nothing, raw kids with little or no experience of football with this amount of bite, seasoned only with a couple of would-be contenders and a past-it up-and-downer hoping to minimise the embarrassment.

The odds are stacked. It's a sorry mismatch.

No Big-time Charlie Squad-Members XI stands a chance against a team of lower-league rejects with a point to prove.

Beat the weather in a top-quality parka

A special offer from Football Monthly Digest

You'll look good—and be well protected against the elements—in these fine quality parkas made of weatherproofed cotton gaberdine. They are quilt lined in red nylon with fun fur surround to the hood. Other features include: zipped front with press-studded covering flap, raglan sleeves for comfort, draw strings at waist and hip and four flap pockets all with press-stud fastenings. Colour: Olive Green.

Mens Small (35"–37" chest) Medium (38"–40" chest) Large (41"–43" chest) Extra large (44"–46" chest) £4·78 (approximate retail price £5·99)

Ladies Sizes 10, 12, 14, 16 £4·28 (approximate retail price £5·50)

Boys and Girls 30", 32", 34" chest £4·28 (approx. retail price £5·50) 26", 28" chest £3·70 (approx. retail price £4·25)

Newcastle United v Hereford U. SATURDAY JAN 15 1972 KICK-OFF 3.00 p.m. ST. JAMES' PARK 5p

Fly Guy: Superwomble Dickie holds out against First Division champions Leeds United.

UNIQUELY SINGULAR AND ONE OF A KIND

Now hold on just a minute, what the bloody heck's going on here?

The player on the full-page picture in my *Striker* comic is from outside the top two divisions – and that's simply unheard of. His shirt is white, with a single, broad hoop running around the middle. Is that even allowed? I'm not sure whether he knows it, but his club badge – with an old ship on it, of all things – has shifted from the left side to the middle of his shirt. Has he no sense of tradition, of self-respect?

Most shocking of all, his hoop, together with the fancy piping around his collar and cuffs... is *green*. And he isn't even a goalie.

And what kind of a name is 'Argyle', anyway?

Suffice to say, the pin-up's weird green kit made a huge impression on my seven-year-old mind – apparently more so than his name.

Plymouth were *special*.

And then, in 2003, Yeovil Town made it into what remains of the Football League, and Plymouth were no longer unique but merely unusual. Yeovil wear green, too. For the first time in a century, Argyle were going to have to sort out an away kit. It wouldn't have been so bad, but the previous season Boston United had clambered aboard the League, insisting that their nickname was also The Pilgrims.

Just when Plymouth fans were coming to terms with being relatively common, they were special again – but not in such a positive, green- or Pilgrim-type way. In 2008, Hull City made it to the top flight, finally ridding themselves of the millstone around their necks, and making Plymouth the biggest English city never to have hosted Division One football.

Tactically changing the subject, did you know Argyle are both the most southerly and the most westerly English League team?

Plymouth Argyle

CORPORAL PUNISHMENT

Portsmouth has strong ties to Britain's martial history dating back to 1194, when Richard the Lionheart granted the city 'a crescent of gold on a shade of azure, with a blazing star of eight points', which he'd nicked off the Byzantine Emperor's standard after capturing Cyprus. No wonder proud Portsmouth FC adopted the motif as their club badge, centuries later. He was the King, after all: it would have been rude not to.

Portsmouth Dockyard is the home of the modern-day Royal Navy and the Royal Marine Commandos, as well as Henry VIII's battleship *The Mary Rose* and HMS *Victory*, Nelson's flagship at the Battle of Trafalgar. At the end of the 1800s, Portsmouth FC evolved out of the Royal Artillery football club. Field Marshal Montgomery was a keen

Pompey supporter and club president – and the outbreak of World War II led to Portsmouth becoming FA Cup holders for longer than any other club, having lifted the trophy in 1939.

So, when Alan Ball was looking for a goalscorer to improve his Pompey side, it was only natural that he should discover Corporal Guy Whittingham, who had scored 93 goals in 110 games for the Army, Waterlooville and Yeovil in a busy 1988-89 season. It cost £450 to buy Whittingham out of the Army, which represented something of a bargain considering that 'Corporal Punishment' netted 99 times in 173 League appearances in three spells at Fratton Park.

That's some fancy shooting. Blue Army!

Portsmouth

118 DEREK HALES

intact. Hunter ended up at Barnsley, Bremner at Hull, while Cooper dived down the leagues to Bristol, City and Rovers. After 747 appearances, Reaney moved on to Bradford – and amazingly won the Aussie Player of the Year award in 1980!

PRACTICALLY ONE-CLUB PLAYERS
Extinct Football Species No. 8

If there were any justice in the world, all these nearly-men would already have made an appearance as a One-Club Player, and you'd still be suffused with a cosy glow at their exemplary, old-fashioned allegiance to a single cause.

But not for any of this crew the timely, handsomely bankrolled bowing-out of a Good and Faithful Servant such as Trevor Brooking, Matt Le Tissier or Tony Adams. After an entire career synonymous with a single club, these poor sods had to blow their record in search of just one more season, suffering reduced wages and – before too long – mutual misgivings with unfamiliar fans. They thought they'd be able to slip gracefully out of the limelight, maybe even drop down the leagues and showboat. But in fact they'd lost more than a yard. They'd lost more than their hair. They'd lost their eternal right to be remembered only in their proper club's kit, battling to the not-so-bitter end.

If only they'd just opened a pub in the Cotswolds instead of going on to prove the dread adage: old footballers never die, they just move to Dundee...

Peter Bonetti – Dundee United

In 1979, after twenty years with Chelsea, Peter 'The Cat' Bonetti handed over his King's Road swinging and spraying duties to Petar Borota – if change must come, then let it be gentle – and headed north to curl up with a well-deserved saucer of warm milk in front of the fire in Dundee. At night, all Cats are grey.

Steve Perryman – Oxford United

Steve's Spurs career spanned seventeen years after signing youth terms in 1969, during which time he clocked up a club record 854 first-team appearances while hardly seeming to age at all. It was moving to Oxford United, and quickly on to Brentford as player-boss, that forced Steve to bring the portrait down from his attic.

Paul Reaney – Bradford City

Of the Damned United, only Charlton and Madeley escaped with their one-club records

David O'Leary – Leeds United

Long before he got into coaching under George Graham and on to the path to management at Elland Road, David O'Leary himself pulled on the hallowed yellow nylon. Having played 558 league games over eighteen years at Arsenal, he managed a paltry ten for Leeds before injury brought down the final curtain on his playing career.

Jimmy Johnstone – Dundee

Think Lions of Lisbon. Think the Battle of the River Plate. But best not dwell on Celtic's greatest-ever player's fall to Earth with the San Jose Earthquakes in 1975, or the threadbare, lonely-looking Jinky from his days with Sheffield United. Or that final extension of JJ's after-life with three League starts for Dundee...

PROPER BEARDIES
Extinct Football Species No. 9

The natural state of man, and therefore footballers, is to be bearded; but the global daily assault by razors (with up to and including five blades) indicates that there are few cultures in the western world where a hairy lower face is the norm. From a high water mark in the mid Seventies, beards have slowly disappeared from the face of British football.

325 ROY GREENWOOD

We're not talking about a bit of lazy Wayne Rooney stubble here, but a proper beard. Months of growth, preferably with the same diameter as a piece of 13-amp fuse wire. A Roger Kenyon... a Trevor Hockey... a Frank Lampard... a Derek Hales... straight off the cover of *The Joy of Sex.*

Proper beards, for proper blokes.

Here's also to those players who binned the razor for a while but couldn't tolerate the fearful itchiness on a long-term basis: Steve Heighway, Martin Chivers, George Best, Colin Todd, Peter Withe .. at least they made a stand.

Life wasn't always easy for Beardies.

In 1976, Sunderland boss Bob Stokoe told his striker Roy Greenwood that he wouldn't be appearing in the pre-season team photo, and all because he'd sprouted some serious bristle.

"I don't care what the manager says," Greenwood hit back. "I keep it trimmed and I think it suits me."

That's right, ignore him, Roy. He's a beardist.

PSYCHEDELIC PROGRAMMES

There must have been something slipped into the Midlands' water supply in 1972, when no less than five of the region's clubs started to vibe up their club programme with some frankly disturbing psychedelic effects.

Could it be that a single hippy mastermind was behind the adoption of the far-out ink-blot look at Blues, Leicester, West Brom, Wolves and Walsall – possibly attempting to saturate the programme market in patchouli oil and clouds of incense?

More importantly, were any of the clubs aware that the others had bought into the same prog-rock look, or did they their programme editors independently happen across the tie-dye technique at the summer's free festivals?

Questions, questions. But none so obvious or as unfathomable as 'how?', and 'why?'.

THE PUNFUL ADVERT

10 Anfield Review

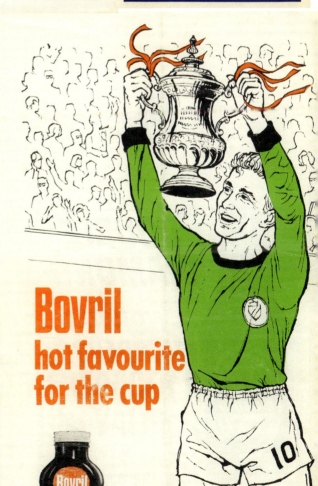

PUNK ROCK FOOTBALL

Noise, freedom and escape. Heroes who played the game by their own rules. Loads of passionate moaning. The long-awaited rise of the underdog.

Shouting and bouncing around to the Undertones seemed to go hand in hand with shouting and bouncing around to the football at the end of the '70s, and within a few years a snarling C-60's worth of crossover anthems had surfaced on *The John Peel Show*.

So what was the greatest football/punk/ New Wave firecracker ever released?

It's hard to look beyond the snot-nosed dead-end whingeing rebellion of 'My Perfect Cousin' (1980) by Derry's finest in muddy Doctor Martens. Apart from a stomping tune that got Peelie up and 'bopping' around the studio, it's the sheer smallness of the Undertones' complaint that makes it a winner. Who cares about 'Anarchy in the UK' in the face of the outrage borne of having a slightly spoiled relative?

PROBE PLUS
TRUM.1-7"
HALF MAN HALF BISCUIT
A
ALL I WANT FOR CHRISTMAS IS A DUKLA PRAGUE AWAY KIT
(HALF MAN HALF BISCUIT)

Stadión Dukly Praha na Julisce
Streda 3. listopadu 1965 ve 14.00 hodin

Disenfranchised Manchester United fans, that's who: they've adopted the Sex Pistols Year Zero classic (1977) as a terrace chant. "I am an FC Fan / I am a Mancunian / I know what I want and I know how to get it..."

On the other side of Manchester, The Fall's 'Kicker Conspiracy' (1983) provided a vital shot of dirty Working Men's Club rockabilly, revolving lyrically about the (at the time) chronically unfashionable subject of football and its attendant hooligan problem. It's the only song in history to namecheck FA bigwig Bert Millichip.

Cherry Red's 'Blue Moon' CD features City songs by Ed Banger, the Freshies and Frank Sidebottom.

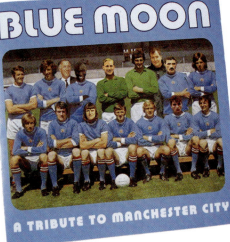

BLUE MOON
A TRIBUTE TO MANCHESTER CITY

Football punk pioneer Ed Banger (late of the Nosebleeds, who did the DIY classic 'Ain't Been to No Music School') was a Manc Blue, too. His first solo outing was a droll, half-spoken football commentary over brilliantly rudimentary bass and drums. 'Kinnel Tommy' (1978) came across a bit like 'Jilted John', minus any suspicion of a tune, but with plenty of extremely cool almost-swearing.

And guess who Chris Sievey out of The Freshies supported? The band's 'Dancing in the Kippax' (1979) featured chants taped at Maine Road – 'Weeeeee'll Drink-a-Drink-a-Drink to Colin the King', 'Oh Manchester is Wonderful', 'Blue Moon' – all over a twangy guitar break of the Buzzcocks school. Sievey was later to don a *papier-maché* head and change his name to Sidebottom.

Powerpop punkers The Boys were the first, on 'Cast of Thousands' (1978) to employ fake crowd noises and terrace chants to firm up the link between loud guitars and football's epic release. "Just because you're losing"? "We are the champions"? And this from Spurs fans.

Norwich stompers Serious Drinking made a short, noisy career out of football, beer and comedy lyrics. Their finest moment was 'Bobby Moore Is Innocent' (1982), Mirror Football's official number 1 footballer namedrop, no less. And their debut 45 'Love On The Terraces' (1982) came as a mighty timely answer to the Cockney Rejects' 'War On The Terraces'. We'll have no fighting here.

Saving the most perverse must-have until last, the Disco Zombies' 'Where Have You Been Lately, Tony Hateley?' (1983) was devoted to the much-travelled Blues, Liverpool, Notts County and Cov striker. Right from the tinny opening drum-machine and contorted one-string *Match of the Day* theme, it lives right up to its big billing as an *Obscure Independent Classic*.

THE BUSH TELEGRAPH

Influenced by the groovy local scene in the 1960s, the QPR programme editor decided to get with-it and adopt a Day-Glo psychedelic look. The result was a lasting classic in terms of design and content.

Never mind local West London rivals Chelsea and their ability to cash in on King's Road associations – fashion, glamour, models, film stars. Shepherd's Bush had a cool thing going, too, being home to The Who, and Goldhawk Road the genesis of the mod scene (witness the revival-sparking *Quadrophenia*). There was a healthy multicultural vibe, multiple music venues around the Green and pop-cultural influences emanating from BBC TV Centre.

So no surprise when QPR tapped into the ultra-mod look of London's Op Art Queen, Bridget Riley, whose geometric black-and-white paintings made your eyes go all wizzy when you stared into their kaleidoscopic depths. Within a few years, the prog ed had used every one of the lairiest colours imaginable on the cover of the so-called *Bush Telegraph*.

Content-wise, it wasn't every football programme that carried front-line dispatches. For those fans who felt aggrieved at having to miss a game due to work or a wedding, a sobering letter:

"Dear Sir,
I am an Englishman who emigrated to the USA in February 1968, by February 1969 I was in the US Army and now I am over in Vietnam fighting this war, but every week I get news clippings of the great QPR from a good friend of mine Bob Thorpe. If I ever get home to England the first Saturday I will be watching the only team – QPR.

Is there anybody reading this who would like to send me clippings or photographs of the great team?
Yours truly, the only QPR supporter in Vietnam –
PFC Nils Guy 171447871 – CoD 1/35th Inf 4th Div."

Instead of watching Rodney Marsh at Loftus Road, this Bush fighter was now patrolling the jungle waiting for a Viet Cong ambush.

According to the letters editor, Nils wrote two messages on the back of his envelope – 'Give Peace a Chance' and 'QPR for the Cup!'

r

RABBIT'S EARS

Back in the Sixties and Seventies much emphasis was placed on the proper tying of shoelaces. It was regarded as an essential life skill and anyone not proficient in the practice would, sooner or later, suffer a terrible injury. No adult would ever pass up a chance to tell you that your untied lace was about as dangerous a hazard as you could ever face in life. They all knew a little boy who had tripped over an untied lace and broken his arm/leg/jaw/sternum and then died of complications.

Even footballers joined the crusade, treating their bubble-gum cards like public information films. For a few years it was all the rage to be nonchalantly tying your shoelaces as the camera pointed at you.

Here, Ron Davies (Southampton) and Sammy Nelson (Arsenal) deliver the subliminal message: "You make two bunny ears, bunny goes around the tree, into the burrow, pull tight…"

Be smart, be safe.

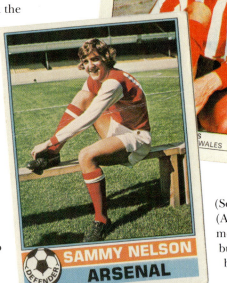

Rangers

COPPING THE CUP WINNERS' CUP IN A CUPBOARD

Rangers' path to the 1972 European Cup Winners' Cup Final did not run smooth, providing a foretaste of events on the big night, when the Gers were destined to meet Dynamo Moscow in Barcelona.

Having drawn 6-6 on aggregate with Sporting Lisbon in the second round, the Dutch ref ordered a penalty shoot-out, which Rangers lost – and only when boss Willie Waddell pointed out that his side had scored three away goals to Lisbon's two was the result reversed.

Rangers were desperate for a European triumph. Celtic had won the European Cup five years earlier and several English clubs had lifted trophies, the latest accessory required to prove that you were a 'big club'.

And Rangers joined their ranks that May night at the Nou Camp, running up a comfortable 3-0 lead with a goal from Colin Stein and two from Willie Johnston. The Russians rallied late on with two goals to test the Scots' nerves but, one pitch invasion later, the final whistle blew and Rangers were triumphant.

The silverware was a little tarnished, however, when thousands of ecstatic fans swarmed on to the pitch to hug the players and get close to the presentation. Skipper John Greig was hoisted aloft without due regard for the Gers hero having played with a broken bone in his foot. Fascist dictator General Franco's baton-swinging *Guardia Civil* were delighted to intervene, and the celebrations degenerated into the so-called 'Battle of Barcelona'.

As war raged outside, Greig was presented with the trophy in a dingy, fluorescent-lit office in the bowels of the stadium, only for the club to be subsequently banned for a season by UEFA. Dynamo's pleas for a replay due to the pitch invasion were sympathetically received but there were to be no more reprieves, or reprises.

The greatest Ranger ever? Undeterred by the KGB's team, a broken foot, fascist guards or a pitch battle.

THE RE-REPLAY

For the 1991-92 season, the Football Association made a change to the rules of their own, historic FA Challenge Cup competition, thereby altering the combative nature of the world's oldest football tournament.

In each of the previous 120 years, the only way to beat your Cup opposition was out on the pitch, no matter how many attempts it took. Two evenly matched sides would replay and replay and replay, clashing antlers like rutting stags until, on the brink of exhaustion, one was finally beaten.

In the new, cheapened version of the Cup, clubs would be spared the effort of a second replay, ties being decided on penalties after just one rematch. Now a team could sidle through the rounds without ever winning a match, hiding behind the artifice of a cop-out shoot-out, and simply poking the ball past the keeper from twelve yards.

Pah.

I remember seeing every minute – well, almost – of a titanic Third Round struggle between Arsenal and Third Division Sheffield Wednesday, when the second, third and fourth replays were all played at Filbert Street within seven days in the filthy winter of 1979.

The first game had ended 1-1 at Hillsborough, where Pat Jennings had been pelted with snowballs by the Kop. The replay at Highbury was another 1-1 draw with Owls' keeper Chris Turner having the game of his life.

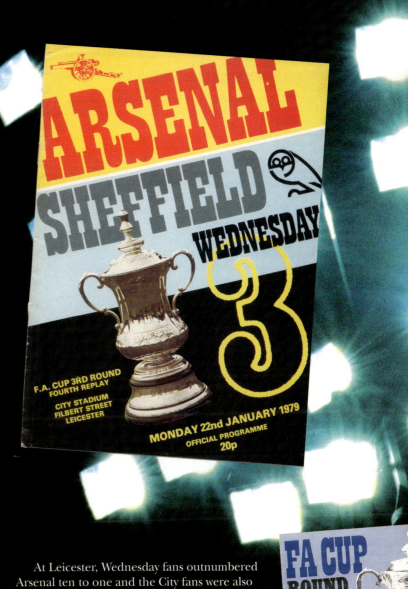

At Leicester, Wednesday fans outnumbered Arsenal ten to one and the City fans were also backing the underdogs, so the Gunners were housed in the away pen. They were great nights, the first match ending 2-2 after extra-time; then the sides' fourth clash looked all over at 2-1 to Arsenal, five minutes into stoppage time. Crowds of fans were out in the street when the roar went up and everyone ran back to watch another half-hour's extra-time, the game finishing 3-3. In the fifth match, the First Division team finally got the measure of Jackie Charlton's battlers, and won 2-0.

Second, third and fourth replays were
all battled out within seven days...

But even this prolonged battle didn't make *The Guinness Book of Records*. That honour goes to Alvechurch and Oxford City who locked horns for eleven hours in the Fourth Qualifying Round of the 1971-72 FA Cup. After 2–2, 1–1, 1–1, 0–0 and 0–0 draws, Alvechurch finally overcame Oxford with a 1-0 win at Villa Park, where Doug Ellis served them Champagne in paper cups...

Unlike Arsenal, however, Alvechurch didn't go on to lift the trophy.

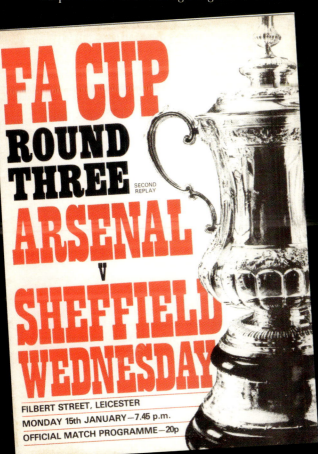

Reading

SCORE AND SNOG A COPPER

This is how Robin Friday first made himself known to Reading fans: as the non-League loudmouth picked out by the local press ahead of their 1973 FA Cup Second Round derby against Hayes. Long hair. Old tracky bottoms. Newcastle Brown Ale T-shirt bordering on the insolent.

It wouldn't be too long before fans had forgiven the swaggering, silky-skilled hippy for stealing the show as Hayes held the Biscuitmen, and only succumbed 1-0 in the replay. Manager Maurice Evans took a £750 transfer punt on the wild kid in the snakeskin shirt and afghan coat. Maybe the lip and the chain-smoking were a warning; but skill this sublime just couldn't be ignored.

Only in time would Friday's true potential emerge – along with his capacity to gleefully undermine his talent with vast supplies of booze, dope and pills. Evans told Friday he could play for England if he would only apply himself, only to be told: "I'm half your age and I've lived twice your life."

Come the Millennium, Friday was named Reading's 'Player of the Century'. But tragically, by that time, he'd been dead for ten years.

Those Reading fans who saw Friday play still dine out on his banana shot against Donny in February 1974; on his infamous goal celebration involving a policeman; on his chest trap and reverse 35-yard thunderbolt against Tranny in '76, of which ref Clive Thomas told the *Sunday Mirror*, "Even up against the likes of Pelé and Cruyff that rates as the best goal I've ever seen." To which Friday suggested Thomas should come down to Reading more often, 'cos he knocked them in like that every week.

Regretfully sold on as a liability to Cardiff City in 1976, Friday was arrested upon arrival in Wales, having travelled on a railway platform ticket. He started just twenty League games for the Bluebirds before resigning from the pro game aged 25, reportedly "fed up of people telling [him] what to do".

Friday on my mind: Robin's faves, the Sensational Alex Harvey Band, headlined at Reading in 1974.

THE REFEREE WHO IS ALWAYS RIGHT

"Sorry, ref, I was a bit late into that challenge."

"Apology accepted, player. But one more slip, and you're in the book."

That's not a conversation you hear too often nowadays, what with refereeing decisions all standardised by FIFA, and any weighing of individual circumstances given a black mark by the Eurocrat filling in his refereeing report up in the stand.

It's even officially frowned upon for a ref to call a player 'player'. It's too democratic, and so potentially demeaning. It's against Euro law on grounds of discrimination against a multi-millionaire shouting spit-flecked abuse into your face. And, of course, a referee can't ask for 'name and number' any more, as that's potentially offensive to female players.

In the Premier League, it's no longer even permissible for a ref to ask a player to turn around to note his number: it's offensive if they don't know all the stars' names.

"Player, you've been warned. Now would you kindly leave the pitch?"

"Yes, sir. And thank you, sir."

Sounds AT READING

READING FOOTBALL SUPPORTERS CLUB

NORTHAMPTON
TOWN FOOTBALL CLUB
OFFICIAL PROGRAMME AND NEWS

3ᴰ

NORTHAMPTON TOWN FOOTBALL CLUB LIMITED

Office: COUNTY GROUND, NORTHAMPTON, Telephone: 31553. Telegrams: "Cobblers," Northampton

Directors: Mr. P. Hutton (Chairman). President: Mr. K. J. Dear.
Mr. F. R. Cutler, Mr. K. J. Dear, Mr. E. C. Hawtin, Mr. W. R. Penn (Vice-Chairman).
Mr. C. T. Wilson, O.B.E., Mr. N. H. Wooding, M.B.E., Mr. R. L. M. Saunders
Secretary/Manager: David Smith. Mr. F. J. York
Hon. Medical Officer: Dr. Jas. Orr.

"COBBLERS" v. ARSENAL
FOOTBALL COMBINATION
SATURDAY, DECEMBER 14th, 1957

This has been
ournemouth, last
me game with

THE RESERVES

The ressies. The seconds – as in shoddy goods. The stiffs – like bodies in a mortuary. And these poor unfortunates plied their trade in a meaningless league known as the Football Combination: Dad said it was so called because it was a 'combination' of has-beens, also-rans, convalescents and kids.

I went once. It was 50p to get in and the teamsheet was free. Two hundred of us sat in an echoing Main Stand, and you could hear the players shouting to each other. I was bored after five minutes and wanted to go home. Most of the players probably did, too.

It was football stripped of its sense of occasion, denuded of its glamour, with the stigma of second-best hanging over the ground like a grey cloud.

Reserve-team football seems to have fallen by the wayside these days. Try telling a millionaire member of your 45-man squad rotation system that he's playing in front of 75 paying customers this Tuesday. And, if he argues, send him on loan to Doncaster, where he'll be treated like a god.

LEEDS UNITED

OFFICIAL PROGRAMME
Price THREEPENCE

LEEDS UNITED A.F.C. TOKEN

Preston N.E. Res 37 1967-1968

VERSUS

Preston North End Reserves
WEDNESDAY, 31st JANUARY, 1968   K.O. 2-15 p.m.

NEXT HOME MATCHES

SATURDAY, 3rd FEBRUARY, K.O. 3 p.m.   C.L.
Derby County Reserves
WEDNESDAY, 7th FEBRUARY, K.O. 7.30 p.m.   F.L. Cup
DERBY COUNTY

LEEDS UNITED FOOTBALL POOL

are you a member?
IF NOT! JOIN NOW

enquiries to
THE POOLS OFFICE, 1 OXFORD PLACE
LEEDS 1 and at THE POOLS KIOSK
WEST STAND CAR PARK

Alf's got the whole world in his hands – the whole world in his hands.

THE REST OF THE WORLD
It Could Never Happen Now

Oh, the splendid arrogance of it all: Us vs. Every Bugger Else. Not even Britain, but England alone against the Rest of the World, including Scotland.

The Rest of the World fielded a strong side.
Hardly surprising, with three billion to pick from...

When the 'FIFA XI' came to Wembley to help celebrate the FA's Centenary in 1963 they had an eye-wateringly strong side, which was hardly surprising with three-and-a-half billion people to pick from. Lev Yashin (USSR), Djalma Santos (Brazil), Karl-Heinz Schnellinger (West Germany), Svatopluk Pluskal, Ján Popluhár and Josef Masopust (all Czechoslovakia), Raymond Kopa (France), Denis Law (Scotland), Alfredo di Stéfano (captain, Argentina), Eusébio (Portugal) and Francisco Gento (Spain) – plus bench-warmers

including Jim Baxter (Scotland), Uwe Seeler (West Germany) and Ferenc Puskás (Hungary).

But were Alf Ramsey's England team intimidated by Chilean coach Fernando Riera's stellar line-up? No way, José.

There were only four players in Alf's line-up who were to claim a place in the World Cup-winning side three years later – Banks, Wilson, Moore and Bobby Charlton – but England still emerged victorious.

In front of a full house of 100,000, Southampton's Terry Paine put England ahead in the 66th minute. Denis Law looked to have earned a draw for the Rest of the World with an equaliser eight minutes from time, but then Jimmy Greaves popped up characteristically to poach an 89th-minute winner.

England 2:1 Earth. Who could we play next?

THE ROSETTE

In the olden days, British males over the age of six were only permitted to wear brown, grey, greeny-brown, browny-green or, in moments of extreme flamboyance, navy.

If a chap had worn a football jersey anywhere other than on a football field he might well have been assumed to be quite insane, and arrested for causing a breach of   the peace. And the same applied to sporting any item of apparel other than a school blazer in a primary colour. Red socks and yellow waistcoats, for example, were only ever sported by show-offs, buffoons and variety acts.

So how to let it be known which side you were supporting in the big Cup game on Saturday? That's where rosettes came in: they were the acceptable face of partisanship in more restrained times.

You don't get them any more.

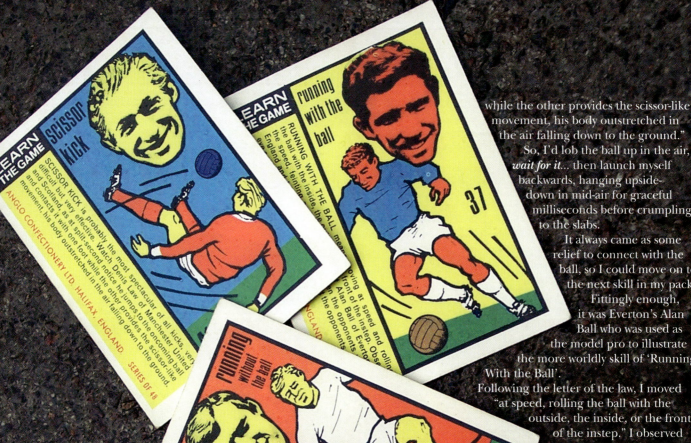

while the other provides the scissor-like movement, his body outstretched in the air falling down to the ground."

So, I'd lob the ball up in the air, *wait for it...* then launch myself backwards, hanging upside-down in mid-air for graceful milliseconds before crumpling to the slabs.

It always came as some relief to connect with the ball, so I could move on to the next skill in my pack.

Fittingly enough, it was Everton's Alan Ball who was used as the model pro to illustrate the more worldly skill of 'Running With the Ball'.

Following the letter of the law, I moved "at speed, rolling the ball with the outside, the inside, or the front of the instep." I observed "the feinting and body swerving", of the cartoon Ball, and mimicked the way he "finds his way between opponents with his eye on the ball, only occasionally glancing at the opponents' positions."

In other words, I booted the ball along and ran after it. Simple.

More troublesome was the accompanying lesson in the series: 'Running Without the Ball', a skill long unappreciated by the schoolboy masses. Running With and Without the Ball are like yin and yang. Halves of a whole. One muddy and exhausting; the other silent and all but unconscious, a product of Zenlike mind training.

As the perfect counterbalance to Alan Ball, you might have expected Burnley's Peter No-Ball to pose for this one, but instead Leeds United's Mick Jones was nominated as the most accomplished... runner. Not necessarily the fastest, you understand: Running Without the Ball is all about anticipation and "moving cleverly into position."

I observed Jones "reading" the pattern of the game "and how intelligently he runs into an unmarked position where he expects his colleague will pass the ball."

I moved cleverly down the garden path as far as Ringo the Rabbit's run, then trotted intelligently back – anticipating that I'd be in for my tea before the Scissor-Kick or Running Without the Ball returned again to the top of the pack.

RUNNING WITHOUT THE BALL

For hours at a time, I would practise my skills out on the driveway, taking a break every couple of minutes to study the little diagrams on my Anglo Confectionery 'Learn The Game' football cards.

The only thing holding me back from performing the perfect scissor-kick was the slight disadvantage of never having seen Denis Law pulling off "the most spectacular of all kicks."

I'd hang upside-down in mid-air for graceful milliseconds before crumpling to the slabs.

Still, the basic idea was there for all to see, and never mind the niceties of cartoon conventions for body movement.

Law "jumps at split-second notice to the oncoming ball and contacts it with one foot

where have all the 'keepers gone?

S

SAINT & GREAVSIE

Not a lot of people remember the BBC's 'Find a Commentator' competition of 1970, which was launched as part of the build-up to the summer World Cup – and still fewer are aware of the repercussions it would hold for televised football in years to come.

Having fielded an unexpected 10,000 entries from individuals keen to book a ticket to Mexico sitting alongside David Coleman and Kenneth Wolstenholme, a final six were selected. A decent class of applicant included Ed 'Stewpot' Stewart from Radio 1's Saturday-morning *Junior Choice* and Gerry Harrison, later to become the voice of Anglia's *Match of the Week*.

The hopefuls were judged by a panel that included England boss Alf Ramsey, dishing out points for player identification and poetic flights, offset by black marks for instances of bias and cliché.

straight man-funny man, catchphrase-driven, down-the-boozer double act has informed TV's football coverage ever since, influencing everything from football comedy shows and the staging of satellite matches to radio call-ins... and even the presentation style of *Match of the Day*.

Unfortunately for St. John and Greaves, their victory is hollow. The double-act was last seen on screen in 1992. They were were too honest, too critical for their own good, and were positively pre-PC in their flagrant disrespect for Scottish goalies. And that would never do.

"The type of work we did changed with the big television contract of the Premier League," Greaves now jests with just a trace of bitterness. "It's become incestuous now. Football wants maximum publicity and all the good things from television, but television is then frightened to adopt any other attitude because they don't want to rock the boat."

Funny old game?

Stain & Greasie blew punditry apart, anarchic and unafraid to rock the boat.

The showcase for skills in sheepskin went to a final mouth-off between two rank outsiders: Idwal Robling, the Welsh sales manager of a packaging firm, and Ian St. John, of Liverpool and Scotland. And that's when Alf made his big mistake.

After claiming his fifteen minutes of fame, presumably during a group match involving El Salvador, winner Idwal was shuffled off to commentate for BBC Wales. Meanwhile, St. John simmered for nearly a decade before getting another chance, finally becoming presenter of ITV's Saturday-afternoon *World of Sport* in 1979.

But it was in 1984, when he teamed up with Jimmy Greaves, that the Scot sowed the seeds for his ultimate revenge.

Although it isn't fashionable to say so today, Stain & Greasie blew the world of football punditry apart. The pair were expert ex-pro insiders, yes; but they also oozed a casual, laddish, fan-friendly charm. And their

Been there, seen it, done it: Greaves scored 44 goals in 57 games for England.

SATURDAY AFTERNOON, THREE O'CLOCK

Before the era of the Premier League, one man alone had the requisite *chutzpah* to fiddle with the time-honoured 3 o'clock Saturday afternoon kick-off.

It wasn't one of Jimmy Hill's finest moments, back in the Sixties, when he changed Coventry City's Saturday-afternoon kick-off time to 2.45, with the avowed intention of guaranteeing his special Sky Blue supporters would catch the rest of the results on *Sports Report* on the way home.

But Hill's ugliest ever decision – even outstripping his whim to make Highfield Road England's first all-seater stadium – came a decade later, as Coventry chairman, in 1977. That's when he

deliberately delayed the kick-off of the end-of-season nail-biter against Bristol City, and then proceeded to flash the crucial result of Everton 2-0 Sunderland – which had kicked off on time – on the electronic scoreboard, urging his boys to play keep-ball for the last ten minutes. Sunderland were relegated. Cov stayed up by a single point, as usual.

It's worth considering the logic of fiddling with kick-off time next Sunday afternoon, when a crowd of 40,000 fans is waiting for the end of an ad break and a thumbs-up from a satellite TV director so the match can kick off, as scheduled, exactly 25 hours and five minutes late.

Go on ref, blow the whistle.

You know you want to.

SCARF ACE

The 1970s brought us so many new technological miracles, most of which had been unthinkable before the advent of the Space Race, the pressurised inventiveness of NASA and the resulting seven-iron shot on the moon. There was the digital watch with the numbers that glowed red; that tennis video game that went *beep boop*; video recorders and non-stick saucepans and portable calculators... and most astonishing of all, the unprecedented ability to print photographs onto fabric.

At first we had Six Million Dollar Man pyjamas and Osmonds T-shirts. Then Major Sports (Leicester) Ltd transferred the hot new technology to the football scarf market and 'picture scarves' were suddenly available for all the top club and Home International sides, up to and including Wales.

Who needed the Bionic Woman, the Bay City Rollers or the Wombles when you could have Brian Flynn, Terry Yorath and Arfon Griffiths portrayed in glorious polyester pixels?

What Happened Next to Mighty Leeds? See front cover...

SCOTTISH SUPERSTARS
Extinct Football Species No. 10

Up until twenty years ago, every great First Division team in football history had included at least one Scot, usually the brains of the operation – the ball player, the stopper who could do more than just stop, or the unstoppable goalscorer.

From the very top: the devastating Liverpool side of the Seventies and Eighties rocked on the fulcrum of Hansen, Souness and/or Dalglish. And the Reds' legendary boss Bill Shankly would never have got away with saying, "Although I'm a Scot, I'd be proud to be called a Scouser," if he hadn't been a Scot.

Once upon a time there were Scottish superstars who played all their best football north of the border. Celtic's wing raider Jimmy Johnstone; Rangers' string-puller Jim Baxter, who led Scotland to their 1967 World Cup victory, beating champions England at Wembley. And every generation used to have a stereotypical Scottish leader who invited clichés like Scottish food invites heart disease: 'fearsome warrior' Danny McGrain in his kilt and big, bushy beard; 'Braveheart' Colin Hendry, possibly the last of his kind.

Entire Scottish dynasties were geared to the production of passion, the players on the pitch often exhibiting a thoughtfulness and vision

"Phew! I haven't felt that good since Archie Gemmill scored against Holland in 1978!" – Renton, Trainspotting.

Dave Mackay was the single most influential player in the Spurs side of the Sixties, and proved it in the supposed twilight of his career when he put off a cushy move, out to grass with Hearts, to slot conclusively into Clough and Taylor's jigsaw at Derby, and lead the Rams in turn to the Championship. Taking over from Clough, Mackay then bossed the Midlanders to the title in 1975, his team including Bruce Rioch and Archie Gemmill.

Cloughie nicked Gemmill for Forest, where he sided with Kenny Burns and John Robertson. Prime-time Everton boasted Andy Gray and Graeme Sharp up front. Leeds had Bremner, the most hated player in British football, but only by opposing teams and their fans. What would we have given to see the dirty wee wind-up merchant in our team's colours, especially alongside fellow Scot Peter Lorimer?

Man U had a brilliant boss in Busby, and a European Footballer of the Year in Law, the most insistent and inventive goalscorer of all time. Next came Gordon Strachan, Joe Jordan and Gordon McQueen: so quake in your boots. Now there's just Alex Ferguson – and he'd never have got away with saying he just wanted to "knock Liverpool off their ****ing perch" upon his arrival from Aberdeen, if he hadn't been Scottish.

that dated all the way back to Queens Park's invention of passing in the 1860s. You know what Shankly believed about the importance of football: Scotland proved it. "Celtic was my

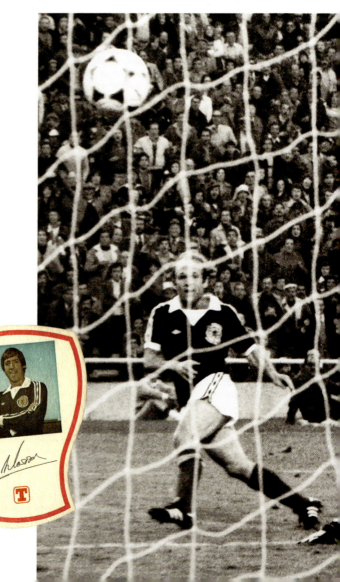

team," Frank McLintock told us, visibly reliving those days. "The whole of Glasgow, more or less, is Celtic or Rangers and they're all football mad. We were brought up on a diet of football morning, noon and night – we didn't even have a TV in those days. I'm not trying to plead poverty, most of Britain was the same. I think there was one car on our street."

McLintock was the skipper of Arsenal's great Double-winning side of 1971 – the archetypal Scot, three moves ahead of the play. If anyone can explain the Scottish malaise, it's Frank.

"As soon as you came out of school you put your jackets down for goals, picked two teams, and you were off in a game. You did it for

If there were a World Cup for value, Avenger would win it.

AVENGER

CHRYSLER
UNITED KINGDOM

The Chrysler Avenger.
Style, toughness. And a Championship performance.

as long as you could get away with it. Your mother would be shouting up the street, 'Hurry up! Your dinner's ready!' as it was getting dark. It's been told by a million people, but that's how it used to be.

"I think that's why Scotland had so many wonderful players coming through. They tell me now that they never see any kids playing in the street at all. They've all got their computers and electronic stuff in their rooms and unfortunately that has changed it all."

For the twelve years between the World Cups of 1970 and 1982, all of Britain took a special interest in the Scots as, time and time again, England failed to take the baby steps up on the world stage. With so many familiar, gifted players, they became everyone's second team.

Well, who were we supposed to support? Iran?

The Scots heap derision on our temporary switching of allegiances thirty years ago. In the same position, they now wear 'Anyone But England' T-shirts, and we wouldn't want it any other way. But how sweet it would be to see Scotland return to dynasty-building form and make their first major championship this century; even back in the Home Internationals, so we can do our level best to beat their pasty bottoms.

Choose fitba.

167

PORTSMOUTH v OXFORD UNITED
Sunday, March 29th, 1981
FOOTBALL LEAGUE DIVISION THREE
Kick-off 3.00 p.m.

TEAM SHEET

PORTSMOUTH
Colours: Blue with White trim

1 Peter Mellor
2 John McLaughlin
3 Keith Viney
4 Bob Doyle
5 Steve Aizlewood
6 Peter Ellis
7 David Gregory
8 Mick Tait
9 Billy Rafferty
10 Leigh Barnard
11 Alan Rogers
12 Steve Perrin

OFFICIALS
REFEREE:
L.F. BURDEN
(Corfe Mullen)
LINESMEN:
A.T. COLETTA
(Epsom) —
Yellow Flag
C. GRADY
(Lightwater) —
Red Flag

OXFORD UNITED
Colours: Yellow with Blue trim

1 Roy Burton
2 John Doyle
3 David Fogg
4 Billy Jeffrey
5 Gary Briggs
6 Malcolm Shotton
7 Mark Jones
8 Peter Foley
9 Tim Smithers
10 Keith Cassells
11 Paul Bury
12 Jason Seacole

PORTSMOUTH FOOTBALL CO. LTD.
NORTH STAND
£1.00 O.A.P.'S SECTION "G"
0734

PORTSMOUTH FOOTBALL CO. LTD.
NORTH STAND
£1.60 MILTON WING
0234

00225

PORTSMOUTH FOOTBALL CO.
NORTH STAND CENTRE
70p SECTION BOYS & GIRLS

JEFF HAMMERMAN ... on target in the third minute

Pompey collision course

Stockport 1, Portsmouth 1

JEFF HEMMERMAN hammered a third-minute goal but Portsmouth could not break a five-month run without an away League win.

Pompey were cruising to victory when keeper Peter Mellor collided with Stockport striker Mike Czuczman in the 75th minute. Two minutes later he hobbled off and skipper Joe Laidlaw deputised.

Laidlaw fumbled a couple of shots and was then drawn out of position as John Rutter whipped in a cross.

Czuczman rose above Pompey's defence and nodded in a 81st minute equaliser.

Pompey had Terry Brisley (foul) and Steve Davey (dissent) booked. But Davey made amends by picking up a long pass from Steve Bryant and shoving it into Hemmerman's path for that vital Portsmouth goal.

Pompey collision course: well, they're in good company with Superman...

THE SCRAPBOOK

In the six million-year interval between man first walking upright and the invention of the 24-hour kids' TV channel, the PlayStation, the Xbox, the Wii and the DS, kids were faced with a bit of a challenge. How to fill all those long, boring hours before it was time to blow their candles out? It was merely hundreds of years ago when the penny finally dropped, and pastimes such as needlepoint, pressing wild flowers and making your own scrapbook at last began to gain popularity.

Scrapbooks had two things going for them – 'UPSs', as Lord Sugar would call them. Most importantly, they were very cheap, and they were also highly, if not wholly, customisable.

Most young football fans had a go at assembling scraps devoted to their football team, but few persisted for very long. The first page of every scrapbook is filled, the last page hardly ever. After a few weeks, cutting your club's match reports and photos out of the paper tended to become a chore, enabling you to later track the ever-decreasing degree of care with which they were Gloyed onto the coarse pages. And then there was that final time you jumped the gun and Dad found a comedy hole in the back of his *Sunday Express* before he'd finished with it.

Although it could feel uncomfortably like homework, my instinctive, desperate need to keep a record of my club's doings meant that I soldiered on for several years. I've still got them now, six wildly up-and-down seasons' worth of lazy headlines and yellowing memories, each game so vital at the time, now meaningless footnotes lost in the enormity of an endlessly repeating fixture list.

Some things never change.

But kids these days, eh? Given a straight choice between:

1 – picking up a Wii zapper and heeding the *Call of Duty* to engage in battle with frighteningly realistic German soldiers on the outskirts of Berlin; or,

2 – a scrapper session, the little blighters rarely seem to opt for the pleasures of ephemera, despite the Pritt in their genes.

I know. I'll get out some examples of my early handiwork and that will inspire them.

THE SECRET ADVANTAGE

Look at the secret advantages these boots have to offer.

And this time you can't just put it down to an obsessive interest in gimmicks and gadgets. It isn't just me saying it, but respected grown-ups from the English Schools FA.

I won't change a word: I'll just type out the information so you can make your own mind up. Let's keep it objective.

"Power-Points are the boots that give you a secret advantage! They're light, flexible, hard-wearing. The only boots recommended by the English Schools Football Association."

See? I told you so.

"Best of all, each pair has REMOVABLE NUMBERED TARGET AREAS – each one specially designed to teach you the professional skills of ball control! And to show you how to take advantage of these unique target areas, Power-Points come with an instructional FREE COLOUR BOOKLET. It's written by a senior FA Staff Coach and cram-full of tips that'll do wonders for your game.

"Hurry and get a pair of Power-Points."

Yes sir, I will.

"You'll find they make winning easy!"

Power-Points don't just come in boys and youth sizes, but in senior sizes 6-12 as well. And how about the prospect of a pair of Power-Points football socks, so from the knees down you can be decked out completely as recommended by your teachers and a senior coach on the FA staff?

Sensational

POWER-POINTS

These fantastic new boots make winning football easy!

Regd. Design

Regd. Trade Mark

Doesn't it make you wonder how you ever managed to backheel a ball without a large '3' sticker stuck on the back of your boot?

And whether the socks had numbers, too?

"Hurry and get yourself a pair of Power-Points!"

"Yes Sir, I will."

Neat neat neat: beware the child with the manically tidy scrapper...

WOLVERHAMPTON WANDERERS 0:3 LEICESTER CITY
Att 15,782
WILSON LINEKER ENGLISH

IAN WILSON

SEVEN-UP . . . City striker Gary Lineker John Burridge as defender John Pender

That'

IT'S A TONIC! CITY BLE LEADERS

OFF THE MARK . . .
mers home his first go
ing at Molineux as W
are

MEL EVES

SEC

Leicester City knocked Wolves off the top of the Second Division, inflicting their first defeat of the season by three goals at Molineux this afternoon.

WOLVES 0, CITY 3

F-A GOALSCORERS

1 2	B Smith	
3 1	Melrose, A Smith, Lineker	
	Lineker	
1 1	Lineker	
0 1	Lynex 3 (2 pens), Lineker 3 (1 pen.)	
0 1	A Smith	
2 0	MacDonald, O'Neill	
0 2		
2 0	Lynex, Lineker	
3 0	Wilson, Lineker, English	

Two first-half goals in a five-minute spell put City in the driving seat. The first came from Ian Wilson, City's best player, and the victory was sealed with Tom English's first goal since joining City from Coventry.

City, unchanged for the third time in a row, should have taken a fourth-minute lead when Wilson sent Friar down the left and his cross fell to English.

by Bill Anderson

minutes later when Eves left the field, having collapsed off the ball.

Eves soon returned and sparked off an attack which nearly brought the opener.

Clarke headed the ball down and Hibbitt's volley was scrambled away by Wallington.

Wolves kept up the pressure. Palmer driving in a 35 yard shot which was deflected wide. Then Livingstone teased his way ... until Mac-

City were in command but had scares when Wallington parried a Hibbitt shot forward — and was lucky that no-one was following up. Then a drive by Palmer was fumbled round for a corner.

When City broke out from a period of pressure, Wilson earned a corner which led to Eves screwing his clearance towards the top corner of his own goal and Humphrey was forced to make a brilliant headed clearance off the line.

City were reduced to breaking out from long periods of pressure and, in one surge for ... Pender obstructed Line... through.

169

SHAME

The ball bobbled slowly to my feet, right in front of goal.

I don't know whether the pain in my chest was my heart leaping or sinking, or maybe momentarily stopping. My mouth was dry and sticky, my throat rasping. I held my breath.

And so, it was going to be me.

I remember the slightly awkward platform-sole feeling of wearing long studs on the baked-hard pitch, bald and uneven in the goalmouth. There were two skinny, scared-looking kids standing on the line three yards in front of me, neither with the presence of mind to rush out and close down my shot. The sun was glaring down on my back and neck and sweat-drenched hair. It was real Cup Final weather. All this time, the goalie was sitting spectating from a nice grassy spot, some twenty yards away towards the wing. The penalty box was full of bodies, but I was all on my own. In the background, the sound coming from the spectators strung down the touchline went up steadily in volume and pitch – a squeal rather a roar of expectation. For this special occasion, an ancient double-decker bus had been hired to carry not only the team but some fans to Belvoir Drive, the Leicester City training ground. As well as the expected complement of dossing, larking, noisy schoolmates, there were girls.

So what do you do when quite literally everything is at stake? Pan it or place it?

When you're Under-15, full-size goals are big, and two scared kids with their shin pads Sellotaped up over their socks are small. But they looked big. There were yards to the right of them, yards to the left of them, a couple of yards between them. But the goal looked small.

And so I half panned it and half placed it – the most important thing was not to miss the target – and I hit the kid on the right.

The shame carried an instant and awful weight, roughly equivalent to getting caught with my mate Claz trying to shoplift a copy of *Knave* inside a copy of *The Topper*, after standing at the magazine shelves for maybe twenty minutes plucking up courage, while all this time the newsagent was watching through his stripy security mirror. Then he made us go and fetch our mums. Except this time there must have been a hundred people watching.

The biggest crowd I'd ever glanced nervously at from the business side of a white line.

I'm not saying missing an open goal in the Leicestershire Schools Under-15 Schools Challenge Cup Final ruined my life, but I can't help thinking things would have been different if I'd scored.

Realistically, I know there isn't another person in the world who remembers that moment, or thinks of me as the kid who missed the open goal. We won the match comfortably enough, after all. We were heroes. But I always felt a bit of a fraud. Jealous, because I wasn't the kid who scored the first goal. Someone else was. I don't remember who.

From the split second I'd known the ball was going to hit the kid on the line, I'd felt physically crushed by the realisation that I'd missed my one golden chance.

Once the ball had bobbled back out to the edge of the penalty box, I did what I always do when I know I've screwed up – I went into a desperate, superhuman rage, charging around after the ball to try and make up. I know there must have been jeers and hoots and moans, but I never heard them. I was in a blur of pulsing shame.

I raced out to the edge of the box, pushed a kid out of the way, dived in, came out with the ball, took one pace towards the goal, shot without looking up, knowing where the goal was, held my breath again. And hit the sodding bar.

Hit the sodding bar.

If only I'd been a pro, I could have ignored the cold eye of the TV camera and told the interviewer that it's all part of the game, that missing a chance can happen to anyone. The important thing as a striker is to be in the right place, making chances happen. That's how a pro earns his thousands of pounds per day, not running around in a desperate rage, trying to make up. No apology required, no passing self-doubt, barely a flicker of concern.

If I'd been a pro, I could probably have got talking to a couple of the girls on the double-decker's return journey; could have convinced the lucky ladies to help celebrate my big win by squirting them with my Cup Final-size bottle of Cristal Champagne. Then it would have been on to a swanky private nitespot where the media turn a blind eye, and so to a courtesy hotel suite with a couple of predatory team-mates and the would-be WAGs in tow – having first watched Mr. Miles (our coach and history teacher) smash the camera lenses on their mobiles.

If only I'd been a pro, I could have been shameless. The missed chance that ruined my life could have made a terrifically funny pizza advert.

A big goal: impossible to miss from three yards out.

171

Lane

recent publicity, ...hoosing, has give... ...ome of the plar... ...ane. After Mr. ...

Sheffield United

PLAYING FOOTBALL ON A CRICKET PITCH

When cricket was first played on Bramall Lane in the middle of the nineteenth century, it was a down a dusty, pastoral lane with a single gateway entrance; but as the steel industry began to sprawl across the city, that rural aspect was swiftly lost. When the Lane hosted its first and last Test Match against Australia in 1902, "murky industrial haze cost hours of play," according to *The Cricketer*.

Sheffield United was a cricket club long before a football offshoot was formed, but cricket and football in the same arena can only ever be an uncomfortable marriage. Football had to suffer with essentially a three-sided ground, while cricket fans had to sit on concrete terraces clearly not designed for a day's play.

In the early Seventies, football announced the divorce. The cricket club were given notice to quit and plans were made to build a whopping football stand, slap-bang on the square.

To even contemplate such a move in the cradle of Yorkshire County Cricket was sacrilege in the eyes of many Yorkshiremen, but it still went ahead and a stark, concrete stand went up in time for the start of the 1975-76 season. The sacred turf was flogged at 20p a square yard.

By 1981 the Blades, crippled by the new stand's costs, had plummeted down to the Fourth Division. Those Yorkshire cricket fans given to a touch of *schadenfreude* will have enjoyed the demise of the stripy heathens... at least those who weren't United fans, too.

Sheffield Wednesday

ERIC THE WED

ERIC LE BRAT! WEDNESDAY TAKE BIG GAMBLE. TREV SWOOP FOR MAD ERIC.

Given the amount of water that's passed under the bridge since 1992 – Eric Cantona's influential genius at Leeds and Man U, the kung-fu kick, the acting career – it now has the feel of a mangled internet fairy tale. But the tall tale of Eric the Blue is, of course, all true.

Having chucked a ball at a ref, called each member of the disciplinary panel an 'idiot', received an extended two-month ban and promptly retired, the 25-year-old French international was personally persuaded by Michel Platini to go on trial –

quite literally – with the Owls, in an attempt to salvage his football career.

The notorious Cantona was a very special talent – "We've never seen so many people at a training session," marvelled Trevor Francis – but a six-a-side turnout against Baltimore Blast wasn't quite enough to convince the level-headed Wednesday boss of the Frenchman's ability and temperament, and he asked to extend the trial by another week.

Meanwhile, table-topping Leeds, in the form of Wednesday old boy and ex-boss Howard Wilkinson, proved less picky, and didn't need to run the rule over King Eric, the decade's greatest player in world football.

Wednesday's Division One push ended in a very respectable third-place finish, while neighbours Leeds lifted the Championship trophy.

If only Eric and the lads had pulled out more stops in that 'indoor soccer' showcase against the wide-eyed American tourists, which they somehow contrived to lose 8-3.

Have a Great Birthday Now You Are 10

2 SHEFFIELD UNITED AWAY
L SIZES

415 LUTON HOME
ALL SIZES

416 LUTON AWAY
ALL SIZES

452 NORWICH HOME
ALL SIZES

454 ABERDEEN HOME
ALL SIZES

457 ABERDEEN AWAY
ALL SIZES

SHORT SHORTS

No matter whether you were playing in the First Division or in a Sunday-morning pub league on a pitch wedged between the elevated M6 and a back line of five dirty skyscrapers, the words every footballer feared most from jocular team-mate, pugnacious high-rise oppo or terrace wit were: "Look! It's Stanley Matthews."

This below-the-belt sleight would result in widespread hilarity among your hobbling, vice-shorted playmates – or, worse still, I suppose, among 15,000 Scousers pointing down from the Kop end.

The source of their amusement? A pair of shorts that clung to your bloodless thighs more than two inches beneath your perineum.

Oh, they were side-splitting, all right.

It was the pros, of course, who can be blamed for starting the Seventies trend for figure-hugging hot-pant micro-shorts. And so, for the next fifteen years, we were all at it, first scrunching our bits into four-inch-square scraps of stretch-nylon – considered sexy at the time for their eye-boggling patterns or an amusing illustration of 'A Nice Pear' – and then rolling up our thighs a further sheath of bone-tight football shorts.

Feeling light-headed due to his crippling XXXS shorts, Wendy grabs a well-earned breather.

The entire Liverpool squad of the Eighties suffered painfully swollen feet as a result of their Speedo-style shorts. The very sight of Gary Lineker at Italia 90 is enough to bring tears to your eyes, never mind Gazza's. But the undisputed king was Spurs' Glenn Hoddle, whose frankly alarming shortness of short was coupled with an unusual length of limb.

Decency campaigner Mary Whitehouse threatened to intervene with a suggested decorous ratio of naked thigh flesh to length of side seam; but Hoddle laughed full in the face of so-called 'decency'.

When Hod went untucked, it was as if he were wearing a baby-doll nightie with nothing underneath. It was excruciating – embarrassing or faintly obscene or eye-wateringly painful, dependent on your perspective.

But, hey. No one ever flicked Glenn Hoddle's arse with a wet towel or shouted over the hoardings from the Pop Side Block 1 Row A: "Ha! It's Stanley Matthews."

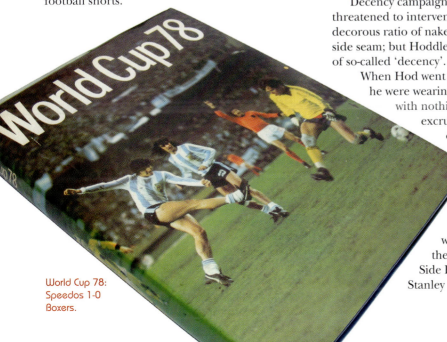

*World Cup 78:
Speedos 1-0
Boxers.*

173

THE SHOULDER CHARGE

"Course, in those days it was legal to shoulder charge the goalie, provided he had both his feet on the ground," Uncle Ken recalls. "Now, Arthur wasn't a dirty player; but he would give a goalie a fair bump."

Arthur Rowley, that is: the Football League's all-time record goalscorer, with 434 from 619 games, stretching from the end of the war right up to 1965.

"It was away at Derby, and I remember the goalie's name was Middleton. He caught the ball up above his head, and Arthur waited patiently for him to land. Then he charged him so hard, the goalie flew into the back of the net, still holding the ball. Arthur was already shaking hands, but the referee disallowed the goal. Arthur tells the ref he was wrong by tapping himself on the arm: 'It was the shoulder'..."

"And then there was a game against Preston at Filbert Street," my dad takes over. "Arthur gave their goalie a nudge, and he was wandering around his six-yard box with a touch of concussion. Else, his name was. But he was fair game, so Arthur gave him one hell of a bump. He ended up tottering round the back of his net, not knowing where he was, but still clutching the ball to his chest..."

SMOKE

Smell: it's the rogue sense, running out of control. At times, your nose can seem almost randomly wired up to your memory. Smells can just creep up on you.

It doesn't matter where I am when I catch a whiff of pipe smoke – I might be on a train or in the street, walking behind a devil-may-care pensioner – and instantly I'm ten again. I'm sitting wrapped

Ogden's Nut-brown Flake? Savory's Baby's Bottom? Stick that in your pipe and smoke it at half-time.

up in the Double Decker at Filbert Street with my dad and Uncle Ken and someone we only ever knew as The Shiverer, and there's an old boy a couple of rows in front of us, struggling to spark up his half-time shag.

It's as if I'm actually there, transported in time by this magic smoky smell. I can actually see and feel and hear, although the Tannoy system is still largely incomprehensible. I can see the muddy pitch, the terrace roofs leading away toward the city centre. Leicester City are 2-0 down. Probably.

"Come on Lenny," shouts an old woman we only ever knew as The Shouter. "I've got five bob on you..."

It takes a million-to-one chemical combination to unlock a memory. You can't just expect to march in and press the right buttons with Chanel No. 5; Brut 33; a dozen red roses. The smells that really do the trick are a less predictable than that. Like Playdoh – that sweet strawberry plastic smell, quite distinct from ordinary plasticine warming up on the radiator.

It can't be long before someone starts marketing the bottled essence of what it smells like to be seven. The smell of weak shandy, drunk outdoors in the sun – like when Dad used to splash a drop of beer into my lemonade in the country pub garden where my big sister wandered off and was chased by a cow.

'Aromatherapy', they could call it... little pots of damp school corridor varnish; the sparking static smell of a nylon jumper being pulled over your head.

No matter where I am when I catch a whiff of pipe smoke, instantly, I'm ten again...

I've found it's possible to use certain smells to take a sniff back in time. Get down on your knees and smell the carpet, close up. It smells exactly like it did when you used to spend half your life playing at ground level. Open a new box of chocolates and take time to smell that corrugated paper sitting on top: that's the smell of Christmas, 1974.

I asked my mum about her great lost smells. She said Yorkshire pudding and beer and clinging smoke – Granddad Green coming home from the pub for Sunday dinner. She could have been describing my dad this Sunday.

Then Dad started to explain how you can fake the long-lost smoky smell of a steam train by snuffing out a candle. But I wanted to remind Mum about my not-so-great lost smell – of lipstick and cigarettes and spit on a damp cotton hanky as she rubbed too hard all around my face. The smell of infant outrage, cut through with a tang of love and safety. And almost incredibly, she denied the practice.

As if anyone would ever make up stories about smoke, beer and spit.

'SOCCER'

People who call it 'soccer' don't know what they're talking about.

Like Bobby Charlton, for example (as in his Casdon Soccer game), Bobby Moore (author of *Soccer the Modern Way*) and Jimmy Greaves (*Soccer Techniques & Tactics*). Then there's the combined legacy of Football on ITV (*Star Soccer*) and the greatest sticker collections of all time (FKS's *Wonderful World of Soccer*). All now discredited in the popular view due to their use of the supposedly 'American' s-word.

Tournament organisers know nothing (Soccer Sixes), neither do respected historians (Jack Rollin: *Soccer at War*), computer gamers (Sensible Soccer), statisticians (www.soccerbase.com) nor managers (Alex Ferguson: *Soccer Training: Games, Drills and Fitness Practices*)...

No, hold on. It's people who call it 'footy' who know nothing, right?

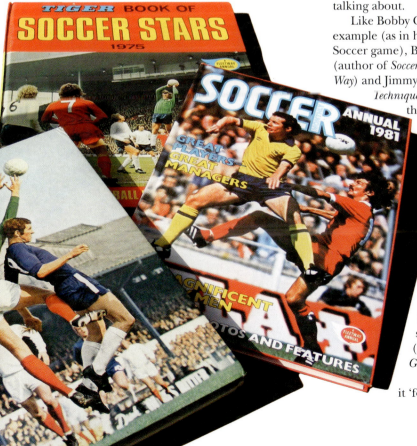

THE SOCCER TRIBE

Now this is a weird one: a footy book by a leather-haired anthropologist best known for the Seventies pseudo-science of 'Manwatching', and for being married to Esther Rantzen.

Just as Desmond Morris's previous bestseller had essentially been about our endless clamouring for sex – how to tell whether the attractive young lady/gent subconsciously fiddling with their bubble perm at the disco bar secretly fancied a snog – so he waded headlong into 1981's second most emotive subject: yobboes at the football.

Managers were witch doctors, refs tribal elders...

There was far more to *The Soccer Tribe* than the standard psychobabble about 'scoring', 'playing away from home', 'banging it in' and 'diving in the box'. To Des, the game wasn't fundamentally about balls and openings framed so invitingly with swathes of fishnet. Football was a tribal mating ritual – and, to prove his point, he drew the whole surrounding culture into an elaborate theoretical model. Managers became witch doctors, players played the part of heroic hunters, and referees were tribal elders. Meanwhile, the adornment, displays and chants of the war-dancing fans were crucial to maintaining high levels of inter-tribal aggro.

In parts, the football jungle theory had to stretch to fit the facts. But mostly it just stretched the reader's imagination.

For example, we'd all probably agree with John Devlin, author of the footy kit bible *True Colours*, that a team's colours "create a unique visual identity for each club and a strong sense of allegiance for its fans."

But Des went further, suggesting that team colours could lend a psychological advantage. Highly conspicuous colours send out the unconscious message: 'I am fearless', he argued. And "'venomous' colour patterns give the wearers' enemies an unconscious sensation that they may be 'stung' or 'poisoned' by too-close contact."

To illustrate the point, Cyrille Regis was pictured in West Brom's yellow-and-green away kit alongside a small but murderous Amazonian frog. And Tony Brown, in the Baggies' home garb, was equated with a 'sickening smelling' skunk.

Southampton

PLAYING IN A DELL

The last time we played Southampton, we travelled for three hours to the St. Mary's Stadium to sit in a ground that was an exact replica of our Walkers Stadium – quite literally from the same page in the architects' catalogue, only in red instead of blue. And we'd thought that naming a ground after a bag of crisps had cheapened our 'matchday experience'...

I couldn't help remembering the first time we'd visited Southampton in the early Eighties, and what a curious, interesting ground The Dell had been. We'd wandered around the away section into what appeared to be a whitewashed cave with a fence at the front. At the other end there were little terrace boxes on stilts above the standing area, and awkward slopes and angles carved into stands wherever you looked.

The Dell had always battled with the problem of being a football ground not only centred around a large hollow but also squeezed into a tight parallelogram of land, hemmed in by Archers Road and Milton Road. Some ingenious designs were employed to accommodate spectators, but the Taylor Report of 1992 spelled the beginning of the end for this sort of quirky, eccentric quality. After making the

place 'safe' enough to satisfy the stringent new standards, the Saints could only fit in 15,000 spectators – not enough for a club who were enjoying a good spell in the new Premier League, with Matt Le Tissier in his prime.

After over a hundred years at The Dell, the Saints moved to St. Mary's in 2001, but it proved to be the beginning of their problems rather than the end. By 2009, they were cast into the twin hells of the Third Division and administration. Many a Saint must have longed for the days when they were crammed into a favourite, oblique triangular corner of their distinctive old home.

SPONSORED MOTORS

In the olden days, the labels on football kit used to be on the inside, out of sight, while now the washing instructions, the manufacturer's and sponsor's logos seem to take pride of place on the front, the back, the hem and both arms.

The inside, tucked-away label had another handy use – kids' mums and footballers' wives could write their charge's name on the tag, so they didn't lose it. This before the watershed when players' names began to appear in big letters on the back of their shirts, for just the same reason.

In a football world turned upside-down and inside-out, sponsorship has now gone haywire, leading to multinational corporations' names appearing on a whole side's shirts – and potential player confusion. Meanwhile, small businesses tussle to place their name next to the goalie's left sock in a largely empty grid in the programme. Everybody's at it.

So isn't it curious that the sole original example of player sponsorship, a sure sign of star status and local community approval, has modestly gone missing from the footballer's driver door?

Stars used to drive proudly to the match in their signwritten metallic-green Ford Escorts. You wouldn't catch old 'Knocker' Powell hiding away behind tinted windows...

SQUASH

Squash was a simple game with simple rules and simple equipment. All you needed was a football and a wall, although a friend could also come in handy to ramp up the excitement. You kicked the ball against the wall in turns, until someone missed. One-nil.

Squash was named after another, similar game played with racquets and a not-very-bouncy rubber ball by angry 1970s sales executives in a large, airtight, transparent plastic box which quickly heated up to thirty degrees and began to take on the sickening smell of skunk. Desmond Morris didn't need to write a book called *The Squash Tribe* to explain why it died out.

Anthropologists tell us the demise of 'football' squash was brought about by the increased popularity of television and indoor games (see 'Kick-the-Goal Soccer', 'Waddingtons Table Football', etc.) although we've just thought of an alternative theory that would have made Des proud.

The next player could then get a fantastic angle and pan the ball forty yards,

deep into skipping-rope country

When you were playing multi-player squash, it was always, like, really bad, when someone deliberately just laid their go up to the bottom of the wall. Then the next player could get a fantastic angle and pan the

ball forty yards away across the playground, deep into skipping-rope country – sometimes even getting evil spin that carried the ball beyond the wall line, calling for an almost impossible bender. The bastards.

STAND-IN GOALIES

In a regularly recurring ratio of one in a thousand matches, a single incident used to signal the end of the ordinary game of football. From that unplanned, unexpected moment, the spectacle at hand took on the atmosphere of a carnival freak show crossed with an old-time, live-ammo duel.

The second it happened – the goalie sent off for rugby tackling the forward strolling past him, one on one; or the goalie on a stretcher, stripping off his green shirt and throwing it disgustedly into his muddy area – all the normal rules ceased to apply. One set of fans held their heads in horror while the oppo rubbed their hands together in glee.

Invariably, it wasn't the 6'4" centre-half, the apparent obvious choice, who took the place of the shamed/crocked shotstopper, but the tricky little flair player who had looked the best hope of salvaging a point. His first, melodramatic,

A rare view of Peter Beardsley: for starters, he's in goals...

defence – a bit like every Premier League match this century. Battling for possession to prevent a single attempt on goal.

As for the attacking side, the rule was to shoot on sight, even from seventy yards. Rough up the stand-in – who often had the temerity to play a blinder.

Out of the thousands of pointless and unpopular changes made to our game over the past twenty years, the introduction of the substitute specialist goalie is the biggest spoilsport.

And all to prevent us ever again seeing what Peter Beardsley looks like in a muddy green shirt pulled over his Newcastle stripes. With his goalie shorts pushed down over his arse, to cleverly distract the oppo attack.

duty was often to face a penalty kick, standing there looking all stiff and funny in his too-big jersey and gloves, swan-diving the wrong way like a dad up the park.

Now it was backs to the wall for the team effectively playing without a goalie. Playing for a point, watching the clock. All ten men in

WHAT WAS LOST IN THE GREAT ROOF BLOW-OFF OF '76

In January 1976 it seemed that Stoke City had somehow angered the football gods. Perhaps it was the fact that they were living beyond their means – racking up debts wasn't quite so fashionable then as it is now – or that they'd lavished a world-record £325,000 on goalkeeper Peter Shilton when the fans knew that what they really needed was a striker to replace big John Ritchie.

Boss Tony Waddington had been certain that success was tantalisingly just around the corner. Stoke had reached the FA Cup semis in 1971 and '72, only to lose out to Arsenal on both

occasions, but had then landed the first trophy in the club's history, beating Chelsea in the 1972 League Cup Final. And then in 1974-75 the Potters had finished just four points behind champions Derby... one more push and surely they could make the big time and recoup their spending?

Then came that January night when a huge gale hit the Potteries, and a large section of the Butler Stand roof was ripped off. An inadequate insurance policy only covered a fraction of a huge repair bill and the club had no choice but to sell some of their prize players.

Every Stokie's favourite player, Jimmy Greenhoff, went reluctantly to Old Trafford; Alan Hudson moved to Arsenal, and Mike Pejic was bought by Everton. Stripped of their best players, Stoke were relegated in 1977 and the club took many years to truly recover their status.

Still, it's an ill wind that blows no good. Mike Pejic sorted through the Victoria Ground rubble and hauled all the useful bits of timber and cladding back to his moorland farm near Buxton.

Stoke City

THE POTTERS
STOKE CITY F.C.
Founded as Stoke on Trent 1863
Champions Div.II
1932 – 33
1962 – 63
Champions Div.III
North Section
1926 – 27

"I didn't care if it was Manchester United, I didn't want to go. I had a marvellous rapport with the crowd at Stoke. They made me the player I was and I owed them so much."

– Jimmy Greenhoff

MAKE THE BALL DO WHAT **YOU** WANT WITH

STRIKER

THE FAST ACTION FOOTBALL GAME WITH A KICK!

FAST SINGLE-HANDED ACTION! PRESS HIS HEAD AND HE REALLY KICKS THE BALL!

STRIKER IS THE FAST NEW ALL ACTION FOOTBALL GAME THAT'S AS REAL AS THE REAL THING, BECAUSE THE PLAYERS REALLY KICK THE BALL AND CONTROL IT. IT'S FAST, BECAUSE THE SINGLE-HANDED ACTION MEANS YOU CAN HAVE A PLAYER IN EACH HAND. STROKE THE BALL FROM A PLAYER IN ONE HAND TO A TEAM MATE IN THE OTHER — HE SHOOTS! AND IT'S FAST BECAUSE THE BARRIER ROUND THE BIG, VELVET-SMOOTH STRIKER BOARD PITCH KEEPS THE BALL IN PLAY.

TRY AND CHIP THE BALL OVER MY DEFENCE!

YOU CAN MAKE THE STRIKER PLAYER KICK THE BALL ALMOST LIKE YOU CAN YOURSELF... CHIP IT, STROKE IT — EVEN PUT A SPIN ON IT...

THE GOALKEEPER HOLDS THE BALL. FLICK HIS ARM AND HE ACTUALLY THROWS THE BALL INTO PLAY....

GO AND SEE STRIKER FOR YOURSELF AT YOUR NEAREST SPORTS, GAMES OR TOY STORE.

PARKER

Reality check: Press footballer's head with fast single-handed action...

STRIKER

My mate Steve and I would have the same heated debate over and over about the various merits of Subbuteo versus those of Palitoy's Striker. There were no more salient points to be made, no new evidence, we just argued out of habit.

Steve maintained that Striker was a far superior game, "because the players actually kicked the ball." And Subbuteo was "too fussy."

I would counter that Subbuteo didn't need a gimmick because it was virtually a sport in its own right. Striker was "only five-a-side" and its players' zones robbed you of the opportunity for a full-blooded clogger's tackle.

That's not to say there weren't Striker

injuries. In fact there were two: the broken ankle or the broken neck, both incurred when you pressed a player's head down too hard.

One of my strongest arguments was floored when they brought out the new Striker goalkeeper. The older version stood cradling the ball in his arms and was supposed to distribute the ball to his team-mates with a swivel from the waist. However, he was just as likely to twist too far and throw the ball into his own net, just like Leeds keeper Gary Sprake had once managed at Anfield. But the new keeper was magnificent, cleverly geared to fling out his arms in a full-length dive when moved to the side.

Time to move on to a new debate: who's better, Steve, the Jam or the Clash?

SUBBUTEO 24-SEGMENT CROWD BARRIER C170

Subbuteo was by far the most popular table-top representation of football, and its '00'-scale figures still hold a special place in the hearts of blokes across the globe. Part of the game's appeal was due to the huge range of accessories which, while unnecessary for the actual playing of the game, did prop up an illusion of realism and 'add to the big-match atmosphere'.

Plastic pitches were one of the ugliest developments in Eighties football. QPR, Luton and Oldham became unbeatable at home because they mastered the art of playing on a surface that had all the properties of lino – sliding tackles were out, except for players wearing motorcycle leathers under their shorts.

Meanwhile, good old Subbuteo exhibited their usual dogged

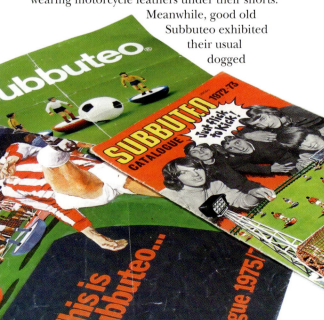

C170

114
121
129
136
144
151
159
166
174
181

determination to keep up with the times, producing their own 'Astroturf' pitch – although, if their 'grass' pitch was made of green baize cloth, and the 'Astroturf' surface from slightly different baize cloth, it's unclear in what sense it was any more 'artificial'.

The rampant hooliganism of the time puts into stark perspective any complaints about plastic pitches, leading as it did to football attendances going down and spike-topped fences going up. Subbuteo didn't shirk its remit to mirroring the game and replaced its friendly green picket fences with prison railings and mounted police to keep any potential plastic yobboes off the pitch.

Although accessories such as the dugouts and the ambulance men, the TV tower with mini-Motty, the floodlights and VIP figures (including Queenie handing over a tiny FA Cup) were affordable and always welcome on a Christmas morning, the ultimate prize had to be the Subbuteo stadium, complete with a decent crowd of ready-painted spectators. Unfortunately, they were beyond the pocket of most kids' parents and you'd count yourself lucky to have a single, foot-long stand with a couple of dozen spectators dotted around it.

While you could buy Leeds, Liverpool and Manchester United teams, your ground was no better than that of the local non-League side. How to construct your own Highbury

or Villa Park on a strict budget? Rather than waiting for our parents to win the pools and buy the sixteen stands required to build a complete ground, some of us took matters into our own hands and constructed cardboard stands using large amounts of glue, paint and perspiration.

Then we bought the much cheaper packs of unpainted spectators – fifty per box, all as naked as the day they were moulded – and painstakingly applied Humbrol paint. There were only five different spectator figures and we got to know them intimately as we toiled with the paintbrush. There was dependable old Fatty in his trilby, a foursquare figure guaranteed not to fall over; Polo-Neck Man, with his arms folded, slim enough to fit in those awkward gaps under the stand roof; Celebrating Man and his equally Celebrating Girlfriend, who added to the atmosphere; while Legs-Crossed Man was always a liability, falling over sideways under the slightest bump or breeze, and taking half a block of his fellow fans with him.

Legs-Crossed Man was always a liability, falling over sideways at the slightest bump or breeze, and taking half a block of fans with him.

Only after weeks of this eye-damaging work did we discover the ultimate irony: with stands on all four sides it was virtually impossible to play the game. Leaning over the terraces didn't help your flick-to-kick technique, and you only had to nudge a stand with a stray elbow and 250 mini-people would be sprawled all over their seats, spilling into gangways and exits.

Oh, come on, let's go up the park and play football.

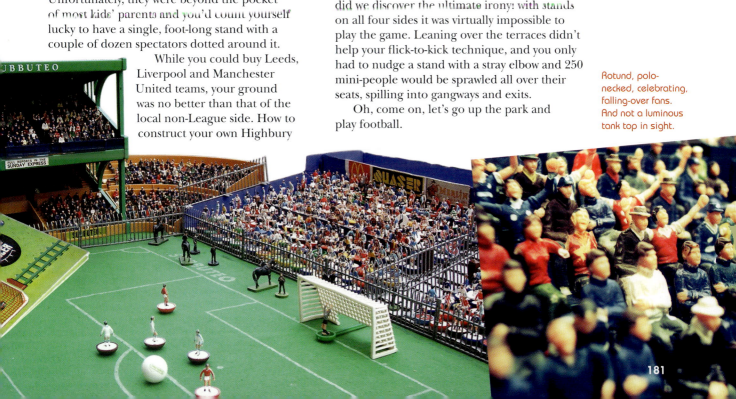

Cult followers: Forest herberts with a deep, dark nature invade the Filbert Street end.

SUEDEHEAD

Through the Sixties, Seventies and Eighties, British youth culture evolved fast, reinventing itself every couple of years. Italian suit- and parka-clad mods begat braced-and-booted skinheads, who became Crombie-wearing suedeheads, who turned into round-collared smoothies who transformed into denim- and scarf-adorned bootboys. Then mods returned, followed by skinheads again, and finally casuals, who brought the whole system crashing down by plundering the dressing-table drawers of middle-aged golfers for their lemon and mauve knitwear.

the Vs up at the stands, blue-and-white scarves tied round their wrists. The old blokes around me all agreed they were a disgrace. Disrespectful silly-buggers.

I recognised the uniforms from school – the Prince of Wales Harringtons and Abercrombie jackets, the Fred Perry shirts, the raised-seam

"Regardless of the do-gooders' claims, some people had an instinct for creating havoc and resorting to jungle savagery..."

These rapidly changing fashion codes were recorded for posterity by Richard Allen, whose *Skinhead* series was published by the New English Library. His tales of terrace bovver and smutty sexual encounters – *Suedehead, Skinhead Girls, Terrace Terrors* – were lapped up by teenage Britain, albeit chiefly by under-age dreamers with as much actual experience of 'knuckle girls' as Richard Allen himself.

I remember looking down in disbelief as a throng of chanting teenagers spilled into the sunny goalmouth below the Double Decker. They were goading the five policemen congregating near the centre line, and flicking

trousers and 'Blakeyed-up' brogues – but had never seen so many people wearing them all together. Now it began to make sense, the older boys lurking in the far corners of the playground, to whom clothes were a new kind of checklist.

Up until that point, the Anglo-Italian Cup friendly against Cagliari had been utterly unmemorable. Now, at half-time, every suedehead in the Kop was legging it over the wall and gathering on the pitch. Slowly they swaggered, chanting, past the helpless cops and the contemptuous Main Stand to take up residence in a cowering Filbert Street End for the second half. They were ace.

At school, I scanned the older kids' *Skinhead* books in a sniggering gaggle. As an adolescent, even my vicarious thrills were vicarious. Likewise Richard Allen, who in reality was a chain-smoking, fifty-year-old journalist called James Moffat. A real pro, Moffat could quickly bang out a book on any anti-social subject, given a suitable supply of fags and booze. He didn't just scatter his titles with authentic accessories, but imbued his teenage alter-ego Joe Hawkins with a hard-drinking, right-wing outsider creed so weirdly individual you couldn't make it up. Unless, of course, you did.

Moffat was like a pulp Dr. Frankenstein, creating a string of frustrated, hard-drinking monsters, each animated by an electric surge of DIY psychology.

Moffat was like a pulp Dr. Frankenstein, creating a string of frustrated, hard-drinking monsters, each animated by an electric surge of DIY psychology.

"Basically, Joe Hawkins had a feeling for violence. Regardless of what the do-gooders and the sociologists and psychiatrists claimed some people had an instinctive bent for creating havoc and resorting to jungle savagery. The club was a front to cover his deep, dark nature. A requirement for his suedehead cultism…"

With his raging prose, Moffat was like a crazy kid trapped in the body of a middle-aged man. For some reason, I can't help but like him. Never could.

Two weeks later, I watched in horror as the disgraceful, disrespectful silly-buggers drawn by the promise of a local derby took to the pitch unopposed. These were red-scarved Forest fans in their late teens and twenties, and they looked threatening.

"Where's our lot from the Caggly-ar-ee match?" I asked my dad.

He explained that the difference this week was an away contingent of 4,000, compared to a travelling Sicilian support comprised entirely of members of the Brucciani family, from the frothy coffee and ice-cream float empire in the city centre.

Sunderland

THE ROKER ROAR

A *Kingdom by the Sea* is our kind of guidebook, a perfect companion to lead you all around the North-East coast with a flappy map, in a sunny historic daze. It's enthusiastic and knowledgeable, by the wonderful Betty James, who also wrote the inspirational *London on £1 a Day*. And, oh yes, it's a little matter of 44 years out of date.

Betty is tempted to Roker Park by the draw of Chelsea, her own 'home town' team, by the question of 'whether football is a game the little woman is ever likely to understand', and by the prospect of being knocked down or lynched (according to some men in a Newcastle pub).

Betty incredulously sucks a hot-dog as reinforced boots trample her frozen tootsies. But the excitement soon hots up.

"The music gets louder, vintage rattles and car hooters are produced. A lethal-looking banner is unfurled under my left ear. Four girls in red-striped boaters take up a stance in front of me and start to yell 'Glorry glorry hey-hey-ha-ha-oo-oo!', like lady cannibals emitting tribal calls at breakfast…

"Two fifty-seven p.m. and excitement has reached fever pitch. The music blares louder, people start pushing. There's a roar, an orgiastic swaying of bodies and they're off, losing a Pools fortune for millions of hopeful humans while I'm smothered in curly hair, old macs and nylon-fur linings…"

Betty is poked in the eye, her tonsure is ruffled and she drops her second hot-dog when her head is caught in a two-man pelvic grip.

"'Oooo stupid! Shocking. Ooooo!'…"

We leave Betty with her pancreas being driven forcefully against a crash bar, the Roker Roar ringing in her ears:

"'Dir-TEE Dir-TEE… Ooooo grotty. It's pa-THE-tic.'

"'Nice ball nice nice nice. OOOOO!'

"'What a bloody way to play!'"

Detective work: Our Betty was among the 32,880 at Sunderland 2-0 Chelsea, 16 April, 1966.

THE SUPERFAN LOUDHAILER

Go green with envy. Google without hope of retail success. Admire open-mouthed our combined electric siren and directional loudhailer – the single greatest invention of all-time (that no one has ever heard of).

Not to be confused with the *vuvuzela*, whose multi-directional din has more recently enabled fans to ruin football matches for everyone within 200 yards (live) or three continents (via satellite), the Superfan represents instead a precision tool for bespoke matchday encouragement

Used according to the manufacturer's guidelines, the ultimate vocal accessory could be aimed directly into the ear of an out-of-form centre-forward, either from the dugout or the pie stall at the back of the Pop Side terrace.

Overdue a comeback, the Superfan enables you to offer words of advice and inspiration – "YOU BIG USELESS CARTHORSE" – in perfect privacy, with no lateral bleed to offend stewards or fellow platinum customers.

The Superfan enables you to offer private words of advice and inspiration –
with no offensive lateral bleed...

SUPERSTARS
It Could Never Happen Now

The BBC's *Superstars* was essential viewing between 1973 and 1985, pitching athletes from various sports against each other in events such as the 100-metre sprint, cycling, weightlifting, canoeing, tennis and basketball, as well as more sadistic disciplines disguised behind the titles of 'gym' and 'obstacle course'. It was a programme made in the spirit of the eternal boy's question: "What would win a fight between a shark and a tiger?"

As things turned out, footballers weren't anywhere near the top of the pecking order, being consistently outshone by judoka Brian Jacks' astonishing performances in the gym; by Jody Scheckter's dubious sunflower oil-assisted squat thrusts, and by three-time champion David Hemery's splendid moustache.

Who would win a fight between a boxer and a footballer?

Football's champs were more often left looking like chumps. Stan Bowles almost maimed himself in the pistol shooting, while he and Malcolm Macdonald both managed to capsize their canoes in the rowing. And Kevin Keegan was involved in the programme's most fondly remembered incident when he wobbled as far as the first corner on the cycling track before falling off his bike and skidding several yards on his back. Keegan bravely shrugged off the mother of all grazes and got back on, eventually winning the heat. However, only once did a footballer manage to finish in the top three of the final: the super-fit Colin Bell in 1974. *Superstars* has been revived by both the BBC and Channel 5 in recent years, but football clubs were strangely reluctant to allow their prize assets to risk friction burns, drowning or a bullet through the foot.

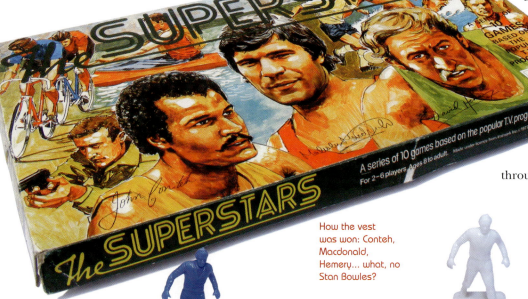

How the vest was won: Conteh, Macdonald, Hemery... what, no Stan Bowles?

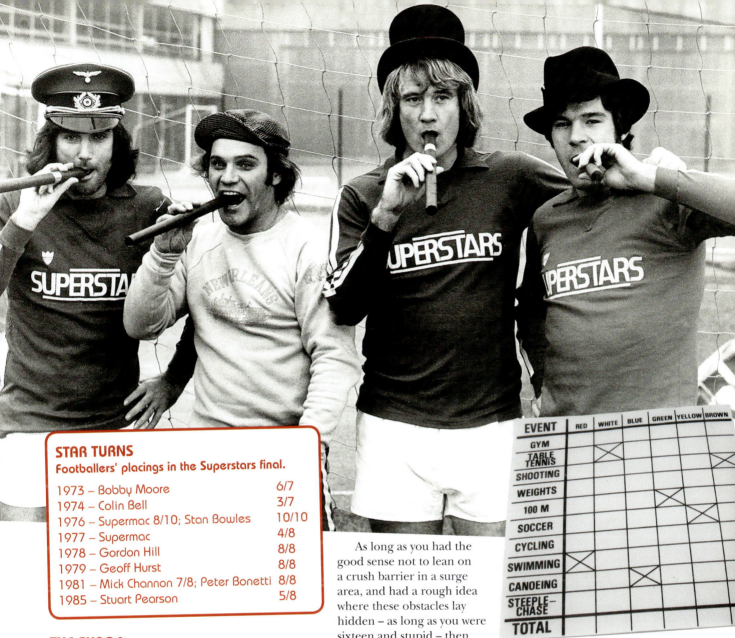

STAR TURNS
Footballers' placings in the Superstars final.

1973 – Bobby Moore	6/7
1974 – Colin Bell	3/7
1976 – Supermac 8/10; Stan Bowles	10/10
1977 – Supermac	4/8
1978 – Gordon Hill	8/8
1979 – Geoff Hurst	8/8
1981 – Mick Channon 7/8; Peter Bonetti	8/8
1985 – Stuart Pearson	5/8

EVENT	RED	WHITE	BLUE	GREEN	YELLOW	BROWN
GYM						
TABLE TENNIS		X				X
SHOOTING						
WEIGHTS						
100 M				X		
SOCCER						
CYCLING						
SWIMMING	X			X		
CANOEING						
STEEPLE-CHASE						
TOTAL						

THE SURGE

The top left-hand corner of Pen 2 of the Kop, tucked in next to the away fans, was the most boisterous part of the ground – where the songs of encouragement and abuse emanated from, along with crowd surges that would ripple down the terrace like a wheat field blown by the wind.

... like a wheat field blown by the wind.

From a distance, the movement of all those heads had a graceful quality, but to be caught up in a surge was a very different experience. First you would hear a low rumble and feel the earth move behind you, then you'd be moving down the terraces at an uncomfortably rapid rate, concentrating hard on staying on your feet. As soon as you'd arrived at a spot with a strikingly different view of the game – hmm, never noticed the self-stripe effect on Ray Clemence's shorts from back there – then an equal and opposite reverse wave would slowly catch you in its undertow, carrying you backwards and dropping you exactly where you'd started off.

As long as you had the good sense not to lean on a crush barrier in a surge area, and had a rough idea where these obstacles lay hidden – as long as you were sixteen and stupid – then you invariably emerged unscathed, having enjoyed the ride.

It was a time when you could go home from the game physically exhausted from surges and pogoing around after a goal, hoarse from shouting and singing.

You really had been the twelfth man.

UNFORGETTABLES

LEAGUE TROPHY

SURPRISE CHAMPIONS

Chelsea, Chelsea, Manchester United, Manchester United, Manchester United, Chelsea, Manchester United...

Okay, we all know Liverpool had a stranglehold on the League Championship in the Seventies and Eighties, but at least that was released now and again for the likes of Derby, Forest and Villa to have a go. The current duopoly is crushingly predictable.

Oh, for the days when an unfancied club needed only a canny manager, a good set of players and the wind blowing in the right direction to carry off the League Championship trophy... like Harry Potts's Burnley in 1960, kicking off a thirteen-year sequence in which ten different clubs won the League.

There was a time when even a newly promoted club could reach the apex of English football, instead of desperately trying to scrape together enough points to survive

– well, provided they had a genius at the helm. Alf Ramsey's Ipswich did it in 1962 and Brian Clough's Nottingham Forest repeated the feat in 1978.

Anyway, back to the future: Chelsea, Manchester United, Chelsea, Manchester United...

Magic Bus: Er, where are the Clarets champs standing?

Swansea City

PRISTINE

Spot the difference between these two Swansea City team groups.

First, we have a Mirrorcard from 1971-72. Underneath a big Sherlock Holmes-style magnifying glass, the Swans live right up to their nickname, gleaming with a pure white, almost heavenly brilliance that looks like something out of a Persil advert. The shirt is completely unadorned apart from the club badge. If you open the image in Adobe Photoshop and use the eyedropper tool it reads: 255, 255, 255 on the RGB colour model. It couldn't be any whiter.

The one design feature on this virginal classic is a double black stripe round the sock turnovers. And you might notice that Barrie Hole (front row, left) has refused even this adornment, choosing plain white socks and white footwear to boot. You'd never find him in a snowstorm.

The picture to the right shows the Swans' 1995-96 strip and, frankly, it's a bit of a dog's dinner. Double pin-stripes, manufacturer's logos, Gulf Oil ads plastered everywhere, horrible red-and-black stripes on the sleeves

– and this far from the worst offender in a time of kit-design excess.

But them hilarious old 1970s, eh? The subject of so many amusing 'Top 100' clip shows. Ridiculous, it was – 'The Decade that Taste Forgot'.

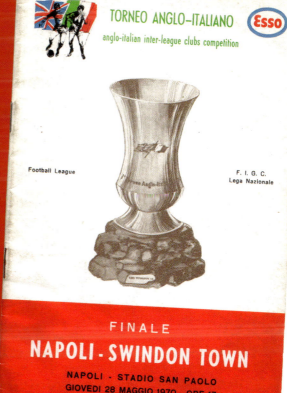

S.S.C. NAPOLI

In piedi da sinistra: **Altafini · Zurlini · Barison · Monticolo · Trevisan · Panzanato**
In basso da sinistra: **Florio · Bianchi · Improta · Montefusco · Hamrin**

THE ITALIAN JOB

Most fans probably think of Swindon Town's victory over Arsenal in the 1969 League Cup Final as the pinnacle of the club's achievements, as a Third Division outfit; but, in fact, they went on to claim a string of high-profile scalps in a European adventure that went largely unreported at the time, and which remains barely recognised today.

Sadly ineligible for the Fairs Cup, a consolation showcase was arranged against Italian Cup winners AS Roma. This was no friendly: the international-studded Italian side only won the away leg thanks to some shocking skulduggery, and then their fans attacked the Swindon team coach. Back at the County Ground, the 4-0 drubbing of the Italian giants seemed a just response.

"We played very much as a team," winger Don Rogers told us of the giant-killers' super-fit set-up masterminded by bosses Graham Williams and Fred Ford. "Everybody's all over the pitch, the front six all covering for each other, with one lone striker. I think we were probably a bit before our time."

That's right: Total Football was invented not in Holland but in Wiltshire.

Total Football
was invented in Wiltshire.

"John Smith dropped in deep to play between Joe Butler and Roger Smart," wing-half Frank Burrows further convinced us. "Roger scored a dozen goals from midfield before it was fashionable, going past John and arriving late in the box."

Next season the Italians wanted revenge, and organised the inaugural Anglo-Italian tournament. But sophisticated Swindon's 4-0 home demolition of Juventus, followed up by away wins at Juve and SS Napoli, only stirred them up even more. And so to the final at Napoli's Stadio del Alpi, in front of a capacity crowd of 55,000.

"With ten minutes to go we were 3-0 up, and it was a comfortable three," Don Rogers chuckles. "The game was all over — and that's what annoyed them, I think. Causing havoc, the crowd were. And all of a sudden, bits of concrete start raining down

on one side of the pitch. Now, I was playing down that left wing, but not for long! I was off, I was — inside one minute I played outside-left, inside-left, centre-forward, inside-right and outside-right!"

The game swiftly abandoned, Stan Harland lifted the Cup while concrete chunks of terrace thudded on to a pitch fogged with choking bonfire smoke and teargas. Once more the team coach was attacked by rioters with bottles and bricks and chased for miles out of Naples (quite possibly to the tune of Quincy Jones' 'Getta Bloomin' Move On', aka 'The Self-Preservation Society'). But, once again, there was no catching Don and Frank and Swindon's long-forgotten European champs...

TORNEO ANGLO–ITALIANO
Esso
anglo-italian inter-league clubs competition

Football League

F. I. G. C.
Lega Nazionale

FINALE
NAPOLI - SWINDON TOWN
NAPOLI - STADIO SAN PAOLO
GIOVEDI 28 MAGGIO 1970 - ORE 17
PROGRAMMA

Strange but true: the Napoli-Swindon final was the first game in Italy to have a programme printed for it.

SWIVEL BOOTS

The first time I ever met my important colleague, we both sported the remains of haircuts, and were young enough to preface our grumbling and reminiscing with a cautious discussion of the trials facing football in the 1990s. Apparently satisfied that we both stood on the same side of the spiky-topped fence, our attention soon turned to love and loss and *Hot Shot Hamish*. But, even so, it isn't easy to ask a new acquaintance if they have a swivel boot-shaped hole in their lives.

"I, er, don't suppose you remember those kids' football boots with the sort of swivelling studs, so you could pivot more easily when you're shooting? It's just that I saw an advert once…"

"Nah, never heard of them – sounds to me like you dreamed them. You're a couple of years older than me, y'see, and that's more like ten years at that age. Swivelling studs? What would've happened if you'd tried to do something other than swivel – like

quality – so even after a lifetime of keeping faith in the holy grail of mod football gimmickry, no evidence has resurfaced to even corroborate the existence of these mythological, mail-order marvels.

It must have been 1971 when the advert appeared in a football magazine – *Shoot!* or *Scorcher*, surely; although it could have been *Goal* or *Striker*. The earth-shattering announcement took the form of a small-ad, about three inches by two, positioned up towards the right-hand corner of the spread. The boots were white with black stripes; but it was the inset diagram of the moulded sole that caught the eye, offering hastily sketched evidence of the manufacturer's claims.

Here was a boot that would enable any boy to swivel quite literally on a sixpence, twisting to bang in perhaps millions of goals past unbelieving keepers just like the one in the ad – and all thanks to the specially patented front four

The comic with the swivel boot ad sank to the bottom of the pile.

run, or walk? You'd have snapped your ankle off. That's why you never saw your advert again – they were probably banned."

Words of wisdom which offered a fresh, grown-up perspective, but little solace. Maybe I'd misjudged the character of this lower-school lunk who had appeared to give a toss about football.

"But, er, while we're sort of on the subject, I don't suppose you know anyone who's got the 1974 World Cup wallchart from *The Wonderful World of Soccer Stars* sticker album? I'd sacrifice everything for that. I'll swap my car for it…"

They were the object of a stomach-churning greed so powerful it led to waking dreams and sleepless nights. A pair of football boots so futuristic, so desirable, they just had to be possessed. And yet, right from the start, they had a taunting, almost illusory

studs under the ball of the lucky wearer's foot, which were inset on a revolutionary rotating plastic turntable.

Casually mentioning the boots at school, it turned out that no one else had seen the advert, and while no one actually came out and said they never existed, there was always a distinct atmosphere of doubt. No one I knew ever got a pair. And, perhaps unsurprisingly, the considered tactics of praying, crying, cursing and hoping against hope failed to bear fruit either in the swivel boot, Action Man minesweeper or Sarah Medhurst departments.

The comic with the swivel boot ad sank away to the bottom of the pile, at first ignored out of pain, then pride, and then lost forever.

It wasn't enough to stop me wondering still whether they made them in a size 9.

C110 Television Tower (60p)
A two-level tower complete with cameraman and commentator to capture all the thrills of your game.

Ipswich and Liverpool stars evacuate the wing beneath the ominously creaking TV tower.

THE TV TOWER

Television was still within the realms of science fiction when the majority of British football stands were built, so when the need to house TV cameras began to crop up more regularly in the mid Sixties, some serious improvisation had to be employed. How to get all that heavy equipment, and the men required to operate it, up to an altitude acceptable to the TV viewer, where no one was likely to wander past pulling faces and flicking the Vs?

The bigger grounds managed to accommodate the cameras either in jerry-built rooftop sheds or hanging under the eaves on a suspended gantry; but for smaller grounds such as Portman Road, the answer was to construct a makeshift tower out of cast-off scaffolding and corrugated iron, the club carrying out a grand whip-round of Ipswich's Meccano sets to complete the spindly legs.

In those days we didn't need safety certificates, because we had blind optimism.

"It'll probably be all right," we believed. And so it always was.

Subbuteo soon brought out their own version, in the swanky Continental Range, no less: the C.110 TV Tower. It may have been an unlikely subject for a toy, two sides of scaffolding with two platforms, a TV camera and cameraman, a monitor and commentator, but it was a top seller and remains one of the favourite Christmas presents I've ever received. I even recall the joy of opening it, undimmed by the fact that I'd already guessed what it was from the size of the box and the rattle of the figures inside.

The tackle from behind is a challenge you don't see coming.

That would only spoil the surprise.

I'm still not sure what made the tower so appealing. Perhaps the fact that my Subbuteo league games would now be reaching a nationwide audience of millions.

TACKLING FROM BEHIND

There would appear to be some confusion regarding the tackle from behind, and whether or not it has been outlawed. In 2005, FIFA removed the phrase "from behind" from the laws of the game, replacing it with "a tackle which endangers the safety of an opponent," which was to be "sanctioned as serious foul play."

With this change, it seemed that uncompromising defenders and combative midfielders would immediately have 180 degrees restored to their field of operations, but sadly that isn't way things panned out.

Because the tackle from behind is a challenge you don't see coming – that would only spoil the surprise – there's no chance, no time to get your feet off the ground, which means an increased chance of injury. And this applies even if the defender does manage to get a toe-end to the ball a millisecond before he sends you twelve feet in the air.

Referees continue to interpret any tackle from behind as 'endangering safety'. In fact, they continue to interpret any tackle as 'endangering safety'. And so gone forever is the sort of 'Welcome to Elland Road' incident that used to give half the crowd such an enjoyable chance to get on their high horse, and the other half an opportunity to ask "What?" and shake their heads in such righteous confusion that they almost convinced themselves it was genuine.

THE TASTE OF FOOTBALL

During last season's deep midwinter, the bitter cold got the better of my old dad, and we were forced to go to the football without him.

I've started taking my son to the odd match now, so I wasn't lacking company, or excited questions to field. What happens if you cross the line where it says you'll be arrested if you cross this point? Who's the best footballer in the world? Can I have a drink? Who works the scoreboard? How many people are here? There must be thousands of them.

I'm weaning him on to the finer points of pessimism, but a natural childish enthusiasm tends to keep shining through. In any case, the sight of the teams trotting out on to the pitch always makes me feel the same as it did in the Seventies – they're the untouchable, responsible, grown-up heroes and I'm a hopeful kid, secretly in awe – and it brought it home all the more, watching again through the eyes of a nine-year-old.

They're less convincing once the game starts, mind, and we struggle through the first half without the car blanket and the usual bag of sweets and chocolate snacks supplied by my mum. And then I'm forced to contemplate half-time without a flask.

Now here's the strange thing: having dived for the relative cosiness of the

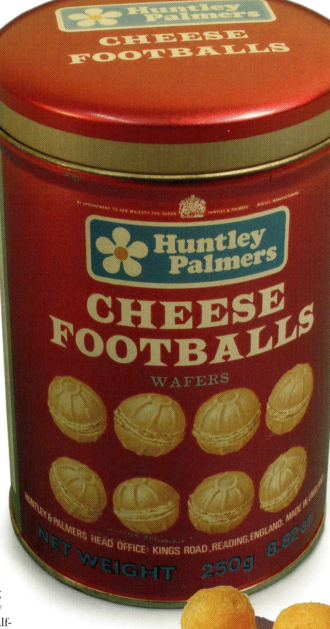

Tunnock's Tea Cakes: on a shelf near you since 1890.

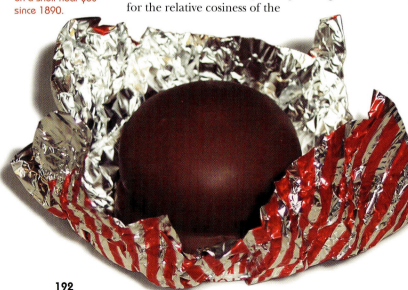

concrete concourse, I bought a Kit-Kat and a Fruit Shoot for Junior... and gave in, on the spur of the moment, to a rogue nostalgic urge of a second-hand nature. In the general confusion of slowly turning into my old man, stepping into his shoes and experiencing the game vicariously as a schoolboy, I bought my first ever matchday pint of boiling gravy.

At the time, Bovril seemed a natural choice for someone having difficulty telling the difference between 1971 and 2011. Millions of middle-aged men have slurped Bovril at half-times immemorial, and now I finally joined their number.

Just for the record, by 'second-hand' nostalgia I mean that peculiar yearning you can feel to return to an era you never even experienced first time around. Like contemporary bands that sound exactly like Joy Division crossed with the Undertones.

The Bovril felt right. Salty meat tea: it's the taste of football viewed from the back of a windy terrace, circa 1966 – when I was three.

If I'd noticed them on sale, I'd probably have bought a Wagon Wheel and a Tunnock's Tea Cake, too. How lucky it is that football has always created an appetite for those less-than-crunchy biscuits which can sit for years in a dank stadium without ever seeming to trigger concerns about their sell-by date.

Bovril seemed a natural choice for someone having difficulty telling the difference

between 1971 and 2011.

The combination of gravy and chocolate was almost enough to make me follow the smell of fried onions to see if they'd got any illegal boiled burgers in their big vats of boiling water floating with flaccid hot dogs and soggy onions.

On a roll, it was now me firing the questions. Why do modern people drink tea through the little slot in their plastic cup lid? Why would anyone ever buy a bottle of water if there was fizzy pop available? What do you mean, you've never tasted Huntley & Palmers' Cheese Footballs?

They were a bit like Wotsits, except shaped like footballs and filled with yellow goo. But what could that stuff have been made out of?

They smelled, and tasted, a bit like old socks. Everybody's fingers ended up dyed bright yellow. As such, they were strangely addictive.

And, for some reason, they were only available at Christmas.

Yes, let's drop by and check the back of Grom and Grompop's kitchen cupboards on the way home...

Bovril keeps you on the ball

...and strength alone won't win a ...e of football. Nine times out of ten ...ory goes to the fitter team. The team ... has put in some hard training. The ...m, more often than not, whose trainer ...nsists on Bovril.
Bovril gives you the stamina that lasts through every second of a ninety minute game. Its concentrated beefy goodness helps build you up to the peak of condition. Whether watching or playing, what a relaxing, cheering drink it is after the game! You can't beat Bovril. Make it a daily habit.

BOVRIL
puts beef into you

BRISTOL CITY

Red/White

1 John SHAW
2 Gerry SWEENEY
3 Geoff MERRICK
4 Gerry GOW
5 Gary COLLIER
6 Norman HUNTER
7 Trevor TAINTON
8 Tom RITCHIE
9 Joe ROYLE
10 Kevin MABBUTT
11 Clive WHITEHEAD
12 Jimmy MANN

TODAY'S

IPSWICH TOWN

1. PAUL COOPER
2. GEORGE BURLEY
3. MICK MILLS (CAPT.)
4. FRANS THIJSSEN
5. RUSSELL OSMAN
6. TERRY BUTCHER
7. JOHN WARK
8. STEVE McCALL
9. PAUL MARINER
10. ALAN BRAZIL
11. ERIC GATES
12.

SATURL

DERBY COUNT

1. BOULTON
2. WEBSTER
3. NISH
4. RIOCH
5. DANIEL
6. TODD
7. NEWTON
8. GEMMILL
9. DAVIES
10. HECTOR
11. LEE
12. BOURNE

RAY CLEMENCE	1
CHRIS HUGHTON	2
PAUL MILLER	3
GRAHAM ROBERTS	4
RICARDO VILLA	5
STEVE PERRYMAN	6
OSVALDO ARDILES	7
MARK FALCO	8
TONY GALVIN	9
GLENN HODDLE	10
GARTH CROOKS	11
	12

LIVERPOOL

(Red Shirts)

1 Ray CLEMENCE
2 Phil NEAL
3 Alan KENNEDY
4 Phil THOMPSON
5 Ray KENNEDY
6 Alan HANSEN
7 Kenny DALGLISH
 (Capt.)
8 Jimmy CASE
9 Steve HEIGHWAY
10 Terry McDERMOTT
11 Graeme SOUNESS

Substitute:

TEAMS THAT YOU CAN RECITE

When teams were teams rather than private contractors of fleeting acquaintance, the first-choice line-up would go unchanged for seasons on end, with the boss blooding a kid or adding perhaps one new face over the close season, but only to replace the arthritic right-back who had just enjoyed his testimonial year.

You knew your team was a team because they piled into a team bath after the match, rather than wearing flip-flops and initialled dressing-gowns and insisting on private shower cubicles. You knew they were a team because their surnames seemed to rhyme when you recited them.

Every year, you'd hear a news story about a fan who had named their firstborn after their whole beloved team. Take a bow, Raymond Christopher Alec Thomas Larry Emlyn Kevin Peter John Ian Blenkinsop. You'll be coming up 39, next birthday. And, of course, it's now a family tradition to name a little one after your heroes. It's vital, living in a street where the Reds vs. Blues balance is so close.

So spare a thought for poor little Brad Glen José Raul Daniel Fábio Luis Steven Andy Joe Maxi Jordan Dirk Stewart Jay Lucas Danny Jamie David Pepe Charlie Christian Jesús Raheem Doni Jonjo Martin Conor Martin John Nathan Martin Andre Jack Blenkinsop.

'Stevie' for short. Smashing little girl.

THE TESTIMONIAL MATCH

When was the last time you went along to pay your respects to a great old servant of your club, putting up with the prospect of a meaningless friendly against your big local rivals – it's never quite the same, on their days off – in order to chip in to the loyal clubman's retirement nest egg as he looked forward to living in temporarily reduced circumstances and having to get a proper job? Eh?

There's no such thing as a testimonial match any more. Lining the pockets of a multi-millionaire with the proceeds of a kickaround against a team with the suffix 'XI' – a Roman digit hasn't been so shamed since they renamed The Great War – doesn't count. The vital elements of long service, need, mutual gratitude and respect are all absent.

Your average club's current longest servant is a seventeen-year-old wing-back, now out on loan at Chesterfield: he signed his life away for an illegal payment of £500 when he was twelve. In the first team, only two players have been at the club for more than four years. A couple more squad players have been on board for nearly three years now, and they're happily sitting out their contracts before moving on.

JOHN PRATT
TESTIMONIAL MATCH
at Tottenham Hotspur Ground
FRIDAY, 12th MAY, 1978
Kick-off 7.30 p.m.

TOTTENHAM H
v ARSEN
WIN A FOOTBALL TRIP

BRIAN STUBBS
TESTIMONIAL GAME

Monday 8th September 1980 - k.o. 7.30 p.m
NOTTS COUNTY
v
NOTTINGHAM FOREST
30p

GLYN PARDOE
ONE MAN, ONE CLUB

TESTIMONIAL MATCH
CITY versus UNITED
FRIDAY, MARCH 25th 1977
Maine Road 7.30 pm

194

But even in the good old days, the testimonial wasn't always a happy love-in. Clubs used the single charity payment to wash their hands of any further responsibility to a player... or even a manager.

Two months after his sacking, a Special Testimonial Dinner was arranged for Alf Ramsey on the eighth anniversary of England winning the World Cup. Prime Minister Harold Wilson, FIFA's Sir Stanley Rous, captains of industry, sportswriters, players and even Eric Morecambe rallied round and speechified in tribute at the Café Royal; but no one from the FA showed.

So tuck into your Mousse d'Arbroath Smokies and your Consommé Madrilene, which translates directly as watery farewell soup. Enjoy your roast lamb.

And then, for afters, it's Bombe Surprise... you'll never work again.

THEY USED TO PLAY ON GRASS

Published in 1971, *They Used to Play on Grass* was a football novel with a difference: for starters, it was set in the future; and, what's more, its author, PB Yuill, didn't really exist, being a composite pen-name for Scottish novelist Gordon Williams and QPR star Terry Venables.

As the pair would prove with their three *Hazell* detective novels, the combination of Williams' sharp storylines (that same year, his *Straw Dogs* got a Hollywood release) and Venables' ear for street-level cockney dialogue held a certain chemistry, and their predictions for the end of the Seventies proved, almost spookily, to hold water.

They got the introduction of Astroturf right, and foresaw a breakaway of the biggest clubs, the action building to the British Cup semi between the Commoners (let's just say QPR's very near neighbours) and Rangers, at Hampden.

In the future, footballers would be free to roam between clubs with no transfer fee (though, unlike today, only at the end of their contracts). Players would even make extra cash on the side by advertising beer. Superstar Wiggy runs a boutique, lives with a model, badmouths TV talk show hosts, and has been denounced

Your club's current longest servant is a seventeen-year-old wing-back, now out on loan at Chesterfield.

by a bishop. The winners of the semi will meet Man U or Leeds at 'New Wembley', with gate receipts set to top £250,000.

Gordon and Tel's marks for crystal ball gazing were certainly higher than those of the more feted futurologists Gerry & Sylvia Anderson. Their *UFO* TV series, also from 1971, foresaw Interceptor spaceships fitted with huge single bullets taking pot-shots at alien invaders, a space base on the moon, cars driving on the right and girls with purple hair... all set in the distant future of 1980.

Oh my gawd – it's the Terry Venables School of Cockernee Argot.

Cascades of bog roll streamed down from the stands and terracing

like tissue-paper comets

TOILET ROLLS

No sooner had the ball sent shockwaves rippling through the net than cascades of bog roll would come streaming down from the stands and terracing like tissue-paper comets. Toilet roll lodged in the net, dangled over the bar and blew around the penalty box.

It wasn't just the wilful mass littering that was at issue, but the waste of resources. Most importantly, all that bottom-related refuse represented a serious Health & Safety hazard. Did you know it's now illegal for pre-school groups to collect up toilet-roll middles for the little kids to make rubbish models with? It's yet more proof of the potential hazards lurking in toilet tissue.

Even so, I still miss the loo-roll deluge, which always seemed a cathartic addition to a goal celebration. Not for us Brits the labour-intensive, flashy South American confetti-storm. A well-aimed Andrex was far more satisfying, plopping down in the mud next to the beaten goalie.

"What I always wanted to know," I threw into a recent round-table discussion of football history, "is how did the yobboes manage to smuggle the loo-rolls in? Up their jumpers? Down their flares?"

Just one look at the delighted face of one fellow symposium member was enough to trigger a *University Challenge* moment – y'know, that penny-dropping sensation when you finally realised the teams aren't really

Steve Coppell (6 games as Man City boss) loses to Trevor Brooking (14 in charge of West Ham).

housed behind double-decker desks. They just shoot it that way for TV.

"They didn't smuggle them in, did they?" I said in a small voice. "They just went and nicked them out of the loos."

"That's right," my colleague confirmed.

And, in turn, he proceeded to let *himself* down in front of everyone in the Turk's Head lounge bar, miming skills previously thought lost to British football – how to obtain maximum backspin, unrolling and streaming effects...

TOP TRUMPS

Right then, here we go: Peter Ward of Forest. One International Appearance; Height 5'7". Best steer clear of those categories.

"League Goals, 81."

"League Goals, 0"
Oh yes! I've won Joe Corrigan. 6'4½"! But now I've turned up David Johnson of Liverpool. Bit average. Take a gamble.

"International Goals, 6."

"International Goals, 4"
Southampton's Dave Watson: he's a good 'un. Next up, Peter Shilton. Virtually unbeatable on League Appearances.

"League Appearances, 557, hand it over."

"League Appearances, 229."

Ray Wilkins of Man United, good card. Now for Arsenal's Ken Sansom: short-arse, doesn't score.

West Ham Unite[d]

Trevor Brooking

HEAD FOR

International Goals
International Appearances
League Goals
League Appearances
Height

Manchester United
Steve Coppell

International Goals	6
International Appearances	33
League Goals	50
League Appearances	295
Height	5'7½"

Nottingham Forest
Viv Anderson

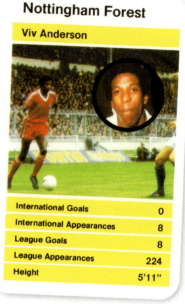

International Goals	0
International Appearances	8
League Goals	8
League Appearances	224
Height	5'11"

"International Appearances, 18?"
"International Appearances, 6." *Arsenal's Graham Rix, I'm on a roll! Now it's Emlyn Hughes of Rotherham, still in his Wolves kit. He's been around forever…*

"League Appearances, 560."
"League Appearances, 347." *Ha! Terry McDermott of Liverpool. He's on the ropes now. For Asa Hartford of Everton, best take a chance on…*

"League Goals, 46."
"LEAGUE GOALS, 101!" *Aargh, no! What's he got now?*

"Height, 5'11"."
"Height, 5'7½"." *Bugger, he's got Steve Coppell off me.*
"League Goals, 32."
"League Goals, 8." *Bye bye, Viv Anderson.*
"League Appearances, 538."
"League Appearances, 364." *Oh my God! I've lost Kenny Dalglish…*

"Peter Shilton.
Virtually unbeatable on League Appearances.

557, hand it over."

THE GLORY GAME

It was one of the first 'behind-the-scenes' football books ever published, and a curiosity at the time, having been penned by a 'proper' writer rather than a sports reporter. Previously known for his authorised 1968 biography of the Beatles, Hunter Davies had a knack for telling which way the wind was blowing. And so to football, and a whole season committed to following 'the richest club in England', from the lads' return for pre-season training to their triumphal lifting of the UEFA Cup.

How jarring it now seems for stars such as Peters, Mullery, Perryman and Chivers to be augmented by just one close-season signing: Ralph Coates from Burnley, for a British record £190,000. Nervous Ralph is dressed in noticeably narrow trousers and pointy shoes, no longer a big fish in a small pool. The season begins with a kickaround on the car park, the players indistinguishable from any football-mad kids with five spare minutes.

Most affecting of all is the attitude of Northern Ireland goalie Pat Jennings, who Davies eventually singles out as his player of the season. Pat is the original gentle giant, a born worrier, and so modest there's a feeling that he's not making the most of his opportunities.

"He's a genuine team man, shy and retiring, with no signs of flash. His fans are always on at him to put a bit of show into his game, make it look a bit harder, just to work up the crowd excitement and draw attention to himself."

The problem comes to a head when Paul Trevillion – sportswear entrepreneur and early football agent (see also 'Dastardly Foreign Tricks') – tries to convince Pat to endorse a pair of goalie gloves: the magic's in the design, not Pat's giant hands. But Jennings refuses to join in the hard sell, and self-consciously even stops catching the ball one-handed. So much for that suggested gimmick.

"They were like spacemen's gloves," Pat declines the easy money. "Ridiculous. They'd tire your hands out just putting them on."

You don't have to be a Spurs fan to enjoy this step back in time to football's Lost World.

Tottenham Hotspur

TOTTENHAM HOTSPUR
MARTIN CHIVERS
CENTRE FORWARD

TOTTENHAM HOTSPUR

STEVE PERRYMAN
INSIDE

And yet even after switching to another new club, Torres was still grumbling, having decided – and who could argue? – "The romance in football is gone. It's different now. People come and leave. When you join a club you want to do the best for yourself and for that club. I never kissed the Liverpool badge…"

THE TWIN TOWERS

It was all mythology, you know. Wembley's spaces weren't really any more wide-open than any other stadium's, and Pelé was just being flowery when he called the old place "the cathedral of football." Seventy years' worth of all-or-nothing matches – Cup Finals, Internationals, even a World Cup Final – were all artificially inflated in the minds of the football fan, sadly blinded by the Empire Stadium's ties with the wrong kind of power, the wrong kind of glory.

When they were erected in 1922 as the twin focal points of the Empire Exhibition, campaigners suggested a gigantic corset be fashioned from scaffold and tarpaulin so as to preserve the modesty of the vast new Wembley and her proud domes. It's probably best for everyone now Britannia's life-giving bounty is returned to concrete dust.

I myself was afflicted with the madness. Four play-off finals and two League Cup finals (including the last to be played at Wembley) stand out among the most memorable occasions in my life as a football fan.

Yes, the old terraces were too shallow, a problem exacerbated when they were converted to all-seating, and the running track set the pitch further away than at most stadiums; but this wasn't most stadiums.

Not long before Wembley was closed, I took the chance to say farewell when I interviewed Alan Hansen, ironically on the future of the game, in the set-piece surroundings of an executive box high over the halfway line. I took time to root about behind the scenes in the doomed stadium, stepping right into the unconvincing waxworks tableau of the 1966 World Cup Final, and joining the moth-eaten players in front of one of the actual goals. It isn't every day you get to be the only customer at a urinal (or a dank, black wall) forty yards long.

Around the same time, I picked up the poison chalice of interviewing FA chief executive Graham Kelly at the FA's Lancaster Gate HQ. He was nervous, intensely passive-aggressive about the controversial plan to demolish Wembley, and didn't realise I just wanted to talk about football, about the man behind the disastrous public image, and the big bag of dirty kit behind his desk.

TRANSFER REQUESTS TURNED DOWN

No greater authority than Jimmy Hill and his encyclopaedic masterwork of 1985 – *Football Crazy! 1,500 Oddball Facts, Amazing Feats, etc.* – delivers one gobsmacking gobbet that knocks all the other *Fascinating Fun for Football Fans of All Ages* into a cocked hat.

"Between 1972 and 1979 Stan Bowles made 34 transfer requests during his stay at Queens Park Rangers."

Can you believe it? There's no such thing as a transfer request today, just a transfer demand. If a player wants to move, he's already gone.

Example: the British record £50 million that Chelsea paid for Fernando Torres, just three days after his transfer request was rejected.

"My commitment and loyalty to Liverpool and to the fans is the same as it was on my first day when I signed," Torres had commented cryptically back in the summer of 2010, after his agent had spoken to the press about a possible big-money move. "I feel the fans love me and everyone knows I am really happy here."

Recently voted 'The Man Who Has Done Most Damage To Football' by *When Saturday Comes*, Kelly had turned up in person to accept the award. It was just the kind of spark he'd shown signing forms for Accrington Stanley as a fourteen-year-old goalkeeper. But now he was needlessly dismissive of his on-field football career, which had progressed as far as the Blackpool third team.

"This is a very cursory discussion, if I might say so," he told me. "You're very poorly researched."

At this point, Mr. Kelly didn't know I was going to ask him what he'd do if he were invisible for the day...

"Stan Matthews was as elusive to catch for an autograph as he was on the field," the lifelong Blackpool fan later enthused like a big kid. "He always used to find a secret exit from the ground! The most exotic autograph I ever got was from Eddie Clamp, who played for Wolves. He always used to sign himself 'Yours in Sport, Eddie Clamp' in a long scrawl!"

And the point of my remembering the man who presided over the demolition of the Twin Towers?

"That's an easy one," he fired back enthusiastically, "I'd score the winning goal in the Cup Final!

"I scored my first goal at Wembley yesterday, in our victory over the MPs. From fully eighteen inches out. It was one of those where you'd so much time you were frightened it was going to bobble under your feet. Too much time. But I stopped it and whacked it in!"

Because scoring under the Twin Towers was special, in a way that scoring under the fat new stadium's Broken Shopping-Basket Handle can never be.

Concrete dust: Twin Towers, domes, thirty-nine steps, funny Olympic Gallery up under the rim...

"Wembley is the cathedral of football.
It is the capital of football
and it is the heart of football."

199

U

UNCHOREOGRAPHED GOAL CELEBRATIONS

Imagine a player scoring a goal this weekend, and somehow *failing* to slide in a headlong swan-dive over to the corner flag, bending it backward under his body like a contestant on *Strictly Come Dancing*, and giving it a cheeky peck right on the club logo – followed by a more earnest snog with the registered trademarks on his shirt, and the revelation of an undershirt with a hand-scrawled message to the glory of God, or his new baby photo-opportunity.

Cue the distorted blare of the PA's virtual 'goal celebration' music – 'Chelsea Dagger' is the curiously inappropriate choice at many grounds other than Stamford Bridge – drowning out any potentially offensive cheers or jeers.

Cue the arrival of his team-mates, who cross themselves in sync and join in a choreographed comedy duck-walk down the touchline, some getting the routine mixed up with last week's and donning imaginary DJ earphones for a spot of air scratching instead of rocking an imaginary baby.

The ref duly arrives and books the scorer for taking his shirt off. No worries, because he only ever gets booked for dissent and taking his shirt off, and so can synchronise another booking in a couple of weeks' time, and get a paid week off with his new arrival at our expense.

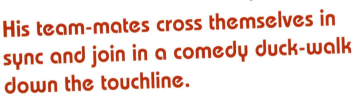

His team-mates cross themselves in sync and join in a comedy duck-walk down the touchline.

They say *schadenfreude* is a uniquely un-British sentiment.

We don't even have a word to describe the way we feel when the lino on the other side of the pitch then disallows the goal for some incidental bodily contact in the box.

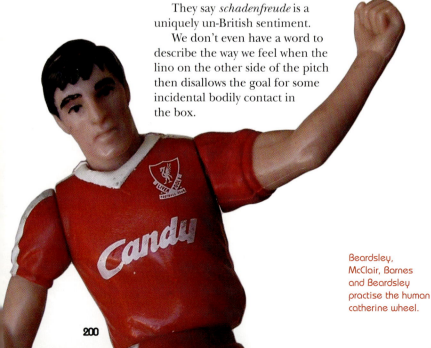

We simply punch the air once in traditional, righteous celebration. A bit like Stuart Pearson, with our arm bolt upright; or 'Sniffer' Clarke, forefinger casually crooked; or even Alan Shearer, himself fast becoming another badly remembered figure from the past.

UNLUCKY BAGS

It must have been 1973 when I dropped into Mr. Sherrard's corner shop for a half-time Vimto and a Bar Six – or maybe the occasion was altogether more after-school and off-the-cuff. All I really remember is the arrival of a new counter box marked with the A&BC logo. Not, this time, the long-awaited new series of football cards, football posters or little tellies with a magnifying lens and a microscopic celluloid wheel of player portraits (could I have dreamt these?)... but a lucky bag instead.

Beardsley, McClair, Barnes and Beardsley practise the human catherine wheel.

200

"What do you get in a lucky bag?" I would almost certainly have asked Mr. Sherrard, an elderly man in his fifties with greased leather hair, a grey moustache and a maroon nylon tunic.

"Sweets and football cards," he would almost certainly have replied – and not just to ensure that he'd get to ring up 3 new pence on his big, chinging till. I'd been running up Fairfield hill for years now clutching a note from my mum ("20 Number 6 Tipped. 4 Lyons fruit pies. 1 pack football cards") and I often helped out by fishing out old shopping lists from under his glass confectionery case. We had a bond of trust.

of horrors, they were black and white, with two retired stars per card, separated by a semi-successful serration. So I tore them all in half, semi-successfully.

Instinctively, I knew I had to collect the set; but the uptake on this innovation was low. Most kids just bought one bag, and sulked. There was no one to swap with. The lucky bag counter box was never replaced.

It was, of course, a cunning ploy to shift some old warehouse stock, and probably a bit of a rip-off; but I wouldn't mind coming across a warehouseful of them now, even if seeing Alan Gilzean with hair does give you the heebie-jeebies. The unseparated cards are worth at least three quid each, and as for an opened pack complete with fossilised gum – we're talking hundreds.

Seeing Alan Gilzean with hair can give you the heebie-jeebies.

Ripping open my lucky bag, I found a handful of sweets, a small plastic toy which couldn't have been football related or I'd have squirreled it away for years before my own kids managed to disperse it to the four winds... and the most curious pack of football cards I'd ever seen.

Tearing into the unfamiliar pack, I found cards printed with players I'd mostly never even heard of, with old-fashioned names like Albert Bennett (Newcastle United). Horror

"Wahey! Er, ouch": Tonka Barnesy celebrates one of his eleven England goals.

RAY CRAWFORD.

ALBERT JOHANNESON

V

CCLX.

18 AUG., 1966.
England's World Cup Football Victory.
CCLX. Chalky paper. Wmk. Type CLXXIX (sideways).
700. 4d., red, reddish purple, bright blue, flesh and black

THE VICTORIOUS OVERPRINT

Readers across the globe from Micronesia to Outer Mongolia will doubtless be chuffed to note that the British stamp overprinted to commemorate England's 1966 World Cup victory appears to feature players in made-up kit. But ours is proper art, ours is, appreciated by the greatest artist of the Sixties.

"What I do find very sexy is the new fourpenny stamp," says David Hockney in Peter Whitehead's swinging documentary *Tonite Let's All Make Love in London*, "with the footballers kicking their legs up."

One day...
I'll convert all my useless boxes of football videos into DVDs.

THE VIDEO AGE

Seldom has a new technology flared so brightly and died so quickly as video.

The race to develop a consumer-level video system was run in 1970s Japan, with JVC and their VHS eventually managing to overshadow Sony's Betamax system, and by 1978 the first video players were available in the UK. Available, but far from affordable for all but the spoilt kids.

We finally got one for Christmas in 1986. I know that because I still have the Kodak E-180 tape that we first used. The first thing I ever recorded was *Saint & Greavsie*, closely followed by *Football Focus* – you see a theme developing? – when the ability to capture moving pictures off the telly box still seemed like something out of *Buck Rodgers in the 25th Century*.

Now we were free from the vice-like control of the programme planners. If we wanted to watch *A Hard Day's Night* more than once a decade, we could. And if we chose to rewind again and again that bit in *Butch Cassidy and the Sundance Kid* where Robert Redford undoes Katharine Ross's blouse, then that was our choice. But apart from taking possession of favourite films and comedy essentials like *Fawlty Towers* and *The Young Ones*, video was all about football.

Whether painstakingly taping goals from the regional news, or building up a video library that could be measured in yards, it was an obsessive, and ultimately a pitifully pointless exercise.

The new century brought the DVD, so superior to videotape in every way that the VCR was almost instantly history.

They're all in the garage now, in several boxes – the season highlights vids, even from crap seasons; the World Cup films narrated by Sean Connery; Danny Baker's *Own Goals and Gaffs* and inferior imitators; classic Cup Finals; the wonderful BBC *Match of the Seventies*... all of them as much use as an ashtray on a motorbike.

But I'm not throwing them out, oh no. One day, I'll get a special machine where you link it up to your computer and convert them all into DVDs. One day.

Virgin VIDEO

TOTAL FOOTBALL
The Official Film of the European Football Championship

VHS MONO

RUNNING TIME
58 MINUTES APPROX

VC2096 VHS

SCOTLAND THE BRAVE
THE GREATEST TRIUMPHS
OVER ENGLAND

the Video COLLECTIO

BBC

MATCH of the 70s
SEASONS 70–75

BBC V 5 87 2

THE **F.A. CUP FINAL GOALS** 1960 TO 1992

WATERSHED
PICTURES
WSP 1117

BELLISSIMO!
Wales 2-1 Italy

BBC Wales
Echo

VHS
GUP1536

DANNY BAKER'S OWN GOALS AND GAFFS

VHS COLOUR
Approx. Running Time
85 Minutes
VVD 1105

VHS HI-FI BBCV 4032

1979 **FA CUP FINAL**
Arsenal v Manchester Utd.

BBC VIDEO

FILM FOUR DISTRIBUTORS

FEVER PITCH
A MATCH MADE IN HEAVEN

VHS VC3606

VC-1

EVERTON v BAYERN MUNICH
European Cup Winners' Cup ■ Semi-final – 2nd Leg
Wednesday 24th April 1985

COLOUR ILC9020 VHS

WORLD SPORTS

RACE FOR THE CHAMPIONSHIP
1988/89
THE OFFICIAL FOOTBALL LEAGUE VIDEO

VHS 2326

CBS FOX VIDEO SPORTS

W

Balance ball on neck, roll ball
down spine, backheel over head,
volley into roof of net.

Let play commence.

WADDINGTONS TABLE SOCCER

Subbuteo had men with wobbly bases; Casdon
Soccer had swivel-action players; Striker had its
push-head-down kick-ball thingy: every game
had its clever gizmo designed to make scaled-
down soccer 'Just Like The Real Thing'.

All except Waddingtons, that is. Their
own branded Table Soccer claimed to be "the
action-packed table football game that brings
the thrill, skill and excitement of the match
indoors!" Translated into English, it was the
Victorian parlour game of tiddlywinks played
on a green rectangle of card.

The instruction manual explained:
"The ball is moved

Wad's Law: "Before
a player takes a
shot at goal he
must say 'I am
going to shoot'..."

about the field by 'flicking' (which in the
remainder of the rules will be called 'kicking')"
– accompanied by an illustration of someone
quite clearly tiddlywinking.

They didn't waste any money on
endorsements, either. A photograph on the box
lid showed an aerial challenge involving four
players, all with their backs to the camera. In
case any of them were still recognisable, their
kits had been coloured in – yellow and black
for one team, fuchsia shirts and green shorts
for the other.

According to the letter of the law,
Table Football wasn't all that realistic
or action-packed, and was actually
better to play on the carpet than a
table.

It didn't stop me spending
close on a million boy-hours
honing outrageous skills
that could see lofted 'kicks'
angling past the 'goalie'
from anywhere on the
'pitch'.

Table Soccer
brought all the skill
and excitement of
winking indoors.

WARMING UP

Not for Frank Worthington, the common, sweaty slog of warming up for a game of football. Frank was always warm, which precluded him from the lesser players' chores such as running and bending. Frank was always cool.

As soon as the 'Post Horn Gallop' had played over the Tannoy, the two teams shot out on to the pitch like greyhounds with greasy legs. There was no lining up, no handshaking, no waving: it was straight into the star jumps and running-and-miming-violent-headers routines. As soon as the goalies had been politely clapped into their goals, had hung their towels and arranged the contents of their voodoo flight bags, the forwards began raining in shots, often four at a time.

Meanwhile, Frank had ambled to the edge of the penalty box for a spot of keepy-uppy, bouncing and balancing the ball around his limbs and extremities with absolute nonchalance. Frank kicked the ball up over his head and caught it on the back of his neck. A flick up into the air from the back of his slicked-back hair, and he carried on as before.

In an episode of ITV's *All in the Game* – think football meets *It's a Knockout* – Frank's tasks included 'head tennis', 'soccer skittles' and 'football golf'. But hold on, Frank wasn't clear on the rules: for how long did the organisers want him to keep the ball up? For how long should he continue chipping balls into a paddling pool 40 yards distant? It never occurred to Frank that he might miss. He dutifully scored infinity in all his disciplines.

Without having to lower himself to look, Frank would sense the ref attracting the skippers to the middle. He now concluded his limbering by again balancing the ball on his neck, this time rolling the ball down his spine, backheeling it over his head and volleying it into the roof of the net.

Let play commence.

And long may Wortho's chilled demeanour, his sense of fun and shining talent act as an example to my firstborn, named in his honour*.

*Hello, Frances! And hello Jimmy, too!
But that's another story…*

HORNETS' NEST

Mysterious goings-on down at Vicarage Road in the mid Eighties…

The Panini 84 album has the bloke with the extraordinary moustache down as 'George Reilly' and the big fella with the blond hair as 'Paul Atkinson'. But by the time of Panini 85 they'd become involved in a mystifying identity swap which could have inspired the film *Face/Off*.

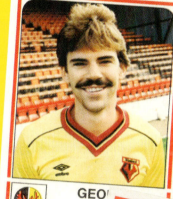

Sadly, George (he's the one on the right) became involved in another mystery as recently as 2003. Working on a building site in Corby (see 'Magazine Shin Pads') long after retiring from the game, he was attacked from behind by a fellow worker. Having being wrestled to the ground, his assailant bit George's ear almost clean off. But why?

His motive only became clear when he leaned over and whispered into the other, fully functioning lughole: "Remember Plymouth?"

Reilly had scored the winning goal that knocked Argyle out of the 1984 FA Cup semi-final and took Watford to Wembley for a meeting with Everton.

The green-hooped maniac had held a grudge for almost twenty years before the horrific attack, when football's lowered standards led him to believe it would be acceptable to vent his spleen in this vile manner.

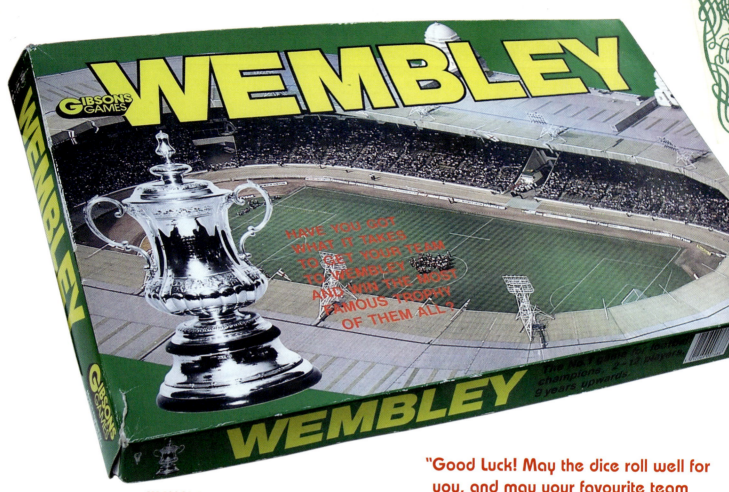

WEMBLEY

"Based on the English Football Association Challenge Cup Competition, the most gripping features and exciting uncertainties of which it reproduces with vivid and truly amazing fidelity…"

It was the thrill of the Cup draw and the possibility of an alternate-universe upset that made Wembley so addictive. The reproduction of all those associations and assumptions that electrify the simple twinning of two clubs' names ("And it's Newcastle United… at home to… *Leeds United*). The tension inherent in the inevitable reduction of 32 clubs to an historic final pairing. The chance to witness a spunky lower-league outfit confound the Darwinian bias that enabled top clubs to make more money, to spend it on star players, to score more goals… and even claim the right to throw loaded dice.

It seemed almost unfair when cousin John's Darlington travelled to face my Liverpool at Anfield, but this intelligent gambling game brought home the hard realities of football.

"Good Luck! May the dice roll well for you, and may your favourite team appear many times in the final of the Cup at WEMBLEY."

"The earning ability of clubs varies greatly, as does their playing ability," stated the Rules of the Game. "Each club has a value (representing gate receipts) and each Division has different colour dice for Home and Away matches. These dice are specially produced to give a built-in advantage both to teams in higher divisions and to teams playing at Home."

The powerful red First Division Home die could roll 0, 1, 2, 3 or two chances

of a 4, while the white Third/Fourth Division Away die was lumbered with two 0s and two 1s – plus a potentially giant-killing 4 and a 5 to spice things up.

I just played out that Reds-Darlo tie as an experiment, and my mighty 'Pule swept the Quakers aside 3-0 at Anfield.

Truly amazing fidelity.

But then, when my swaggering, odds-on Arsenal used to fall 4-1 at home to cousin John's Rochdale… well, that would never happen in the real world, would it? It's all just down to luck. Stupid blinking game.

THE THIRD DEGREE

Now hold on just a minute. How can we hope to prove that football used to be better in the past – and would benefit from a smart U-turn in most respects – while acknowledging the racism and violence that lurked in the wings, marring British society during what were otherwise golden years for footer? Simple: let's be thankful that there are now considerably fewer Nazis throwing bananas at black players, fewer weekend Commandos using matches as an excuse for a punch-up… and proceed forthwith on the other 250 points.

West Brom were the first team in the League to field three black players, which in retrospect proved to be one small step in the right direction. For years, the lone black player had been treated as fair game – as a figure of fun, a lesser person to whom the normal rules of bullying didn't apply – by some proportion of every mostly white, mostly male crowd. Even when fans sympathised with lonely Clyde Best or Garth Crooks, and recognised their bravery in the face of thousands of monkey chants, the best we felt we could do was not join in.

But West Brom boss Ron Atkinson did more than just go along with the crowd. He picked Laurie Cunningham, Brendan Batson and Cyrille Regis on merit – a meaningless act now, but a bold move in 1977, especially in the Black Country where the National Front vote was high, and black heroes and role models scarce.

"Our presence was a radical statement," says Regis. "Here we were, playing well and helping to break down serious barriers in the

First Division." But still there were torrents of abuse. "Nobody knew how to deal with it. There was no vehicle to use to speak out."

History tells us Big Ron blotted his copybook by rechristening the trio 'The Three Degrees', after Britain's adopted Motown girl group. But, again, Cyrille's "great man-manager and motivator" didn't accept the targeting of any of his team as the Baggies rose to third in the League. Instead, he set out to humanise his black players, to bring home to ordinary fans the personal nature of their mass weekly torture.

"How could I fight back? Through my talent. And when you've won the game you can say: 'That's my response'."

Cyrille Regis

Yes, dressing up his lads in feather boas (and the real Three Degrees in football shirts) caused some clenched bottoms at the time. But ultimately such larks only poured ridicule on the notion that the British Way of Life was under threat from the Baggies' new heroes: the quicksilver Cunningham, from Archway, the first black player to wear an England shirt at any level; Batson, the intelligent ex-Gunner, snapped up cheap from Cambridge United; and the powerful, pacy, hugely impressive Regis, fresh off a West London building site.

West Bromwich Albion

CYRILLE REGIS

207

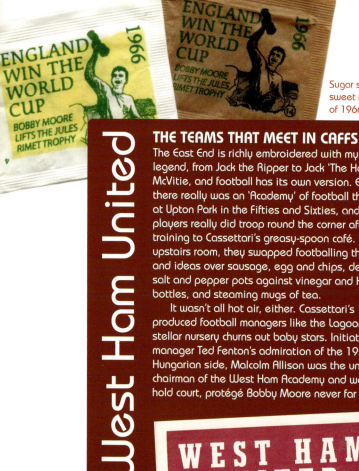

Sugar sugar: a sweet reminder of 1966.

West Ham United

THE TEAMS THAT MEET IN CAFFS

The East End is richly embroidered with myth and legend, from Jack the Ripper to Jack 'The Hat' McVitie, and football has its own version. Except there really was an 'Academy' of football thinking at Upton Park in the Fifties and Sixties, and the players really did troop round the corner after training to Cassettari's greasy-spoon café. In the upstairs room, they swapped footballing theories and ideas over sausage, egg and chips, deploying salt and pepper pots against vinegar and HP Sauce bottles, and steaming mugs of tea.

It wasn't all hot air, either. Cassettari's produced football managers like the Lagoon Nebula stellar nursery churns out baby stars. Initiated by manager Ted Fenton's admiration of the 1950s Hungarian side, Malcolm Allison was the unofficial chairman of the West Ham Academy and would hold court, protégé Bobby Moore never far from his side. Allison went on to coach and manage all around the world in a thirty-year career, most famously at Manchester City and Crystal Palace.

The tentacles of influence in the game spread far beyond West Ham. Around the chequered tablecloth were: Noel Cantwell, who took Coventry City into Europe; Frank O'Farrell, who led Torquay and Leicester to promotion before landing the Manchester United job, with Malcolm Musgrove his assistant at all three clubs; John Bond, who guided Bournemouth and Norwich to promotion before replacing Allison at Manchester City; Ken Brown, Bond's Carrow Road assistant, who went on to lead the Canaries to promotion and Milk Cup success; Dave Sexton, who built QPR's best ever side, before managing Manchester United, the England Under-21s and Coventry; Jimmy Andrews, Cardiff manager for four seasons; and Andy Nelson, who won promotion with Charlton...

The nature of the Academy changed over the years, but through the long managerial eras of Ron Greenwood and John Lyall the philosophy remained the same.

Fifty years on, we went on one of our nostalgia trips to take some snaps at Cassettari's, but found it had closed down just a couple of months before. The building had been taken over by a firm of solicitors, always good to blame.

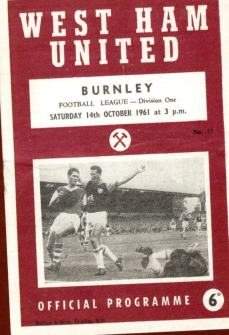

WEST HAM UNITED

BURNLEY

FOOTBALL LEAGUE — Division One

SATURDAY 14th OCTOBER 1961 at 3 p.m.

No. 17

OFFICIAL PROGRAMME 6d

"The crowds at West Ham have never been rewarded by results but they keep turning up because of the good football they see. Other clubs will suffer from the old bugbear that results count more than anything. This has been the ruination of English soccer."

Ron Greenwood

THE BEST-BEHAVED CUP WINNERS

We had a meeting in London that morning, 1 June 1985, and noticed in the morning paper that Brentford and Wigan Athletic were contesting the Freight Rover Trophy at Wembley. It was on the way back to the M1... hey, we might as well.

We strolled down a sunny Wembley Way as neutrals, but the blue-and-white colours and the fact that they'd brought far fewer fans than the London side swayed us in favour of the northerners.

It was the first time we'd ever stood among lower-league fans, and perhaps it was just that Wigan were so new to it all, only having entered the League in 1976, but their attitude was refreshing. Instead of the threats and taunts towards opposition fans that we were used to, the Latics proudly sang, "We're the best-behaved supporters in the land."

Those fans were rewarded with a 3-1 win, and we celebrated along with them, cheering their canny Irish manager Bryan Hamilton, rock-solid Man of the Match Steve Walsh and goalscorers Mike Newell and David Lowe.

What we didn't realise at the time was that we were watching the future of our own club in action, as a year later Hamilton arrived at Leicester. His first signing was the big centre-half who became a legend over fourteen years at City, followed the next season by Mike Newell and, a few years later, his fellow Scouser Lowe.

But nowadays Wigan are in the First Division and we're the plucky outsiders – the best-behaved platinum customers in the Upton Steel West Stand.

Wigan Athletic

GOING OUT OF EXISTENCE

While football media attention was focused on celebrity hair transplants and the Champions League's billion-dollar carnival, one of the game's greatest ever stories recently reached its climax, as AFC Wimbledon returned from the dead.

Back in 2001, the long-homeless club's chairman, Charles Koppel, announced plans to relocate seventy miles north in Milton Keynes. However, fans in south-west London were distraught, pointing out the move's alleged illegality and drumming up mass support from every other club's fans. For another year the FA debated doing the decent thing and blowing the insulting scheme – or 'lifeline', as Koppel called it – out of the water.

In 2003, a Wimbledon side in name only, undead, unloved, played their first home match in Buckinghamshire.

But, by this time, the real Wimbledon had been re-established by its fans in the Combined Counties League Premier Division, the ninth level of the football pyramid.

What an epic battle ensued as the Dons fought their way back from the non-League depths, claiming five promotions in eight seasons, finally bursting back into the bigtime with a play-off victory over Luton Town in May 2011.

It's an inspirational tale for all fans now that tales of corruption, mismanagement and bankruptcy are so commonplace, and most of our clubs are at risk from coolly disinterested owners.

You might secretly yearn to see AFC Coventry playing on mud with you as centre-forward, but remember... it's a long road back.

Wimbledon

Wolverhampton Wanderers

FOCUS ON THE DOOG

What sort of nutcase would take on the Damned United in unarmed combat?

Answer: just the sort of character who would sport a mohican hairdo in the conservative Sixties, leaving behind a trail of heartbroken fans (if not managers and owners) as he skipped from club to club before settling at Wolves – and then recommencing battle as a spiky World Cup TV pundit, as the PFA Chairman campaigning for freedom of contract, as Kettering Town manager pioneering shirt sponsorship, as the head of the consortium that saved Wolves from liquidation, as parliamentary candidate for East Belfast and representative of UKIP.

It looks as though he's winning too, with Terry Yorath disabled by the eye jab and Peter Lorimer suffering the double discomfort of a Vulcan death grip and hoof up the backside.

Not for the effervescent Wolves and Northern Ireland goalscorer, Alexander Derek Dougan, any of the dull stock answers to *Shoot!* magazine's weekly Q&A session: 'steak and chips'; 'my father'; 'a gym teacher', 'Dick Emery'...

Biggest thrill: Meeting Ian Paisley.

What person in the world would you most like to meet? Bernadette Devlin.

Best friend: My bank manager.

Best country visited: Ireland.

Favourite food: Irish stew.

Miscellaneous dislikes: Irish stew cooked by my German wife.

Professional ambition: To get over to Russia to visit a few friends.

If you weren't a footballer, what do you think you'd be? Jimmy Hill's assistant.

Biggest drag in soccer: Arsenal's Bob McNab.

THE WOODWORK

As the venerable Sarf London songsmith Max Bygraves would once delight in telling us, 'Fings Ain't Wot They Used T'Be'.

Example: the woodwork – as in the once-common phrase, "Coh, he's lost his head and smacked it against the woodwork."

For no good reason whatsoever, the woodwork is now obsolete, replaced by horrid hollow metal – and it doesn't take a Sarf London songsmith to tell us that the phrase, "Coh, he's lost his head and smacked it against the metalwork" lacks poetry and is never going to catch on.

You used to get a nice solid *thweck* when a ball hit the post full on, and an exciting *thoi-oi-oing* when a thunderbolt set the bar wobbling.

Now you get the tinny, unsatisfying little *ping* of plastic on thin steel.

Almost inevitably, FIFA Führer Sepp Blatter will one day prove to have been behind this outrage, yet another downgrading of the simple pleasures once inherent in watching a game of football. It's hard to imagine how he'll have cut a percentage, fixed the bidding, shaved a corner or helped out his brother-in-law in this case, but the evidence is there for all to see – he found a way.

Lovely shooting: right in the top left corner...

AUGUST DIARY 1972

TUE 1
WED 2
THU 3
FRI 4
SAT 5
SUN 6
MON 7
TUE 8
WED 9
THU 10
FRI 11
SAT 12
SUN 13
MON 14
TUE 15
WED 16

10

WORKING CLASS HEROES

Tricky bugger, class. Things used to be simple when the sides in the big game were us against them: everybody who worked versus the lucky chancers who paid us tuppence a week for making their millions. But things aren't so simple now that half of us spend our lives staring at little screens, colouring in with our cursors or clicking to move pointless crap around the globe, providing 'services' for people we never even meet instead of getting out in the fresh air and digging a bloody big hole or making something useful like a boat or a gun or slogging out into the middle of a muddy field and kicking a ball around to make people cheer.

Everyone who ever bought shares in something they used to own outright, everybody who can afford a football season-ticket. Drug dealers, pop stars, the lady behind the counter in the grocer's.

Confusion reigns now nobody's working.

Sometimes, when you're driving at 80mph down a packed motorway at 11 o'clock on a Tuesday morning, it makes you wonder what everybody does to earn their shiny little runarounds and those important executive motors that look like big silver slippers.

Whatever it is, they're not at work. Maybe they're all footballers...

"I was up at 6.30 every morning, cycling to work," Frank McLintock tells us. "I was serving my apprenticeship as a painter and decorator and doing two nights a week training at Filbert Street. Plus I was going to night school to study signwriting. When we got to the FA Cup Final, I finished work on the Friday and cycled home. I got washed, showered and shaved, cycled down to the ground and got on the first-team bus down to London. I stayed at the Dorchester Hotel, met Elizabeth Taylor and Richard Burton, played at Wembley in front of 100,000 people and then was back at work on the Monday morning.

"You can't see David Beckham doing that now, can you?"

"I stayed at the Dorchester, met Liz Taylor and played in the Cup Final, but I was
back at work on Monday morning..."

When work was more easily recognisable, the working-class hero always used to have two jobs, sometimes even three or four. Back in 1950s, they didn't call Tom Finney 'The Preston Plumber' for nothing. Jimmy Greaves wasn't just the greatest goalscorer of all-time, he also ran a removals company throughout the 1960s. Dave Mackay's Ties are still in business to this day.

Now work is a four-letter word, it isn't us against them but rather us against us. We're all middle class now, even if we worked in a factory before it closed down and we went up in the world. Everyone who has ever watched BBC2 or passed an exam, fancied their chances on *The X Factor* or been shopping is middle class.

Frank McLintock

THE WORLD CUP SQUAD SINGALONG
Mexico 1970
England World Cup Squad:
'Back Home'

Even at the age of seven, I knew it wasn't the done thing to well up and blubber along to an England squad singalong. To cover my lapses, I improvised diversionary routines, snorting manfully or loudly stating the obvious – that the players couldn't sing and looked a bit embarrassed, swaying out of time.

Right from the big *cha-cha cha-cha-cha* intro, 'Back Home' epitomises everything an England World Cup song should be. There's an instant, exotic Latin flavour, albeit sensibly watered down to suit the domestic tastes of the time, like Vesta 'just add boiling water' paella. The big horns signal a muscly romp, but one magnificently constrained by dinner jackets under the sweaty *Top of the Pops* studio lights.

It's still affecting today, Jeff Astle's finest moment leading the line for England. The message from the players was certainly rare in its personal perspective: while we're watching

them on the box, battling in the sunshine far away, they'll be thinking about us... the folks back home.

Lodged all summer at number 1, the message of 'Back Home' was to change in meaning as events unfolded in Mexico, initially making my eyes prickle at the sheer hopefulness of England's mission, then making my bottom lip wobble with the terrible time-lapse power of a postcard from the front. Even after we'd lost to West Germany, the song lingered around the top of the chart. That's when it finally dawned that our boys had been doomed all along –

"We'll give all we have got to give" – only ever destined for an early plane back home.

Of course, not all the songs on the *World Beaters Sing the World Beaters LP* carried on the big themes of war and death. According to the notes on the circular gatefold sleeve, the famous single's flip-side, 'Cinnamon Stick', features Brian Labone and Francis Lee "letting their hair down on this 'bubble-gum' song". 'Lovey-Dovey' is "your actual reggae music with Gordon Banks in true Caribbean form." And 'Sugar Sugar' gets a first-rate duffing-up at the hands of Working Men's Club soul veterans Bobby Moore and Frannie Lee.

THE WORLD BEATERS SING THE WORLD BEATERS

℗ 1970
NSPL 18337-A

SIDE I
NSPL 18337

1. Back Home (Martin, Coulter) (2.07)
2. Sugar Sugar (Barry, Kim) (2.33)
3. Lovey-Dovey (Martin, Coulter) (2.25)
4. Lily The Pink (Gorman, McGear, McGough) (4.14)
5. You're In My Arms (Martin, Coulter) (2.42)
6. Puppet On A String (Martin, Coulter) (2.10)

ENGLAND WORLD CUP SQUAD "70"

Produced by Martin and Coulter
Arrangements by Phil Coulter
MEWS MUSIC (1, 3, 5), WELBECK (2),
NOEL GAY (4), PETER MAURICE (6),
N.C.B., B.I.E.M.,
G.E.M.A.

Germany 1974
England World Cup Squad with Magnum Brass: 'Here We Are'
Scotland World Cup Squad: 'Easy, Easy'

It's shocking how the England set-up could have been so complacent, so presumptuous, to record a World Cup song for Munich 74 long before their dismal flop in the qualifying stage. Few fans will remember the resultant coupling with Magnum Brass, let alone the ironically titled 'Here We Are', where a tiddly-om-pom-pom military band from another age drowns out a grudging squad performance.

"England's having a ball / What a day for one and all": that was the imagined outcome of England's first World Cup qualification campaign since 1962; but even without the intervention of Poland and Peter Shilton, this fixed-grimace perkiness would never have made the charts. Even now, the misplaced optimism still has the power to wound.

Meanwhile, the Scotland World Cup Squad's effort was 'Easy Easy', a Bay City Rollers cast-off notable only for the rhyming of "Yaba-daba-doo" with "We are the boys in blue."

ENS1 STEREO
OFFICIAL
INLINE
ENGLAND FOOTBALL SONG
'HERE WE ARE'
sung by
THE SQUAD
accompanied by THE MAGNUM BRASS

Argentina 1978
Rod Stewart (featuring the Scottish World Cup Squad): 'Olé Ola'

With England now making a habit of missing the World Cup trip, it was again up to Scotland to carry all our hopes for Argentina – and curiously they chose to get us in the mood with a Brazilian samba sung by a Londoner.

The Auld Enemy at least warranted a mention in dispatches in professional Scotsman Andy Cameron's 'Ally's Tartan Army', which swaggered famously about 'the greatest fitba team's' impending victory, and stuck the boot in quite magnificently with the pay-off line: "We're representing Britain, and we're gaunny do or die / England cannae dae it, 'cos they didnae qualify."

30p

ARGENTINA HERE WE COME!

8,320 miles

PRESTWICK

CORDOBA
MENDOZA
BUENOS AIRES

OFFICIAL
SOUVENIR
PROGRAMME

SCOTLAND'S WORLD CUP SEND-OFF AT HAMPDEN PARK,
THURSDAY, MAY 25, 1978. GATES OPEN 5.45 p.m.

EASY! EASY!
Scotland World Cup Squad

Easy!: Scotland were unbeaten in '74 but were on the first plane back home from West Germany.

Spain 1982
England World Cup Squad:
'This Time (We'll Get It Right)'
The 1982 Scotland World Cup Squad:
'We Have a Dream'

When it comes to that particular brand of patriotic heroism best exemplified by a choir of thirty non-singers clenching their buttocks, England's last great moment came in 1982. It's the very beginning of the record that does it – not the folkie opening bars with the twiddly accordion or the circus drum lead-in, but the squad's balled fist of a mission statement: "We're on our way / We are Ron's twenty-two…"

Like 'Back Home', the song captures a sense of togetherness and courage in the face of a vastly superior enemy; but it goes downhill after the big kick-off. The kitchen-sink arrangement layers up crowd chants and calypso drums with oompah and 'The Dambusters March', while the blokes seem to get steadily shriller as the Germans loom. "Hear the roar / Of the red, white and blue…"

In retrospect, they should have let chorus-leader Kevin Keegan loose on a follow-up to his top-drawer Anglo-disco hit 'Head Over Heels In Love'. Still, the FA's resolute refusal to acknowledge disco, punk or even New Romanticism was partly tempered on the 'This Time We'll Get It Right' LP, where Justin Fashanu's frankly astonishing 'Do It 'Cos You Like It' predated the thrust of Frankie Goes To Hollywood's 'Relax' by at least a year.

The Scotland squad, meanwhile, swayed in the background while actor John Gordon Sinclair recalled a dream about them winning. It was an attempted cash-in on still-warm memories of the delightful *Gregory's Girl*; but surely Clare Grogan – the film's titular heart-throb – and her band Altered Images might have whisked up a more rousing anthem to nocturnal teen reverie and ultimate disappointment.

Mexico 1986
England World Cup Squad:
'We've Got the Whole World at Our Feet'
Scotland World Cup Squad:
'Big Trip to Mexico'

Where the unofficial 'Official Colourbox World Cup Theme' showed the way forward, pumping up the volume with new-fangled hip-hop samples over a juddering BBC Radiophonic Workshop *Doctor Who* vibe, the two British squads stuck to the same old booted-and-suited formula.

Scotland's 'Big Trip To Mexico' was a snaking, mariachi-driven street party with a vibe that brought to mind locations as far south-west as Lossiemouth. And would you believe the same songwriting team, under Tony 'Brotherhood of Man' Hiller, was also commissioned to produce England's flop, which only reached number 66?

With the pack nervously following Captain Marvel's homicidally patriotic lead, no doubt anticipating a disastrous sprained tonsil, the song casually ripped off 'We Got the Whole World In Our Hands' by Paper Lace & Nottingham Forest – "There's Spider and Needham, they'll never yield / There's Archie the Gemmill all over the field" – but this slack, sad effort made Cloughie's mob seem like soulful poets. The end of an era.

Chart glory: all these rousing anthems are collected on Cherry Red's England Squad comp.

X Y Z

THE XXX PRINTER

If aliens with big veiny brains were to stumble across a post-apocalyptic Earth 50,000 years from now, they'd soon begin to assemble a picture of what life was like back in the day. Overgrown roads, dotted with rusty engine blocks, will still link up crumbling towns; settees and chairs will remain crowded in front of screens; and, of course, all plastic packaging will be as good as new. Some irradiated treats will still be edible past their sell-by date, perfect loot for a Sunday rocket-boot sale.

The football stadium will clearly have been a gathering place for the city's inhabitants, a rectangle of jungle surrounded by sloping walls to keep the prey inside. Traces of nuked balti pie will lend our futuristic visitors an uncanny insight into the culinary options once available.

However, any curious ET who comes across my rubber X-stamper will be letting himself in for one giant throbbing headache.

It's a small wooden block with a rubber underside textured with tight rows of 15 x 18 tiny Xs, all dyed black. Accompanying the block is a shallow plastic tray holding a thin pad of inky foam rubber.

The alien's head will begin to throb wildly. Experimenting with the block and foam, he might successfully print out 270 microscopic Xs in a neat oblong block. But *why?* It's *impossible* to guess what use it could have had!

"DoEs NoT cOmPuTe! OvErLoAd!"

And so the Earth will be saved from invasion by my Spot-the-Ball X-printer, which mum bought for 99p off the pools man in 1983.

Not a bad investment, looking long term.

NOW YOU CAN ENTER 540 X'S ON ONE ENTRY FORM

ASK YOUR COLLECTOR FOR DETAILS OF A

Rubber Stamp & Pad

LIMITED OFFER! STAMP + PAD ONLY 99p

ORDER NOW! WHILE STOCKS LAST!

I require ....

Stamps .... Pads .... Total Cost £ ....

Name ....

Address ....

YOUTH ENVY

"This word football, and the thing it stands for – when we were small boys, we knew what it meant, all right."

So they harangued, Maurice Edelston and Terence Delaney, in *Masters of Soccer,* a passionate dissection of the modern game and its greatest exponents. No stiff, self-conscious analysis, this. In order to put into context the exploits of their heroes, the football writers first underwent a kind of primal scream therapy, remembering the way it had felt to play in pitch-dark parks, to loose rocket shots between chair legs, and to dispute every decision.

"We were unruly, but we were devoted," they recalled. "Football was what we did when they set us free."

Football without innocence is still all but impossible. Roll a ball to the feet of the most cynical mercenary and he'll instinctively weigh the old options, like a caged jaguar seeing only the horizon. Every football fan can still undergo the same kind of childlike reversion, grabbing on to a single split second's magic in ninety minutes: a tale to tell, a memory to savour.

When I was a kid, I couldn't wait to be an adult and do all those exciting, grown-up things like stay up for *Match of the Day* every week and tinker with a £200 sports car and buy a season ticket and get into X-rated films without having to assume a casually gruff voice. However, now I'm old enough to go to the pub without having to sit in an alcove out of sight of the bar, and even own a car with a futuristic electric seat, I find myself the victim of a comic reversal: I spend ever more time, effort and money attempting to escape into the apparent simplicity of the past.

Nowadays, we spend ever more time, effort and money attempting to escape into the apparent simplicity of the past.

Even though my own selective memories of football are threatened by the shadows of Hillsborough, Heysel and Bradford, by the European ban, monkey chants and flying bananas, by reported stabbings, fighting and falling walls, I still wouldn't swap them for a modern child's experiences of the game. The era of youth envy is over.

It's nothing new, this feeling that our football was best, and is now being left behind, taken over. Edelston and Delaney's *Masters of Soccer* was published by Heinemann in 1960.

"Some people, it seems, were not like this," they concluded. "To them, the word means something else; something more solemn, more proper, connected with national honour and the upright life. To others still, who came to the game presumably late in life, football is an industry, best regulated by the application of what are called sound business principles."

THE ZX SPECTRUM

When software came on compact cassette and you plugged your £129, 48-bit console (so much more than just a cassette player – we're talking 48 whole *kilobytes* of onboard RAM here) into the living room TV, the virtual world made accessible by Clive Sinclair seemed very real. More real, in many ways, than the actual mid Eighties envisioned by the inventor from the viewpoint of his C5 executive go-kart.

Fully loaded, Addictive Software's prototype *Football Manager* came closer than ever to mirroring real-life football, the number of variables written into the game a thrilling new high.

You could buy and sell and juggle your team using basic lines of text, putting up with injuries and chairman pressure and crowd trouble.

Football's virtual world is now worryingly difficult to discern from the real thing. In today's *Soccer Director* game, you can buy a club with shadowy offshore funds, hire star players who have no contact with society, and ignore the rules of economics and authority.

The games used to be little clips of stick-men scoring goals.

So much more than a cassette player, the Speccy packed 48 whole kilobytes of onboard RAM…

Wanted!

Your treasure, your stories... and some proper football.

Please do get in touch with your own memories of football back in the day, with your most cherished treasures from the shrine under your bed, or with any incisive pub grumbles on the state of the modern game. We want to hear, and see, anything that adds to the overwhelming proof that *football used to be better in the past.*

Send us a photo or a scan of the precious childhood clutter that survived your mum's Great Spring Clean of 1987. Send in your old pics of stars snapped in the street or from the stands, your souvenirs, DIY banners and memorabilia – anything with a great story or memory attached – and share them with other fans on the Got, Not Got blog.

You can contact us direct via gotnotgot. wordpress.com – and don't forget to also look out for Got, Not Got posts on MirrorFootball. co.uk, Facebook and YouTube.

Mail us if there's anything *else* you miss about football in the past. Like rattles, for instance. How did we go and forget rattles? And Kaliber lager, as advertised by Lawrie McMenemy. "It's *grairght*, man." And football dynasties – you don't get them any more, do you? And no one these days ever takes their boots to the match, just in case. Not like John 'Budgie' Burridge used to whenever he went

to Wembley. And what about footballer poets, like John Toshack. Progress charts. The Anglo-Scottish Cup, eh?

You can even get in touch about the future of football if, like us, you still haven't managed to wean yourself off your first love. On that score, thanks go out to Michel Platini for a heartfelt note admitting that he, too, "can see lots of red lights flashing," and is "afraid for the future of football, which is going pear-shaped in some areas." The UEFA president's early contributions to *Got, Not Got 2* include "match fixing, corruption, illegal betting, violence on the pitch, racism and hooliganism," all topped off with suicidal debt and pay strikes, the influx of foreign owners, coaches and players, and the ensuing loss of clubs' identities. It can only be a matter of time before mud, ungentlemanly

> **"Maybe it's old-fashioned, but I like those clubs that belong to their members. The only ones who give a club its identity are the fans.**
>
> ## Everything else has changed; but they stay."
> Michel Platini

conduct and players called Nobby make a comeback.

Most importantly, get in touch if you remember swivel boots, especially if you have concrete evidence of their existence. Or if you've got the World Cup wallchart out of the 1974 FKS sticker album in unused condition (except for the usual few first round scores, before you made a scribbly bodge and Scotland got knocked out).

Yours in sport,

Derek Hammond.

Gary Silke

The Authors

Derek Hammond & Gary Silke

Got, Not Got is based on Derek and Gary's blog on mirrorfootball.co.uk. They have also written on the 'stuff' of football fandom for many magazines, club programmes and fanzines, and even supplied the football cards for BBC1's *Match of the Seventies* and *Match of the Eighties*. They were recently major contributors to TalkSPORT's *100 Greatest British Sporting Legends* (Simon & Schuster, 2011).

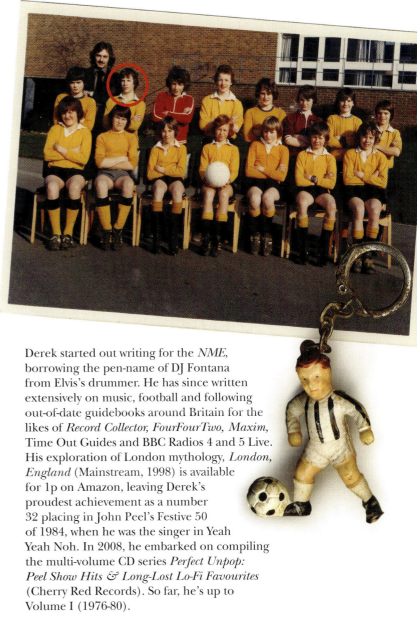

Gary is editor of *The Fox* fanzine – at 24 years and counting, one of the oldest original football fanzines still in existence. He has written a weekly *Leicester Mercury* column since 2003, and has contributed to *When Saturday Comes*, retro football mag *Backpass* and the *Leicester Chronicle* retro newspaper. It's probably fair to say Gary likes old stuff. He is also the author of the *Fanatical Frank* and *Thirtysomething* series of comic-strip books, and the *Big Blue Leicester City Scrapbook* (all Juma, 1999-2006).

Derek started out writing for the *NME*, borrowing the pen-name of DJ Fontana from Elvis's drummer. He has since written extensively on music, football and following out-of-date guidebooks around Britain for the likes of *Record Collector, FourFourTwo, Maxim,* Time Out Guides and BBC Radios 4 and 5 Live. His exploration of London mythology, *London, England* (Mainstream, 1998) is available for 1p on Amazon, leaving Derek's proudest achievement as a number 32 placing in John Peel's Festive 50 of 1984, when he was the singer in Yeah Yeah Noh. In 2008, he embarked on compiling the multi-volume CD series *Perfect Unpop: Peel Show Hits & Long-Lost Lo-Fi Favourites* (Cherry Red Records). So far, he's up to Volume I (1976-80).

Gary and Derek both live with their delightful young families in sunny Leicestershire. Not all in one house, like.

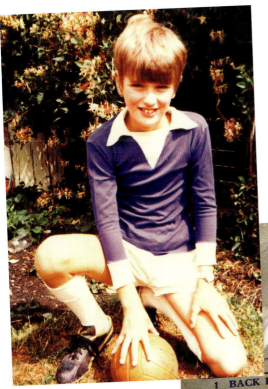

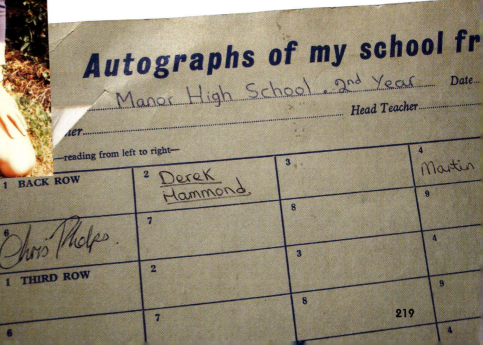

Acknowledgments

Special thanks to Steve Anglesey, Deputy Publisher, Trinity Mirror Digital; Gordon Banks; David Barber, FA historian; Andy Betts for his list of clobber at Leicester-Cagliari; Frank Burrows; Dermot Carney, the Villa Poet; Dan Davies for the *Football Handbooks*, rescued during the last days of Rivals.net, and yet to be returned; Gavin Hadland for his Pardoe prog; Half Man Half Biscuit for permission to reproduce the lyrics to 'Even Men with Steel Hearts'; John Hammond for the big piles of programmes, 1971 and 2011; Henry, Freda and Lynda Hammond for the memories; Ken Hammond for more memories;

Cyril and Kay Hammond for the 1966 sixpence; Peter Hammond for his World Cup memorabilia; Graham Kelly; Simon Kimber for his help and support; Andy Lochhead for his FA Cup runners-up medal; Ian Long for his memories of Dennis Rofe; David Luxton at Luxton Harris Limited; Frank McLintock; Robert Nichols at *Fly Me to the Moon;* Emma Prigmore for her retro inspiration; Don Rogers; 'The Shed' Chelsea fansite; Simon Trewin at United Agents; Sid Waddell; Pete Watts for his notes on Pat Nevin; *When Skies Are Grey* for the Everton hitchers' story; and – last and by all means most – Frank Worthington.

Picture credits

MirrorFootball.co.uk / Mirrorpix – main picture page 8, 24, 25, 26, 29, 33, 35, 39, 47, 49, 52, 63, 65 (both), 73, 80, 81, 88, 90, 93, 97, 98, 100, 107, 121, 126, 133, 136, 147, 148, 158 (both), 160, 166, 177, 179, 185, 212. Thanks to Fergus McKenna, Mirror Group Head of Syndication & Licensing, and Patrick Purcell, mirror.co.uk picture editor.
Neville Chadwick Photography – main picture page 7, 13, 75, 111, 165, 182, 191, 204; both main front-cover.images.
David Morcom Photography – main picture page 56, 100 (Manor), 114 (Schmeichel), 185 (surge); Twin Towers on inside covers.
Simon Smith and Russ Carvell – Unforgettables illustrations.
Derek Hammond & Gary Silke – all other photography, except for the following.
A huge thank-you to our many picture contributors:
Graham Aldred – Man City memory board; Richard Banyard – Anglo-Italian programme – visit swindon-town-fc.co.uk; Bristol City FC Supporters Trust – Ashton Gate Eight plaque – contact info@bristolcityst.org.uk; Cherry Red Records – 'Blue Moon' and 'England's Glory' CD covers – these and many more great football club and country song CDs available from cherryred.co.uk/football/index; Ron Crane – Burnley team bus – for similar items visit nickopendle on eBay; Simon Dack – Steve Foster; Ralph Davidson – Man City ECWC tickets; John Devlin – Norwich & West Brom kit illustrations – visit truecoloursfootballkits.com; Andy Ellis – Cloughie door sign and campaign sticker, Centenary Ale, Baseball Ground model, Robert Maxwell share certificate, Watney Cup ticket – see also *Relics of the Rams* (Breedon) and *Derby County: From the Nineties*

(DB Publishing); Kevin Freer – Boothferry Park; Stephen Grinnell – Luton Astroturf; Ian Guildford at *The Ram* matchday magazine – *League Liner* dancers; Dave Hartley – Nan and Granddad's Villa coaster; John Hutchinson at the Leicester City Digital Archive – Scotland shirt, England badge, vintage rattle; Rickey Lacey – Fulham wallet; Steve Marsh – West Ham mugs, 1966 sugar wrappers – visit theyflysohigh.co.uk and enjoy the biggest, most beautiful online collection of memorabilia for any club; Neil Jeffries – sock tag; Richard Maskell – George Best flexi-disc; Nigel Mercer – A&BC counter box, 'Norman Bites' card jigsaw, FKS stickers unwrapped, Findus badge, *Lion* and *Victor* league ladders – visit the finest historical football card website on the planet at cards.littleoak.com.au; *Leicester Mercury* – Fans on the Roof – with thanks to Jeremy Clay; Andy McConachie – Cloughie mug transfer, Tennents beermats – visit footballcardsuk.com for 15,000 football cards on offer, and even more programmes at football-programmes.net; Tom Morris, Charlton Athletic FC photographer 1969-2005 – the derelict Valley; Duncan Olner – Twerton Park, signed Cov programme; Andrew Ormerod – Wedding Present *George Best* Hama art, Pompey scrapbook, Stockbridge 'No Ball Games' – visit Andrew's hilarious blogs at pleasurecityavenue.blogspot.com (indie pop) and hoppingaroundhampshire.blogspot.com (football); Merv Payne – Wembley facade; Nick at ITV Football 1968-1983 – ITV regional idents and Notts County *Post Football Guides* – more Sunday soccer nostalgia at homepage.ntlworld.com/carousel/ITVfootball68-83.html; Patrick Quinnelly – Action Man; Reading Museum Service – Cheese Footballs – thanks to Angela Houghton, and for more biscuitabilia visit huntleyandpalmers.org.uk; Keith Stanton – Rangers magazine – for similar items visit keithstanton14f0e on eBay; Toffs – Blues, Hibs, Plymouth and Wolves shirts plus 'Cotton' and Sheff U shirt badges – thanks to Dale Robinson at Toffs, number one for quality, authentic, nostalgic football shirts; Vectis Auctions Ltd of Stockton-on-Tees – Ford Cortina model; Vocalion Records – 'Hardcore' film soundtrack CD cover – visit duttonvocalion.co.uk.

Checklist
What We Miss in Modern Football

Perhaps needless to say, no tick appears against any item in this checklist of contents. However, we're going to leave a copy of our plans with the FA – those nice men we entrusted to take care of every aspect of football on our behalf – so hopefully it shouldn't be too long before we're ticking things off, football card-style, as they begin to reappear…

- ☐ A&BC
- ☐ Action Man
- ☐ Action Transfers
- ☐ Admiral
- ☐ After the Match
- ☐ Animals on the Pitch
- ☐ Applying for Re-election
- ☐ **ARSENAL** North Bankers in the First Team
- ☐ **ASTON VILLA** The Football Cathedral
- ☐ Astroturf
- ☐ The Autograph Book
- ☐ Avoiding the Score
- ☐ Baldies **EXTINCT FOOTBALL SPECIES No. 1**
- ☐ The Banana Shot
- ☐ **BIRMINGHAM CITY** Über Alles
- ☐ **BLACKBURN** Uncle Jack's Title
- ☐ **BLACKPOOL** When the Wind Blew
- ☐ Bloodied but Unbowed
- ☐ **BOLTON** Goal of the Century
- ☐ **BRIGHTON** And Smith Must Score
- ☐ **BRISTOL CITY** The Ashton Gate Eight
- ☐ **BRISTOL ROVERS** The Nickname Strike Duo
- ☐ Bully for England **IT COULD NEVER HAPPEN NOW**
- ☐ **BURNLEY** The Football Factory
- ☐ The Car Blanket

- ☐ **CARDIFF CITY** Jekyll & Hyde Adventures in Europe
- ☐ **CARLISLE UNITED** On Top of the World
- ☐ Casdon Soccer
- ☐ **CELTIC** Winning in a Wood
- ☐ Chancer Chairmen
- ☐ Charles Buchan's Football Monthly
- ☐ **CHARLTON ATHLETIC** Back Home to The Valley
- ☐ Cheap Admission
- ☐ **CHELSEA** Blue Is the Colour
- ☐ The Clogger **EXTINCT FOOTBALL SPECIES No. 2**
- ☐ The Close Season
- ☐ Clubcall
- ☐ Coffer
- ☐ Comic Underdogs
- ☐ The Copper
- ☐ Cossack
- ☐ Cotton
- ☐ **COVENTRY CITY** Sky Blue Revolution
- ☐ **CRYSTAL PALACE** The Fedora
- ☐ Cuff Clutching
- ☐ Cup Final Build-up
- ☐ DIY
- ☐ Dangerous Training
- ☐ Dastardly Foreign Tricks
- ☐ **DERBY COUNTY** Bring Back Cloughie
- ☐ Divisions One to Four
- ☐ Doing the Pools

- [ ] The Donkey Kick **IT COULD NEVER HAPPEN NOW**
- [ ] Do's and Don'ts
- [ ] The Dugout
- [ ] Dutch Courage
- [ ] England 4-2 West Germany **IT COULD NEVER HAPPEN NOW**
- [ ] ertiM
- [ ] Escape to Victory
- [ ] The European Cup Winners' Cup
- [ ] **EVERTON** Hitching Abroad
- [ ] Exotic Foreigners **EXTINCT FOOTBALL SPECIES No. 3**
- [ ] The FA 'Tactical Guru'
- [ ] The Fancy-Dress Photo Op
- [ ] Fans on the Roof
- [ ] Fanzines
- [ ] Fergie's Dons Storm Europe **IT COULD NEVER HAPPEN NOW**
- [ ] Fiddling with the Rules
- [ ] Flicking the Vs
- [ ] The Football Card Engine
- [ ] Football League Review
- [ ] Footballers' Wives who Aren't in Pop Groups
- [ ] Fossilised Football Card Bubble Gum
- [ ] **FULHAM** NASL by the Thames
- [ ] Garden Goals
- [ ] Genuine Showbiz Fans
- [ ] Girl of the Match
- [ ] Glorious Amateurism
- [ ] Goal! Lollies
- [ ] Goalhanging
- [ ] Goalie Gear
- [ ] Goalkeepers Are Different
- [ ] The Goalpost Tree
- [ ] Groovers **EXTINCT FOOTBALL SPECIES No. 4**
- [ ] Halfway Flags

- [ ] Hastily Recoloured Kit
- [ ] **HEARTS** Friendly Fire
- [ ] **HIBS** Turnbull's Tornadoes
- [ ] Helix
- [ ] Home
- [ ] Home Internationals
- [ ] Hot-Shot Hamish
- [ ] **HUDDERSFIELD TOWN** Playboy
- [ ] **HULL CITY** Fer Ark
- [ ] ITV Sunday Afternoons
- [ ] In for Free
- [ ] In the Buff
- [ ] Injuries Before Cruciates and Metatarsals
- [ ] International Honours
- [ ] **IPSWICH TOWN** Osborne Overwhelmed
- [ ] Jam Jar Lids
- [ ] The Jock-Strap
- [ ] Joker in the Pack **EXTINCT FOOTBALL SPECIES No. 5**
- [ ] Jossy's Giants
- [ ] Jumble-Sale Stadiums
- [ ] Jumping Over Minis
- [ ] Junior Fags
- [ ] The Kays Catalogue
- [ ] Keepy-Uppy
- [ ] Kick-the-Goal Soccer
- [ ] The Landlady
- [ ] The Landlord
- [ ] League Ladders
- [ ] The League Liner Disco Train
- [ ] The League of Ninety-Two
- [ ] **LEEDS UNITED** 100 per Cent Beef
- [ ] **LEICESTER CITY** The Tent
- [ ] Liniment
- [ ] **LIVERPOOL** Champagne Magnum
- [ ] Look At Me
- [ ] Lost in Space
- [ ] Lower-League Signings
- [ ] **LUTON TOWN** The Futuristic Masterplan
- [ ] Magazine Shin Pads
- [ ] The Magic Sponge
- [ ] The Manageress
- [ ] **MANCHESTER CITY** Inflatables
- [ ] **MANCHESTER UNITED** Life Before Prawn Sandwiches
- [ ] The Manual Action Replay
- [ ] Men Only
- [ ] **MIDDLESBROUGH** Champions At Last
- [ ] **MILLWALL** Only a Game?
- [ ] Mind the Gap
- [ ] Model Professionals
- [ ] Mud
- [ ] My First Shoot!
- [ ] NASL
- [ ] Nameless Shirts
- [ ] **NEWCASTLE UNITED** Stadium Fraud
- [ ] Newspaper Programmes
- [ ] Nicknames Unsuitable for a Modern, Go-Ahead Club
- [ ] **NORWICH CITY** Bayern Munich Away
- [ ] **NOTTINGHAM FOREST** The Million Pound Man
- [ ] **NOTTS COUNTY** The Old-School Gaffer
- [ ] Numbers 1-11
- [ ] The Observer's Book of Football
- [ ] One-Club Players **EXTINCT FOOTBALL SPECIES No. 6**

- Other Avenues **EXTINCT FOOTBALL SPECIES No. 7**
- Oversize Third-World Stamps with Players in Made-up Kit
- Panini
- Parklife
- Pet Scottish Second Division Teams
- Peter Barnes Football Trainer
- Petrol Station Giveaways
- Players Called Bobby and Jimmy
- Players Living on Your Street **IT COULD NEVER HAPPEN NOW**
- The Plucky Giantkiller **IT COULD NEVER HAPPEN NOW**
- **PLYMOUTH ARGYLE** Uniquely Singular and One of a Kind
- **PORTSMOUTH** Corporal Punishment
- Practically One-Club Players **EXTINCT FOOTBALL SPECIES No. 8**
- Proper Beardies **EXTINCT FOOTBALL SPECIES No. 9**
- Psychedelic Programmes
- The Punful Advert
- Punk Rock Football
- QPR The Bush Telegraph
- Rabbit's Ears
- **RANGERS** Copping the Cup Winners' Cup in a Cupboard
- The Re-Replay
- **READING** Score and Snog a Copper
- The Referee Who is Always Right
- The Reserves
- The Rest of the World **IT COULD NEVER HAPPEN NOW**
- The Rosette
- Running Without the Ball
- Saint & Greavsie
- Saturday Afternoon, Three O'Clock
- Scarf Ace
- Scottish Superstars **EXTINCT FOOTBALL SPECIES No. 10**
- The Scrapbook
- The Secret Advantage
- Shame
- **SHEFFIELD UNITED** Playing Football on a Cricket Pitch
- **SHEFFIELD WEDNESDAY** Eric the Wed
- Short Shorts
- The Shoulder Charge
- Smoke
- 'Soccer'
- The Soccer Tribe
- **SOUTHAMPTON** Playing in a Dell
- Sponsored Motors
- Squash
- Stand-In Goalies
- **STOKE CITY** What Was Lost in the Great Roof Blow-off of '76
- Striker
- Subbuteo 24-Segment Crowd Barrier C170
- Suedehead
- **SUNDERLAND** The Roker Roar
- The Superfan Loudhailer
- Superstars **IT COULD NEVER HAPPEN NOW**
- The Surge
- Surprise Champions
- **SWANSEA CITY** Pristine
- **SWINDON TOWN** The Italian Job
- Swivel Boots
- The TV Tower
- Tackling from Behind
- The Taste of Football
- Teams that You Can Recite
- The Testimonial Match

- They Used to Play on Grass
- Toilet Rolls
- Top Trumps
- **TOTTENHAM HOTSPUR** The Glory Game
- Transfer Requests Turned Down
- The Twin Towers
- Unchoreographed Goal Celebrations
- Unlucky Bags
- The Victorious Overprint
- The Video Age
- Waddington's Table Soccer
- Warming Up
- **WATFORD** Hornets' Nest
- Wembley
- **WEST BROM** The Three Degrees
- **WEST HAM** The Teams that Meet in Caffs
- **WIGAN** The Best-Behaved Cup Winners
- **WIMBLEDON** Going Out of Existence
- **WOLVES** Focus On The Doog
- The Woodwork
- Working Class Heroes
- The World Cup Squad Singalong
- The XXX Printer
- Youth Envy
- ZX Spectrum

Dont Forget!

MANCHESTER CITY F.C.